Issues
In
Sexual Ethics

Biblical, Theological, Ethical
and Scientific Perspectives
on Human Sexuality

Issues In Sexual Ethics

Editor: Martin Duffy

Contributing Editors:
Gerald M. Sanders
Leslie C. Wicker

UNITED CHURCH PEOPLE
FOR BIBLICAL WITNESS
SOUDERTON, PA.   1979

COVER DESIGN BY ARMAND L. WELLER

PUBLISHED BY UNITED CHURCH PEOPLE FOR BIBLICAL WITNESS,
276 W. CHERRY LANE, SOUDERTON, PENNSYLVANIA 18964

Printed by Indian Valley Printing Ltd.,
16 Harbor Place, Souderton, Pennsylvania 18964

To Our Beloved
United Church of Christ

"Bear one another's burdens, and
so fulfill the law of Christ"

Contents

Introduction

The Eleventh General Synod of the United Church of Christ, working through early July of 1977 in Washington D.C., witnessed a unique event. Reacting to the advance report *Human Sexuality: A Preliminary Study* with associated recommendations, a minority caucus with delegates from 36 Conferences gathered to present a minority resolution to General Synod. Although General Synod received *Human Sexuality: A Preliminary Study* and commended it to the whole United Church of Christ for study and response, when 34% of the delegates voted in the negative the minority resolution gained official recognition. Texts of the minority resolution and of the Policy Statement of the United Church People for Biblical Witness, formed out of the minority caucus, are printed in the *Appendix*.

The central concern of the minority resolution was the "limited theological, biblical, and ethical viewpoint reflected in the Study which does not characterize the diverse perspectives of the United Church of Christ." While the resolution expressed appreciation for the opportunity the preliminary Study provided to engage in significant discussion about human sexuality, it called upon the local churches, Associations and Conferences to seek additional study materials with viewpoints not reflected in the Study. The United Church People for Biblical Witness has prepared *Issues in Sexual Ethics* to meet the above concern and trusts that, together with the preliminary Study, it will provide the church with the wide range of materials required for extensive inquiry and discussion.

Having described the origin and intent of this book, we would like to share some of the convictions of the hundreds of persons and churches who made it possible with their comments, prayers and giving.

We believe that the Biblical Witness must have precedence in all areas of the church's life and teaching. A genuine dialogue and debate on issues of human sexuality has to be engaged throughout the United Church of Christ *before decisions are made* in order to prevent schism and loss and to ground our ministry in the mind of Christ. Study and dialogue are useless unless we are willing to speak the truth in love, to agree or disagree according to our convictions but *to listen carefully* to all sides of the issue.

We commit this work to the people of the United Church of Christ with deep love and concern. Our church—indeed the whole Christian church—needs profound renewal to minister the gospel of Christ in the final quarter of the twentieth century. In faithfulness to Scripture, genuine renewal will combine a ministry of social justice with a call to repentance, faith and personal holiness. It will portray the Lord who practices justice, kindness and righteousness in the earth. "Righteousness and justice are the foundation of thy throne; steadfast love and faithfulness go before thee."

Great sections of the church are trapped in a new Babylonian captivity to secular views and practice. Once again the Word of God powerfully challenges our idolatry. We are a pluralistic denomination with a tradition of theological freedom. But pluralism cannot mean believing whatever one wishes to believe and going our separate ways. Pluralism makes sense only if we share our spiritual gifts, if we grow up in every way into him who is the head, into Christ, if we keep the unity of the Spirit in the bond of peace. This kind of pluralism requires the most intensive and searching theological inquiry on the grass roots level where ordinary Christians live and work. Executives, theologians, pastors and teachers have to be servants to the awesome prospect of discerning the mind of Christ in the midst of our parishes and communities. Failing intense inquiry and renewal among the great body of members, we will become a church without a community of vision and ministry—a church without a future.

We trust that *Issues in Sexual Ethics* will serve with many other resources and movements in the church to stimulate Biblical and theological reflection, deepening our common life and bringing our covenant of ministry into clear focus. Reviewing the Contents, our book divides into three general areas. The first addresses Biblical, theological and ethical issues raised in the preliminary Study. The second examines the crucial matter of Christian family living against a backdrop of social change and alternate life-styles. The third reviews homosexuality in the light of Scriptural teaching and new programs combining psychiatric and Christian healing.

Elizabeth Achtemeier begins *Issues in Sexual Ethics* with a warm and sensitive treatment of human sexuality from her book *The Committed Marriage*. The major Biblical teachings on human sexuality are carefully interpreted.

Gabriel Fackre explores "the new morality" advanced by secular and Christian thinkers in a delightful and searching critique of situation ethics. His essay first appeared in *Storm Over Ethics* in 1967. While some references to "the new morality" are dated, the issues with which the author struggles are as current as the other questions addressed in this volume.

Donald G. Bloesch, in an excerpt from his book *Essentials Of Evangelical Theology,* reviews what the Fathers, the medieval theologians, the great Reformers and the reformed tradition have to say about the authority of Scripture. His work reveals a convergence of reformed Protestant and modern Catholic regard for Scripture as sovereign over the church.

Gerald M. Sanders contributes two chapters. In the first he questions the principles of Old Testament exegesis and hermeneutics used in our denomination's preliminary Study. In his second chapter he clarifies the difference between scientific and ethical statements, takes a hard look at relativism and subjectivism, and questions the Bultmannian disregard for the historical Jesus and his teaching.

Martin Duffy follows with an examination of Jesus' relationship to the Law—the Law seen as commandment, Scripture, Jewish tradition and the whole content of God's revelation. This chapter interprets Jesus' teaching on human sexuality.

John C. Shetler uses Scripture, the reformed tradition and U.C.C. documents to provide an overview of ordination in the United Church of Christ. The bearing of sexual practice upon ordination, an issue raised in the preliminary Study, cannot be decided without a firm grasp of the meaning and standards of ordination. This chapter lays a foundation for in depth study and discussion by the whole church.

In the middle section of our book, Robert L. Stogner and Leslie C. Wicker devote three chapters to the crucial subject of Christian family living. Leslie C. Wicker provides a wealth of sociological data describing what we face as we attempt to structure Christian living patterns. Robert L. Stogner strongly relates Christian marriage and family life to an experience with God; he suggests helpful marriage enrichment ministries and resources.

The final chapters explore the issue of homosexuality. We have given considerable space to this topic because it is the most acute sexuality issue facing our church. We have attempted not to polarize the issue with extreme positions. Martin Duffy's chapter on civil rights, for instance, seeks to establish a balance between the rights of homosexual persons and the rights of society at large. We have attempted rather to blend sound Christian theology with sound medical and psychiatric opinion to show that the church can minister to homosexual persons with justice, love and healing.

Robert M. Nuermberger, in an essay he wrote for the magazine *Christian Life,* examines homosexuality in the light of Scripture and informed medical opinion, finding good news for the homosexual and the church.

William P. Wilson and Robert Abarno describe six case histories, affirming the need for principled Christian therapy in the treatment of homosexual persons. Their paper first appeared in *The Bulletin* published by the Christian Association for Psychological Studies.

Jim Kaspar and Mike Bussee engage in an arresting dialogue based upon their personal experience as they explode the myth that constitutional homosexual persons cannot change.

Issues in Sexual Ethics concludes with an *Appendix* and *Suggested Readings.* The *Appendix* contains statements by members of the United Church of Christ, including a short paper by Barbara Weller, Chairman of the United Church People for Biblical Witness. We take this occasion to thank Mrs. Weller and her husband Armand for their countless hours of devoted labor on behalf of our study and church renewal. We direct the reader's attention to the statement in the *Appendix* by Frederick W. Schroeder, former President of Eden Seminary. Our contributors represent several positions on the theological spectrum, from evangelical to neo-orthodox and even unorthodox! In this sense we represent the constituency of the United Church of Christ. But we all agree with Dr. Schroeder that we have to take the Bible seriously. As Dr. Schroeder eloquently says, "Everything in Scripture is a part of what St. Paul called 'the whole counsel of God' (Acts 20:27). By its very nature the church is obligated to teach and preach the whole counsel of God."

THE EDITORS

1 The Unique and Tender Knowledge

by Elizabeth Achtemeier

This is the will of God, your sanctification: that you abstain from immorality; that each one of you know how to take a wife for himself in holiness and honor, not in the passion of lust like heathen who do not know God; that no man transgress, and wrong his brother in this matter, because the Lord is an avenger in all these things, as we solemnly forewarned you. For God has not called us for uncleanness, but in holiness. Therefore whoever disregards this, disregards not man but God, who gives his Holy Spirit to you.

—I Thess. 4:3-8

How should we regard sex? If couples are confused about the answer to that question these days, there is ample reason. They are being barraged by a variety of views concerning sexual activity, its importance, its meaning, and its method.

If the marriage manuals are to be believed, then good sexual adjustment, frequent intercourse, and simultaneous orgasm on the part of both partners are the ideal goals of every marriage. If popular books are the guide, then bizarre methods and changing locales are the spice of sexual life. If clinical studies are what one reads, performance is all-important. By all of these, couples are given the idea that they should get in bed and achieve! The American view of achievement and performance as the basis of worth has been transferred to the bedroom.

On the other hand, the radical women liberationists are loudly proclaiming that sex as it has been practiced in American society is basically an evil, a tool of male power and manipulation used against dependent females to turn them into sexual objects and unthinking physical beings. Sex therefore in this view is to be avoided when it symbolizes male domination. Females are better off with masturbation

Elizabeth Achtemeier is Visiting Professor of Homiletics and Hermeneutics at Union Theological Seminary in Virginia and a minister of the United Church of Christ. This chapter is from her book *The Committed Marriage* (The Westminster Press, 1976).

or homosexual relations, although they too can seize the initiative and use their sex as a sign of their freedom.

Among our youth, sexual relations are often the natural and "friendly thing to do," a means of getting to know someone more intimately and personally. Sometimes it is a protest against the depersonalization and materialism of our bureaucratic society, but certainly a natural and necessary part of human relations.

In the daily newspaper, sex is an ugly and aggressive side of our society. It is the rising incidence of rape of women on our city streets, the horrible sexual torture and murder of adolescent hitchhikers, or the perverted motive of the kidnapper or of the child molester.

For some, sex is the X-rated movie showing at the local drive-in, the topless waitress serving drinks at the all-night bar, the massage parlor or the go-go girl or the porno film at the stag club.

Sex takes a multitude of forms in our multifaceted society. From all sides couples receive the stimuli of its differing definitions. Unless they wish to fall victim to our society's warped views of sex, unless, as Ephesians puts it, they wish to be "tossed to and fro and carried about with every wind of doctrine, by the cunning of men, by their craftiness in deceitful wiles" (Eph. 4:14), couples must have, in this area too, a sure foundation for their relationship. Once again the word of God forms the rock upon which we can firmly build.

That sounds immediately repressive and prudish to a lot of couples, and not without reason. If any institution has a bad record of teaching with regard to sex, it is the Christian church. For centuries, the church abandoned the Scriptures and considered the sexual urge as evil. One has only to read some of the statements of the early church fathers to find how negatively they treated the subject.[1] To be sure, they defended marriage and procreation as good, over against those heresies such as Gnosticism which regarded fleshly life as evil, but the passion connected with the sexual urge always made it suspect. To give only one example, Roland Bainton describes Augustine's position this way:

> Since procreation is definitely approved, the sexual act as such cannot be wrong. Nevertheless it is never without wrong accompaniments. There is never an exercise of sex without passion, and passion is wrong. If we could have children in any other way, we would refrain entirely from sex. Since we cannot, we indulge regretfully. Augustine almost voices the wish that the Creator had contrived some other device.[2]

At the same time that it frowned on the passion of sex, the earlier church also exalted celibacy as a higher state, a position still held by Roman Catholicism today. In Protestantism, on the other hand, while there were occasional rejections of the physical relationship in marriage, even the Puritans affirmed the goodness of the sexual relationship.[3]

Nevertheless, there is in Protestantism another movement that has had a subtle effect on our views of sex. Whether we are conscious of it or not, we tend to value things spiritual more highly than things physical. This is a legacy we have received from Pietism. I shall never forget the time when our daughter was in kindergarten. Shortly before Thanksgiving, the teacher asked the class what they should be thankful for, to which our daughter innocently replied, "Money." "Well," responded the teacher hesitantly, "I'm not sure we should be thankful for money." Money, politics, jobs, sex—these are all of the material world, having little to do with spirituality and holiness and the higher reaches of the soul. We never think of a "spiritual personality" as being at the same time a sexual creature—hence our shock over Mary Magdalene's love song to Jesus in *Jesus Christ Superstar.* Sex and religion, to our way of thinking, are incompatible opposites.

In short, Protestantism too shares to some extent the view that sex is sinful, if not downright "dirty." Protestants therefore often react to sexual expressions in our society with a good deal of prudery. The worst sinner in our eyes is often the one guilty of a sexual offense, and we point first to increasing promiscuity as the sign of growing immorality. Indeed, sex and sin are often synonymous in our minds. It does not bother us half so much that people are proud or selfish as it does that they have committed some sexual trespass.

Human sexuality can be viewed in such fashion only by abandoning the Biblical faith. As we pointed out before, sex is understood as a good gift of God in both creation stories. In the first, God makes both male and female in his image (Gen. 1:27); the sexual distinction is built into the structure of creation, and God pronounces it "very good" (Gen. 1:31). In the second creation story, the woman is made from the rib of the man—originally they were one—and after the creation of the woman they long to become one again. Some commentators have suggested that Adam's ecstatic cry in Gen. 2:23, "This at last is bone of my bones and flesh of my flesh," follows upon his sexual union with his wife. Whether the text is to be interpreted in such a fashion or not, it witnesses strongly to the fact that sexual desire and oneness are good gifts of God, given to human beings out of God's love for them. Thus the Old Testament celebrates sex and stands in wonder before its mystery:

> Three things are too wonderful for me;
>   four I do not understand:
> the way of an eagle in the sky,
>   the way of a serpent on a rock,
> the way of a ship on the high seas,
>   and the way of a man with a maiden.
>   (Prov. 30:18-19.)

One entire book in the Old Testament, Song of Songs, is made up of nothing but love poetry, and some of that contains the most explicit sexual imagery. For example:

> How graceful are your feet in sandals,
>   O queenly maiden!
> Your rounded thighs are like jewels,
>   the work of a master hand.
> Your navel is a rounded bowl
>   that never lacks mixed wine.
> Your belly is a heap of wheat,
>   encircled with lilies.
> Your two breasts are like two fawns,
>   twins of a gazelle.
>   (Song of Songs 7:1-3.)

In Gen. 18:12, Sarah speaks of sexual intercourse as "pleasure" (cf. Ezek. 16:37; Ps. 147:10), and the word comes from the same root as that used for "Eden" or "paradise." In the New Testament, I Tim. 4:1 ff. attacks those who counsel ascetism, "who forbid marriage and enjoin abstinence from foods" (I Tim. 4:3). The reasoning is that "everything created by God is good, and nothing is to be rejected if it is received with thanksgiving" (I Tim. 4:4). In both Ex. 21:10 and I Cor. 7:3 ff., sex is necessary to marriage, and husband or wife is not to deny the mate conjugal rights. There is nothing in the Bible that would condone the Victorian commandment to wives to indulge in intercourse, but never, never to enjoy it. The Biblical writers revel in the goodness of God's creation, and sing and shout out their praise to God for the way he has made it.

It must also be realized that in the Biblical faith, there is never any split made between the material and spiritual worlds. In fact, Christianity is one of the most materialistic religions known to man. Consider, for example, how often the message of the New Testament centers around eating.[4] Or think of the earthly rewards that are promised to those who are faithful (Mark 10:29-31 and pars.; Deut. 28:1-14), or the emphasis put on the physical nature of the resurrection (Luke 24:36-43; John 20:24 to 21:14). Or consider that in the Kingdom of God, there will be eating and drinking (Mark 14:25 and par.; cf. Matt. 22:1-14 and par.). Think of all those times when Jesus healed not only souls but bodies. The stuff of the physical world is very much of concern to God, and while Jesus does not wish us to put our trust in material things, he is concerned with our material welfare and promises physical as well as spiritual wholeness (cf. Rev. 21:3-4). His healings, for example, are the firstfruits of life in the Kingdom of God.

In the Biblical view, human beings are always considered as psychophysical wholes. They cannot be split into separate parts of soul and body, mind and spirit. They are always one, with the whole person engaged in any act. When the psalmist hungers after fellowship with

God, it is with his flesh as well as his spirit:

> O God, thou art my God, I seek thee,
>   my soul thirsts for thee;
> my flesh faints for thee,
>   as in a dry and weary land where no
>   water is.
>
> (Ps. 63:1.)

The psalmist's flesh cries out in praise to God:

> How lovely is thy dwelling place,
>   O Lord of hosts!
> My soul longs, yea, faints
>   for the courts of the Lord;
> my heart and flesh sing for joy
>   to the living God.
>
> (Ps. 84:1-2.)

This flesh trembles before the awesome presence of the Lord:

> My flesh trembles for fear of thee,
>   and I am afraid of thy judgments.
>
> (Ps. 119:120.)

As these quotations show, a person's flesh is understood in The Psalms as one and synonymous with a person's being, and to talk about a person's spiritual relationship to God is at the same time to talk of that person's body. Deutero-Isaiah can therefore say that in the last days, all flesh will see the glory of the Lord (Isa. 40:5), all flesh will know that the Mighty One of Jacob is Savior and Redeemer (Isa. 49:26), all flesh shall come to worship before the Lord of Israel (Isa. 66:23). In such passages, "flesh" is synonymous with "person."

For this reason, the New Testament never speaks of the immortality of the soul, but only of that resurrection of the body in which the whole person is included. It knows nothing of a spiritualized Jesus, condemning all who would deny that the Son of God really lived life fully in the flesh (I John 4:2; II John 7). To speak of human beings in Biblical terms means to include the body, and when Paul opposes the life in the flesh to life in the Spirit, for example, in Rom., ch. 8, or Gal. 5:16-26, he is speaking not of separate parts of a person but of human beings redeemed or unredeemed. For Paul, too, human beings are one, and they are related to God not only in their spirit but also in their bodies, which are understood as an essential part of their being (Rom. 8:23; I Cor. 6:12-20). "Glorify God in your body," writes Paul (I Cor. 6:20), because it is the temple of the Holy Spirit. Human beings, to be understood in the context of the Biblical faith, must be seen as psychophysical wholes.

This means that the life of sex can never be separated, for the Christian, from the life of spirituality. It is fully as possible to violate or to fulfill our relation to God through sexual activity as through prayer or service. We are involved in what we do with our bodies and cannot separate our selves from their activities.

This is one of the reasons why the Biblical witness stands opposed to all "casual" views of sex. Premarital intercourse, or fornication, is uncompromisingly opposed (Ex. 22:16-17; Matt. 15:19; Acts 15:20, 29; 21:25; I Cor. 6:15-20; I Thess. 4:3-4), because it is an attempt to engage in sexual activity apart from the total commitment of the self in marriage, and that is a perversion of God's intention for us. In ancient Israel, the woman who engaged in premarital relations was stoned to death (Deut. 22:20-21), while a man was forced to marry any virgin whom he violated (Deut. 22:28-29). Today, such laws would pretty well decimate the population. But the point is that the Biblical writers will settle for nothing less than the involvement of the whole self in the sexual act. Thus, Israel also forbade bestiality (Lev. 18:23; 20:15-16; Deut. 27:21), that perverted act which would satisfy sex only as a biological urge and which would thereby turn a human being into an animal. We are not to use our bodies in a manner that would deny our spirit.

Indeed, Paul says that it is actually impossible to do so. We are always involved in every act we do with our bodies, and if we pervert the God-given function of our bodies, we pervert also our souls: "Do you not know that he who joins himself to a prostitute becomes one body with her? For, as it is written, 'The two shall become one.' . . . The immoral man sins against his own body. Do you not know that your body is a temple of the Holy Spirit within you, which you have from God?" (I Cor. 6:16, 18-19). Paul is arguing here that we may think we can indulge in sexual intercourse with no commitment of our inner selves, but actually our total self is involved and will be perverted by our immoral act. The truth of Paul's insight is perhaps evidenced by the fact that the result of illicit relations is often disgust, repulsion, even hatred of self, because the self has been so cheaply valued and used. It is also the case that premarital sexual relations often have a negative effect on subsequent marital relations, resulting in guilt or frigidity or other personality disturbances.

God does not intend us to descend to the level of animals, nor does he wish us to join bodies without joining lives. Karl Barth has put it this way:

> Coetus without co-existence is demonic. What are you, you man and woman who are about to enter into sexual relations? What do you really want of each other? What is your business with each other? What do you have in common? Is there any meaning in it? Is it demanded and sustained by your real life together? . . . This is the challenge of God's command in relation to this particular human

activity.[5]

On the basis of such arguments, however, some theologians have maintained that premarital or extramarital sexual relations are not improper if they truly involve the commitment of the self. The title of "the New Morality" has been given to such views, and they are represented by Harvey Cox in his earlier book, *The Secular City:*

By definition, premarital refers to people who plan to marry someone someday. Premarital sexual conduct should therefore serve to strengthen the chance of sexual success and fidelity in marriage, and we must face the real question of whether avoidance of intercourse beforehand is always the best preparation.[6]

Bishop J. A. T. Robinson concurs:

The decisive thing in the moral judgment is not the line itself [between marital or extramarital sex] but the presence or absence of love at the deepest level.[7]

Such views really leave couples standing on quicksand. They assume that a man and woman, inflamed by sexual desire, can judge whether or not love is present "at the deepest level," or whether or not premarital intercourse will better prepare them for marriage, or indeed, whether or not they are committed to each other at all. With our human propensity to rationalize in order to gain our own selfish ends, it is doubtful that couples in such a situation can make such judgment accurately. It can certainly be said, as we stated in Chapter 3, that couples before marriage have not really committed themselves to each other fully because they have not in fact acted out that commitment. They have not left father and mother behind and cleaved to each other alone. They have not taken on the responsibility of housing and clothing and feeding each other, of bearing each other's burdens and faults and of answering to society for each other. They have not become primarily responsible for the welfare and happiness of another human being, and they have not committed themselves irrevocably to a relationship that they cannot at some future point abandon. To enter into sexual relations with such a lack of commitment is therefore to pervert oneself, to misuse one's spirit by the misuse of one's body, to violate the intention God has for the relation of male and female.

If we ask just exactly what God's intention is for us in sexual activity, certainly we have to answer that procreation is one of his purposes (Gen. 1:28). Yet, in the Biblical witness, that is not God's primary purpose. The primary purpose of sex according to Genesis, and to Jesus, who quotes Genesis, is to unite two people: "The two shall become one. So they are no longer two but one. What therefore God has joined together, let not man put asunder" (Mark 10:8-9; Gen. 2:24). The function of sex is a unitive function. Sex is to be a "knowing," a way of intimacy that can be realized in no other way. Just as we know God in a unique way through the Sacraments, so also we know each other in a unique way through sexual intimacy.

At its best, sexual intercourse is a kind of flowing together: an overwhelming hunger and drive to join bodies as one, a feverish working together for realization, ecstasy so great it is almost painful, and then release, deep contentment and security and happiness in the arms of each other. In the process of sexual intercourse, we feel as if the most hidden inner depths of our beings are brought to the surface and revealed and offered to each other as the most intimate expression of our love. All we are as male or female becomes open to the other, and is made complete by being joined with the inner self of one's mate. We know each other and become one with the other and are fulfilled by each other in a way otherwise utterly impossible, and that knowing and that fulfillment carry over into our whole married life, and strengthen and deepen and periodically refresh it.

The Biblical writers witness to this unitive function of sex by the very vocabulary they use. Throughout the Old Testament, sexual intercourse is described as a "knowing": "Adam knew Eve his wife" (Gen. 4:1) or "Elkanah knew Hannah his wife... ; and in due time Hannah conceived and bore a son" (I Sam. 1:19-20). Indeed, this vocabulary is carried over into the language about God, and the intimacy of God's relation with his people is expressed by this "knowing":

> I am the Lord your God
>   from the land of Egypt;
> you know no God but me,
>   and besides me there is no savior.
> It was I who knew you in the wilderness,
>   in the land of drought.
>   (Hos. 13:4-5.)

In order to express the promise that he will redeem his people Israel in the future, God uses the metaphor of marriage: "I will betroth you to me in faithfulness; and you shall *know* the Lord" (Hos. 2:20, italics added). When Israel becomes a faithless adulterer toward her divine husband, it is said that then there is "no *knowledge* of God in the land" (Hos. 4:1, italics added).

We must be clear about how the Old Testament intends this sexual language, however. When it is used of God it is only metaphorical, and there is never any thought in the Bible that sexual intercourse can be revelatory of God, a fact that many contemporary writers on marriage have failed to realize, but a fact that is important for our understanding of sex. The reason for this, moreover, is very clear: Israel was surrounded on every side in the ancient Near East by peoples who practiced fertility rites in their religion. It was thought in those pagan religions, just as it is thought in many religions today, that the life of nature and of man were one, and that by the exercise of cultic prostitution, the fertility of nature could be magically coerced. Human fertility affected the fertility of the gods of nature. Through sex, it was thought, humans participated in the life of the divine. This thought is emphatically rejected by the Old Testament writers (cf. Hos. 2:2-13; Amos 2:7-8; Jer. 2:20-22, 2:23-28; 3:1-5; many other references). There is nothing of God revealed in the sexual act, and knowledge of him is not communicated in the mystery of sex. There is no doubt that the sexual life of human beings has a wonder and mystery about it, and the Biblical writers acknowledge this mystery, as we have said. They also warn us against calling that mystery "God," just as they warn us against giving God's name to anything in all creation (Ex. 20:4-6;Deut. 5:8-10). The teen-agers who think they have discovered something "divine" and beautiful in the backseat of an auto are not only kidding themselves; they are breaking God's commandments and blaspheming his holy name.

Sexual intercourse in marriage does bring with it knowledge of our mates and of ourselves, however, and that knowledge is such a profound communication and touches so deeply the center of our selfhood that it can be given in no other way. It is this which makes nonsensical so much of the sex education offered to our young people. We think we are going to teach them, openly and fully, about sex, and to be sure, the physiology, psychology, and theology of sex should be taught to them. But we delude ourselves if we think we have thereby exhausted the subject and prepared our young people fully. Try as we will, we cannot communicate the knowledge that is given in sexual intercourse.

This is one reason so many parents have difficulty talking about the sexual life with their children. They cannot express that which they have known, and in fact that knowledge is inexpressable outside of the situation. Yet, without the knowledge and communication that are given in sex, it seems like a bestial and abhorrent thing to many of our children. When confronted with the mechanics of sex, they often cannot believe that their parents would do such a thing. Sometimes they break into tears. And we parents are left stammering and stuttering in embarrassed confusion.

Perhaps the only way children can be taught about sex, having once been given the basic facts, is to see that their parents have a joyful and good conscience toward the subject. Then the children can believe that sex is good and that it is a mystery known only to married adults, who hold it in trust for them until they themselves marry and enter into it. Sex can only be presented to children fully as a promise to believe, because it involves a knowledge and communication of the self which children cannot possibly grasp.[8]

Because the sexual life of man and wife does involve this knowing, this communication of the self at its deepest levels, this also means that sex cannot be separated from the rest of married life. It is bound up with everything that husband and wife do in relation to each other. When sexual difficulties enter a marriage, they are very often symptoms of a deeper disturbance of the relationship. It must be emphasized, however, that this is not always true. There are some couples who simply lack essential sexual knowledge, or who suffer from specific fears or inhibitions and guilt as a result of childhood training or earlier experience. Just the common factors of fatigue and lack of time play an enormous role in sexual adjustment. Nevertheless, if a marriage is disturbed on other levels, new sexual techniques alone rarely will help it. Far too much emphasis has been placed on techniques and performance by popular articles and books. The sexual relation is only one part of the total marital relation. It alone can never carry or preserve the relationship, although it can certainly help. It is a tool that is given for the purpose of expressing the total relationship between man and wife, but it does express the relationship in a marvelous and joyful way, which adds to the intimacy and appreciation of a husband and wife for each other.

Sexual relations do not always have to be ecstatic and profound, of course. Sometimes they may be comfortably humdrum, or enchantingly playful. Patting, snuggling, touching, also deepen marital intimacy, and certainly are a pleasurable method of communication. Nevertheless they seem to mean most and are most satisfying, when the couple also are able at other times to enter into the ecstasy of orgasm. There is no substitute for the intimacy of that form of knowledge.

Because sexual intercourse is a means of communication at the deepest level, it is almost axiomatic that a couple cannot achieve their most satisfying sexual life together overnight. Sexual satisfaction, as with other forms of communication in marriage, is a gradual achievement, a process in which the couple learn and grow together in their appreciation and understanding of each other over the years. As in other areas, words are important here too—the frank and open discussion of each other's needs, of what is pleasant sexually and what is not, of any fears or problems that seem to interfere.

There is no marriage manual that can or should lay down rules for everyone. Every couple is different. Every individual has different needs, with respect to frequency, manner, and method of sexual activity. For example, some marriage manuals have held up simultaneous orgasm as the ideal for every couple, but it is perfectly possible to enjoy a satisfying sex life and never to have experienced such simultaneity. A wife may find that she needs the release of orgasm only occasionally and yet may thoroughly enjoy simply furnishing pleasure to her husband in between times. In sex, as in every other area of life, "the written code kills, but the Spirit gives life" (II Cor. 3:6). It is the heart, the love, the spirit of caring expressed by sex that is the most important. Trying to follow someone else's rules can turn the caring into an exercise in frustration. Sexual life, as all life, is given us as a good and merciful gift of God. He gives it to us that we may have joy —joy in the vitality that surges in us, joy in the closeness of the relationship with our mate, joy in the marvelous mystery that makes the two of us one, and binds us together in a unique and tender knowledge.

When a couple achieve such joy in such intimacy together, when through their years of living and working, of laughing and weeping, of celebrating and worrying together, they achieve that oneness of flesh that turns their marriage bed into a haven of security and tenderness and comfort, then they come to realize that God has indeed provided marvelously for them in marriage. They recoil in horror at the thought of ever spoiling that provision by breaking their covenant of faithfulness with each other. Inconstancy in the exercise of such a gift would be as horrible as if Christ were to say to his church, "I no longer faithfully love you; I am rejecting you and giving my love to another." That Christ would ever prove untrue is simply unthinkable. Equally unthinkable therefore should be the unfaithfulness of Christian mates, for Christ's love is the pattern of what our love for each other should be in marriage.

Unfortunately there are those who misuse and abuse God's good gift of sexuality. Rather than enjoying sex as a unique and tender means of loving communication, they employ it as an instrument of pride or power or aggression. We are all aware that some men use their sexual prowess as a tool of conquest. Whether we speak of the college man, sowing his wild oats among the local high school girls, or of the middle-aged man who sets out to prove that he is still sexually desirable to his secretary, we know that sex can be employed as a tool of power. There is no consideration in such a use of sex for the good of the other, much less of communication and lasting intimacy with her. She is being viewed simply as one to be conquered, like a trophy of war to be later exhibited and bragged over.

Females too are not exempt from the use of sex as a tool of power, for many are the women who employ their sexuality to manipulate a male. This is a use of sex that is widely advocated in American advertising, and women are urged every day to make themselves glamorous in order to control their men. ("Use Maybelline—for eyes a man can get lost in," or "Gentlemen prefer Hanes.") The women who seek such control give love or withhold it, in reward or punishment of their captive mates. Sometimes the marriage bed is turned into a battlefield, or the wife becomes a bait that always must be caught. As ludicrous as such games appear, they are widely practiced in the American home, and many are the subtle methods women use to set them up.

In any misuse of sex, it is obvious that the mate is considered little more than a thing. Certainly this is the case also where sex is pursued purely for selfish animal pleasure, where the physiological release afforded by orgasm becomes the all-important goal of one partner, apart from all consideration and concern for the needs of the other. Such selfish pursuit is little more than rape, and breeds in the partner so being used a feeling of disgust and repulsion.

Sometimes, in extramarital relations, sex is employed as a means of social approval, or even as a way of overcoming boredom. Similarly, sex can be an aggressive tool for wreaking vengeance on a lover or spouse or relative. ("If he's going to play around, then I'll show him two can play at this game.")

Perhaps we should also say a word about the perversion of God's gift of sex in homosexual relationships. Homosexuality has been loudly touted by radical members of women's liberation groups as a substitute for heterosexuality, and apparently it is freely practiced, not only within gay groups, but also in youth communes of various types. Certainly there is more acceptance of it in our society today than at any other time in our history. Some psychotherapists no longer consider it to be an illness, but simply a form of sexual behavior at variance with the norm. Homosexuality can assume as many forms as heterosexual relations and may be practiced for many differing motives. There is little doubt that some mature homosexual couples enjoy an intimate and loving relationship, in a lasting commitment to each other resembling heterosexual marriage. On the other hand, adolescent homosexual relations are usually of temporary duration, and within the women's movement, some homosexual relations are pursued purely for selfish physical pleasure.

Whatever the type of homosexual relationship involved, it is sheer fantasy to think that it can be an adequate substitute for the heterosexual relationship of a happy marriage. When a husband and wife know each other sexually, it is precisely their sexual difference which is communicated, both to themselves and to each other. They learn deeply what it means to be male and female, apart and together. The way male and female know each other is far different from the way male and male, or female and female, know each other. This is one of the stumbling blocks of the "sisterhood" of women's liberation. The "sisters" form close relationships, and the women may get along beautifully with each other. But they have not thereby developed that further communication of getting along with males or of entering into the most intimate relationship with the opposite sex, in the one-to-one intimacy of marriage.

For this reason, homosexuality, no matter how loving its nature (and far too often it is not loving at all, but a psychological aberration spawned by previous distorted relationships with parents in the home), must always be viewed as an aberration and often as a perversion of God's gift of sexuality. Certainly Paul understands it as an unnatural perversion (Rom. 1:26-27), and while we may not be as condemnatory as he, we should understand homosexuality as a use of sex not intended by God and therefore not finally to be encouraged or glibly accepted. One of the tragic aspects of modern gay groups is that they often lock young persons into lifelong homosexual behavior, when those persons might grow and change and eventually achieve the true intimacy and joy of a happy and heterosexual marriage.

The methods of misusing God's good gift of sex are almost numberless, but as someone has wisely said, the best way of guarding against the abuse of sex is to put it to its proper use.[9] That takes time, it takes words, it takes consideration and concern for one's mate. Above all it takes the love that cherishes and honors for a lifetime. Only those who responsibly use God's gifts inherit the joy that comes from them, but oh, how tender and unique is the knowledge that mates have of each other in their unity of one flesh!

NOTES

1. For brief but good presentations, see Roland H. Bainton, *What Christianity Says About Sex, Love and Marriage* (Association Press, 1957), or David R. Mace, *The Christian Response to the Sexual Revolution* (Abingdon Press, 1970).

2. Bainton, *op. cit.,* pp. 42-43.

3. *Ibid.,* pp. 93 ff.

4. See Mark 2:13-17, 18-22, 23-28 and pars.; 6:30-44 and pars.; 7:1-23, 24-30 and par.; 8:1-10 and par.; 9:49-50; 14:3-9 and par., 17-25 and pars.; Matt. 6:25-34; 22:1-14; Luke 12:35-46 and par.; 14:7-14; 17:7-10; 17:22-37.

5. Karl Barth, *Church Dogmatics,* III, 4, pp. 133 f.

6. Harvey Cox, *The Secular City* (The Macmillan Company, 1965), pp. 214-215.

7. John A. T. Robinson, *Christian Morals Today* (The Westminster Press, 1964), p. 42.

8. I am indebted for these insights concerning the sexual education of children to Helmut Thielicke, *The Ethics of Sex* (Harper & Row, Publishers, Inc., 1964), pp. 69 ff.

9. Mace, *Whom God Hath Joined,* p. 39.

2 The New Morality

by Gabriel Fackre

*Does situation ethics do
justice to facts and faith?*

Newspaperman Tom Wolfe reports on a recent visit to the planners of a popular television panel program:

> They showed me a big board with topics of prospective shows pinned up all over it. One of the topics was "Adultery—For or Against." One of the TV people told me, "We're having a problem with that one. We have some terrific people lined up to talk in favor of it. Norman Mailer and a lot of terrific people, but we haven't got anybody against!"[1]

The revolution in patterns of sex morality is too well known to require documentation. The old codes are being put into radical question by new theory and practice. An umbrella term for the changing style is "the new morality."[2]

Squeezed under this covering idea is a variety of notions as to what newness means. Two major theses are au courant, one expounded by an articulate "secular" spokesman, and the other finding its protagonists in the "religious" community. The first can be called the *detached new morality* and the second, the *involved new morality,* or for shorthand purposes, the *cool* and *warm* moralities.

COOL MORALITY

Hugh Hefner, *Playboy* magazine, and the Playboy Clubs around the country are the prophet, scripture, and church of the detached new morality. As Harvey Cox points out in his perceptive *"Playboy's* Doctrine of Male,"[3] the picture of masculinity that comes through the magazine's stories, advice columns, photographs, advertisements,

---

Gabriel Fackre is Professor of Theology at Andover Newton Theological School and a minister of the United Church of Christ. This chapter is adapted from *Storm Over Ethics* by John C. Bennett et. al. (United Church Press 1967).

cartoons is that of a cool, casual character who knows how to mix a drink with finesse, has just the right stereo set, sports car, and necktie, and makes use of these accouterments with skill and detachment. The call to prayer he hears from the muezzin in the *Playboy* tower is, "Play it cool, man."

The cool posture applies, of course, to sex. Sex is for fun. It's good recreation. It's play. A real man needs his collection of "playmates"—in his monthly magazine foldout, and in real life. The worst thing that could happen to him is to get involved, entangled in the clutches of a woman who wants to tie him down with talk of love or marriage. Principal target of ridicule is the traditional code morality, which is portrayed as somber anti-sex and anti-joy.

In the cool play notion of sex, the woman emerges, as Cox observes, as a kind of accessory. The real man has his "in" cuff links, stereo, sports car, and playmate. Each is to be used as long as it is in style and doesn't get worn out. When no longer fun as a plaything, it may be disposed of. A woman is detachable like other items in the playboy's ensemble. It's no accident that the "bunny" has become the chief symbol of the cool morality.

WARM MORALITY
Sex is not something about which you can be detached. It is a matter of deep personal involvement. So affirms the warm new morality.

The condition for the sex act, according to proponents of the involved new morality, is the wholehearted commitment of two people to each other. Sex cannot be torn from love. The casual, nonchalant, recreational use of a woman is dehumanizing. Where there is a humanizing, caring relationship between two people, there sex finds its proper home.

This powerful critique of the thingifying of sex has been part of the long history of Christian reflection on the meaning of the relations between men and women. What, then, is new about this version of the new morality? Joseph Fletcher puts it this way:

> We cannot dogmatize. . . . Any sexual act (hetero-, homo-, auto-) engaged in, in or out of marriage, will sometimes be good and sometimes be bad, depending on the situation. . . . Sex for procreation or sex in marriage only is to me . . . warmed-over natural law. . . . The new morality would deny this and say rather that the right of any sexual act is to be determined by responsible calculation in the situation, not by prefabricated calculations.[4]

Or again:

> This neocasuistry repudiates any attempt to anticipate or prescribe real-life decisions in their existential particularity. . . . We are always . . . commanded to act lovingly, but how to do it depends on our own *responsible* estimate of the situation. Only love is a constant;

everything else is a variable. Is adultery wrong? . . . One can only respond, "I don't know. Maybe. Give me a case. Describe a real situation."[5]

Agape, understood as a "benevolence," which seeks the deepest welfare of particular persons in particular situations is the one absolute for this "situational" sex morality. One gets a fix on the polestar of love and looks afresh at each new occasion in the light of it. The mandates in the Christian memory that have to do with hetero-, homo-, and auto-sex behavior are, of course, in the background as "social wisdom" or "maxims," but one holds this "prefabricated" baggage lightly, being guided essentially by the decision-maker's careful assessment of the meaning of love in each context, by "responsible calculation in the situation."

SOME FACTS OF LIFE

Since the love-oriented involved morality is an inviting alternative to the code rigidities of the past and speaks persuasively of the humanizing of sex, let us begin our evaluation of the new morality with this warm version. And the beginning will be a very homely one.

Several years ago, my family and I launched an experiment in the doing of household chores. Husband and wife and five children reasoned: In this busy world in which there is such a varied traffic pattern in the home—after-school Girl Scouts, choir, athletic programs, meetings, and different arrival and departure times for work and school—we could not possibly keep a rigid schedule for tablesetting, dishwashing, and cleaning responsibilities. The situation changed each day, and the situation of each person in the family was different. Why not then be fair about it and let each new day's context determine who does what? We became situationalists in our ethical theory. Let the doing of daily meal cleanup chores be determined by neighbor-love in each day's new context, a love which takes into account the needs and availability of each, seeking "the deepest welfare of particular persons in particular situations."

The experiment proceeded. Here is a typical slice of after-dinner conversation:

Mother: Well, Judy and Gabrielle have to get ready for Girl Scouts and Bonnie says she has a big test in English tomorrow that she has to study for, so I guess Skye is the logical one to wash the dishes tonight.

Skye: Mommy, I washed them last night! How come I have to wash them again? That's not fair. Bonnie always gets out of the hard jobs by saying she has homework or something. I've got homework too!

Judy: Oh, Skye, stop whining. I got cheated all last week when you were sick in bed with a cold. Actually, you

	could have done more then, but you goofed off.
Skye:	You be quiet! You haven't washed the dishes for three days. Besides you and Gabrielle aren't going to Girl Scouts until 6:45 and you both would have plenty of time to wash them. You're just giving excuses!
Gabrielle:	We are not, Skye. We are supposed to be in charge of the program tonight and we have to get all the leather tools lined up and everything.
Mother:	Bonnie, I just realized that you haven't washed the dishes now for a couple of weeks. Just when is your test?
Bonnie:	Well, it's really not for two days, but it's a very hard test and I have to start now studying for it.
Mother:	I thought you had it tomorrow! You can take fifteen minutes off and do the dishes. Skye has done them for the past two nights.
Bonnie:	But, Mother, I just can't! Do you want me to flunk the test?
Mother:	Well, you should have thought of that last night. You were downstairs watching "Hullabaloo" when you could have been studying.
Bonnie:	Mom, I'm going to flunk that test and it will be your fault!
Father:	Stop! I'll do the dishes.

Let me make a theological appraisal of what transpired. In seeking to operate with neighbor-love alone as a guide, certain things became apparent. To implement love in an open situation, there has to be objectivity in the assessment of the facts of the situation. Skye, for example, should be able to see that Judy and Gabrielle did, in fact, have many preparations to make for the Scout program. Not being in their shoes, however, she was unable to see it. Mom, not sitting in Mrs. Musselman's English class as Bonnie does every day, could not possibly understand the heavy assignment that did in fact require two days' work. People look at a situation from their own vantage point. And because this is so, no one (except God himself) can see all the facts that are necessary to be seen in order to decide what love dictates in a given situation. This is the human condition that Christian theology has called "creatureliness," or finitude. We human beings are finite, limited creatures shaped by our peculiar past and present. Everything we see, therefore, is colored by this partial perspective, a fact which is driven home every time a group of witnesses positioned at different points on a street give conflicting reports of an accident. What we see is not "the situation," but *our version* of the situation.

There is another factor that extrudes itself in the process of living with the situation. Bonnie indeed could have given up the viewing of

"Hullabaloo" the night before, knowing that she had an important test forthcoming, aware also that she had successfully avoided dishwashing for several weeks with her smallest sister Skye regularly absorbing the punishment of double duty. The fact is she chose to watch the TV program. Again, could not Gabrielle and Judy have done their preparation that afternoon instead of waiting until the last minute? Also, it is interesting to observe the self-righteous fury of Dad. A closer look reveals that he had a burdensome writing deadline to meet that night, and was looking for a good excuse to postpone it, and at the same time throw up a pious smoke screen around his irresponsibility. In short, our *personal interests* as well as our particular angle of vision enter into the definition of a situation in which one is counseled simply to mate love to fact. This, of course, is what Christian theology means by "sin." Its interesting subtleties are also evident in the way it expresses itself. No character in the little drama announces that he or she is selfishly asserting their own interests. No, each has a high-minded reason for the course of action taken—Bonnie is studying for a test, Gabrielle and Judy have "Girl Scout duties," and Dad is "bringing peace to the household." Such piety neatly obscures the personal interests at stake and demonstrates why self-righteousness is the most dangerous sin in the biblical catalog.

Eight months of the warm new morality in household affairs drove our family to a code of household conduct. On Mondays, "Judy, thou shalt do the chores"; on Tuesdays, "Bonnie, thou shalt do the chores", and so on. To live out neighbor-love in the household situation, to assure some degree of justice to all, and to avoid the chaotic result of ignoring our finitude and sin, we bound ourselves to a set of rules.

Certainly there are exceptions. When Judy is sick on Monday, or Gabrielle is at Girl Scout camp on Wednesday, the rules have to be set aside. There is a wise saying that there is an exception to every rule— and further, that the exception proves the rule. To acknowledge the fact of exception, however, is one thing. To erect that fact into an absolute which insists each situation is an exception allowing for no "prefabricated" rules, is quite another. In short, situationalism is a perfectly legitimate position if it is used itself situationally. This kind of *radical situationalism* applies its own judgment to itself: The theory cannot be made into an absolute, but is to be applied only in contexts where it is germane, and those contexts are the exceptions.

The great and good point made by the warm new morality is that human beings are the important thing in the Christian style of life. This is a telling blow against the detached posture of playboys. But the problem is not solved simply by affirming that neighbor-love is our absolute. The question remains: What in fact serves neighbor-love in sex relations? Does the assertion that we should get our heart in the right place first, and act responsibly in the situation, work to this end?

Indeed it would, if we were wise enough and good enough to see all the facts in a given situation and act accordingly. Humans, however, are not angels, with omniscience and purity. The *Time* magazine reporter commenting on Fletcher's entreaty not to be bound by "rules" but instead to seek out "in every decision-making moment" the neighbor's good observes, "Which is quite a long thought for an eighteen-year-old during a passionate moment in the back seat of a car."[6] This secular savvy neatly exposes the naivete of moral counsel which ignores basic facts of the human condition.

The role of codes in Christian teaching is to do precisely what situationalists plead for—to make and keep life human, yet to do it in full awareness of the facts of finitude and sin. The biblical commandment "Thou shalt not kill" was hammered out in the covenant community because the God of the covenant honored human life. The mandate "Thou shalt not commit adultery" is also a judgment derived from the conviction that there is something so precious about the sex relationship that anything less than faithful love is dehumanizing. We shall return shortly to these positives after canvassing further the rationale for the negatives.

THE LEGISLATION OF MORALITY

In its rejection of codes, the warm morality makes some strange bedfellows. The belief that "love will find a way" without benefit of law (sometimes Augustine's declaration "Love God and do as you will" is inaccurately quoted in support of this),[7] is not unlike the refrain heard currently from segregationists and others seeking to resist social change: "You can't legislate morality." The pious plea that accompanies this dictum is: Forget the laws and confine yourself to the task of changing hearts.

It is true that one cannot make a bad person good by a new law.[8] But one can keep a good person safe. A traffic law is not going to convert a reckless, thoughtless driver into a considerate, humane one, but it may well deter that driver from running someone down as the car screams to a halt before a red light. The point is that Christians cannot wait until they convert all the reckless drivers into Christians. We need to set bounds to the chaos and injustice that irresponsible people can inflict on society—hence the need for laws. In the case of the struggle for the dignity of black citizens, this means laws that will protect their elemental rights in voting, work, housing, and education from those who would deny them.

By the same token, moral law, as such, will not change a heart. Obviously we need more than legal mandate, particularly in Christian faith, which declares we are not saved by law but by grace. While law will not save, a generation that is nourished in respect for its wisdom will have some standards to keep its impulses in check. When we take as seriously the need to set boundaries to our self-love in personal sex morality as we do in public civil rights, the utopian assumption that all that is needed is to get one's heart in the right place is properly exposed. Law is not the enemy of love. It is the expression of it. This is as true in sex rights as it is in civil rights.

JESUS, PAUL, AND THE LAW

A favorite text of the warm morality is Mark 2:23-28—Christ's breach of a rigid interpretation of sabbath law, and his explanation of the action, "The sabbath was made for man, not man for the sabbath." Does not freedom in Christ mean this kind of freedom from the law for us as well?

There is a wealth of meaning in this passage. Ironically, its central intent may well be precisely the opposite of the interpretation given to it by the situationalist. The mechanical observance of the sabbath requirement, and the heavy barnacles of interpretation that grew up around it, had virtually obscured the central motif of the fourth commandment. The letter had killed the spirit. How does one shake people out of this mesmerism of the minutia? Christ opted for a demonstration in the grainfields in which the intent of the law was dramatized at the expense of attention to its details. The point made was that this ritual observance had a human meaning. It was on the books *for* humanity; the sabbath was made for human beings. Or putting it another way, love is the ground and goal of the law; Christ is Lord of the sabbath.

As well as pointing to the humanizing source of the law, this passage is an affirmation that rote observance of the letter, or its casuistic refinement, are not enough, for Christians are called to commitment to the Love that is the ground and Lord of the law. And further, it means that the motif of sabbath rest must be brought under the critical scrutiny of its source to assure that its going usage is indeed *for human beings.* In short, Christ is the fulfillment not the negation of the law. In the encounters with the rich young man and the adulteress, Christ does not disregard but presupposes law. The full power of his compassion is brought home in the latter case precisely because he takes adultery seriously as sin, yet finds it in his heart to accept the unacceptable sinner.

What then of Paul's insistence that we are not saved by the law, but by faith? Yes, this is a central theme of the gospel. To transcend law, however, is not to dissolve it, any more than the presence of the New Testament abolishes the significance of the Old. (There is an interesting correlation between the Marcionite rejection of the Old Testament and its lawgiver God in favor of a properly expurgated New Testament with its God of love, and the zeal to replace law by love in ethical theory.) Paul's declaration that the law is "holy, just, and good" is intimately related to his bout with it. Out of his own profound struggle to live up to the law (vis-a-vis the commandment against covetousness, for example, Romans 7:7-25), as that law was animated, internalized, and radicalized in love by the Lord of the law, Jesus Christ, he was driven to his knees in penitence. In that confrontation the world of divine mercy and the meaning of grace was born for him. Hence, law for Paul is a "schoolmaster" preparing us for the coming of grace, and in our half-and-half Christian life, *simul iustus et peccator,* serving as a continuing guideline.

Law is a fundamental theme in the teaching of Christ and Paul. To understand its penultimate role in the life of faith is no mean task, the difficulty of which is amply demonstrated by the constant appearance in Christian history of legalisms which seek to elevate it to ultimate significance as the way of salvation, on the one hand, and antinomianisms on the other, which eliminate it altogether on the grounds that faith and/or love render it unnecessary.

CODE, CREED, AND COMMUNITY

That no human being is an island is a familiar note in both contemporary theology and sociology. We are born, nourished, and become a person in the network of interrelations that make up the human community. So too, a human being is born, nourished, and becomes a believer in the supportive fabric of the faith community. The Christian faith community, in particular, speaks of the marriage of Christ to the church and disavows any individualistic claim that the Christian life can be fully authentic in abstraction from the Christian life together.

One expression of sensitivity to the corporate note is the use in Christian history of shared testimonies of faith. A "creed" is the fruit of communal reflection on the meaning of faith. To recognize the value of the classic confessions of faith, such as the Apostles' and Nicene Creeds, and the continuing need for the church to hone new statements of faith relevant to a changing world, is to affirm that Christians cannot simply write their own religious ticket. As a member of a larger community of Christians, you and I are partners in its heritage and its continuing struggle to bear a shared witness to its times. We do not operate "by our lonesome," developing our own version of Christianity in lordly isolation from our brothers and sisters.

A code, like a creed, is the product of the covenant community's reflection on its mandate. To take the communal dimension of Christian faith seriously in the sphere of morality is to respect the research the community has done, is doing, or ought to do, in that sphere as well as in the area of Christian doctrine. Where there has been a research consensus that points to code guidelines in sex ethics, a Christian committed to a communal view of faith will not lightly dismiss them. A "play-it-by-ear" morality that speaks of love finding its own way in each situation is really the same kind of rugged individualism in morality as the rejection of testimonies of faith is in the area of doctrine.

Neither takes seriously the organismic nature of Christian faith.

The need for developing new codes is as manifest as that of the need for restatements of faith. Where fantastic new moral questions surface, ones for which there is no fund of communal wisdom (such as the issues of prenatal genetic control, the creation of life in the laboratory, and the possibilities of the indefinite extension of human life with its attendant questions of "death management" and the like), the church has a responsibility to muster its reflective resources and develop guidelines for decision-making in these areas. No one is an island that can afford to neglect the insights of either the mainland of the human community or the faith community.

GOD'S KNOWING AND OURS

Up to this point we have dwelt on the negatives—the need for guidelines in sex ethics necessitated by the facts of creatureliness, sin, and community, and in faithfulness to the biblical teaching about law itself. The presence of a firm "no" has its roots ultimately in the biblical "yes" to sex. The fact that sex is precious, lovely—yes, fun!—is the positive at the heart of the matter.

"A man leaves his father and his mother and cleaves to his wife, and they became one flesh. And the man and his wife were both naked, and were not ashamed." That is not from *Never on Sunday* but from the Bible—Genesis 2:24-25. This frank and exuberant report is echoed in the biblical description of the sex act: "Adam knew Eve . . . Cain knew his wife . . . Elkanah knew Hannah." Sex is *knowing* another person. The mystery of the other's being is disclosed. The two are no longer separate, but are "one flesh." In the coming together of a man and a woman the secret of the universe is let out. The alienation that is everywhere apparent is challenged by the oneness here embodied. Mystics talk about knowing God in contemplative ecstasy, but the Bible speaks of knowing in the sex relationship. The Bible is an earthly document that speaks about an earthy God—creator of matter, enfleshed in Jesus, present now in the solidities of history and its institutions, and ultimately transfigurer of it—who is the farthest thing from the hazy spirituality of present or past gnostics. God is for humanity, and this means, in the present context, for sex.

The seriousness with which the Bible takes sex is manifest in commentary on its indelibility and the wound it leaves theologically when it is abused. Paul says, "Do you not know that he who joins himself to a prostitute becomes one body with her? For, as it is written, 'The two shall become one' " (1 Cor. 6:16).

Another thing comes clear in the biblical understanding of the one-flesh union. It is a jealous relationship, taking place between just two people. We do not hear about Adam and Eve and Jane, or Adam and Sam and Eve. Sex is a closed corporation. How is it possible to have this deep personal knowing passed around? The parallel here to the relationship with deity is striking. God does not tolerate competition. Separated by only a few lines are the declarations "The Lord your God is a jealous God" and "Thou shalt not commit adultery." In fact the Old Testament speaks of a person or nation faithless to God as one that goes "awhoring after other gods."

God seals the singular relation between his chosen people and himself with covenant vows. So, too, the one-to-one bond between a man and a woman is made firm in the covenant of marriage. As God's unconditional, steadfast love is promised through thick and thin, so the wedding vows mirror this in-spite-of love which persists through sorrow as well as joy, sickness as well as health, want as well as plenty. Again it is no accident that the marriage service begins with the moving words "Compared by St. Paul to the mystical union between Christ and his church," for the union between husband and wife is a broken reflection of the divine action itself. As Roger Mehl says:

> If scripture accords to marriage, among all other human institutions, an exclusive privilege, if it compares the love of a man for his wife to the love of Christ for his church, it is because it well perceives that mysterious bond between conjugal union and the kingdom, the prefiguration of reconciliation and the final recapitulation in this very humble, very banal, and very impure encounter of a man and a woman.[9]

CREATION AND PROCREATION

God is Redeemer and he is Creator. He knows and makes humanity. Marriage is a mirror of God's redemptive I-Thou love, and his creative love as well. The covenant union between two people is for knowing, and also for making. God is Creator. Humanity is procreator.

The Roman Catholic Church has long insisted that the basic reason for marriage is procreation. Its misgivings about birth control follow naturally. However, in the ferment of renewal current in the Roman communion there is being heard a growing plea to consider the profound significance of conjugal togetherness—one flesh knowing—as a companion purpose. If this receives formal endorsement, a reconsideration of the birth control position may eventuate.

Do we Protestant Christians have something to learn here from our Roman Catholic friends? If they are beginning to see the conjugal love dimension of sex—a point made strongly by Protestant Christianity —we ought to take a second look at their firm commitment to the bearing of children as a fundamental purpose of marriage.

Protestant Christians have always acknowledged the importance of the biblical injunction to "be fruitful and multiply." To take it with greater seriousness, as is urged by Paul Ramsey, is to shed considerable light on both the moralities of detachment and involvement. For one, any detached sex relation to another, embarked upon as simply a natural extension of the handshake, or for the gratification that goes with the use of a plaything, is a clear abuse of the purpose which includes responsible bringing of new life into the world. For another, to use the gift of procreation in a sexual relation outside of marriage on the grounds that it is a humanizing act of neighbor-love is as faithless to the procreative purpose of marriage as is the morality of detachment. The humanizing, neighbor-loving expression of sex *includes* the responsible bringing of life into the world, and its nurture in the bosom of a family (not in every sex act, of course, but as an intrinsic part of the total relationship of two persons in marital covenant). Whether sex is engaged in outside of marriage "for kicks" or "because we love each other," it plays havoc with the divine intent for a man and a woman to beget and take responsibility for the fruit of the womb.

Marriage in its creating as well as its redeeming dimension is a mirror of the life of God himself. God's creativity and divine love are, for Christian eyes, reflected in the procreativity and human love of a man and a woman sealed together in the marriage bond.

INSIGHTS OF THE NEW MORALITY

While we have dwelt here on the shortcomings of the new morality, cool and warm, implicit in this critique is an appreciation for the genuine biblical themes which are underscored by both in the face of their neglect by over-eager defenders of the old morality (the "hatpin brigade," as Hefner calls them). One such insight is the note of joy in the facts and processes of the created order, specifically the sex facts and processes. A somber puritanism is rightly criticized by all forms of the new morality, for it is more gnostic and docetic than Christian.

Another genuinely important accent of the involved new morality is its reminder of the "for human" style of the Christian faith. On the one hand, in its plea for persons it has helped to shape the indictment of the dehumanizing sex represented by the cool morality and all forms of human exploitation at work in the current "sexplosion." On the other hand, it has properly rebuked the thoughtless rote observance of law, and the authoritarian defense of it resorted to so frequently by proponents of the old morality. A healthy response to that attack is not blind defense of codes, but a serious look at their purpose and a consequent interpretation of the intent that lies behind the sex disciplines of the Christian community.

The corollary of this is the willingness to scrutinize all the moral baggage of the church, and all the new issues, in the light of the neighbor-love mandate. This will mean the restatement of inherited notions that have had a relevance in another day but no longer are instruments of neighbor-love. It will mean the development of guidelines for new kinds of decision-making pressed upon us by new moral issues for which there is no fund of research in the Christian treasury. And it will also reinforce our awareness that the higher law of love may require an exception to the very rules that are the normal structures of that love.

Another dissatisfaction properly aimed at the old morality, one inadequately developed by either version of the new morality we have here discussed, is its "angelism." A moral stance consisting simply of a plea to live up to the codes, or for that matter to live out "benevolence," which does not at the same time take into account the creaturely setting of the person who is so addressed (for example, his or her embeddedness in a ghetto where the normal family patterns are shattered by the long-standing scar of slave days, and where the desperation of slum-living and discrimination easily precipitate those not far advanced in saintliness into frenzied escape routes, the most convenient being promiscuous sex) is an unbiblical notion which assumes that a human being is a disembodied spirit, detached angel-like from the vicissitudes of physical-social rootage. While no one is a complete captive to the environment, loud moral exhortation is not the answer. On the basis of the doctrine of humanity as enfleshed spirit, Christian faith recognizes that the plight of the oppressed and disadvantaged cannot be overcome by pleading with them to pull themselves up by their bootstraps. We challenge the voting, housing, work, and educational patterns that are the springboards to their demoralization.

The same is true of those who abuse the gift of sex. From mass media that commercialize and exploit sex to the ghetto despair which propels its victims into the anodyne of promiscuity, the structures of society are indeed part of the question of sex morality. Any version of old or new morality which feels its job is done by finger-wagging entreaties is talking in the air to disembodied angels, not flesh and blood men and women, and consequently is irrelevant to the problems of human conduct.

BEYOND THE OLD AND NEW MORALITIES

"Neither . . . circumcision nor uncircumcision, . . . but Christ" (Col. 3:11, KJV). One who is in Christ is chained neither to the old legalisms nor to the latest "in" styles of thought and practice. The Christian believer is free enough to move into an open future, full of unresolved questions, free also to choose the yoke of discipline of the Body of Christ, a community whose research and wisdom is affirmed and honored. The believer is captive neither to the loveless code of the legalist, nor the codeless love of the new morality which has not adequately measured the depths of the human problem of creatureliness, sin, and individualism, nor the heights of knowing and making. True freedom is the way of faithful love, a love that finds its embodiment in a joyful, responsible, caring, sharing union—the one flesh mystery of a man and a woman in lifelong covenant.

NOTES

1. Tom Wolfe, "Speaking Out: Down with Sin!" *The Saturday Evening Post* (June 19, 1965), pp. 12 ff.

2. The fact that the phrase new morality is usually interpreted as new *sex* morality reveals our preoccupation with the private sector and gives force to the allegation that many today are in retreat from the great public issues of morality: war and peace, poverty, race. The attempt by some to restate the meaning of obscenity so as to include the public as well as the private arenas of morality is a wholesome corrective to this, as is the effort to place the question of sex in the context of the more wide-ranging public issues. In order to make contact with popular usage, and in recognition of the importance of sex ethics in its own right, I do confine my discussion of the new morality here to the issues raised by the new sex morality.

3. Harvey Cox, *"Playboy's* Doctrine of Male," *Christianity and Crisis,* XXL, 6 (April 17, 1961), 56-60, and available in reprint. Essentially the same treatment can be found in Harvey Cox, *The Secular City* (New York: Macmillan, 1965), pp. 199-204.

4. Joseph Fletcher quoted in James L. Hofford, "Harvard Conference on the 'New Morality,' " *The Christian Century,* LXXXII, 13 (March 31, 1965), 409.

5. Joseph Fletcher, *Situation Ethics: The New Morality* (Philadelphia: Westminster Press, 1966), pp. 29 f., 45, 142 f.

6. *Time,* LXXXV, 10 (March 5, 1965), 44.

7. Cf. the exegetical discussion in Lindsay Dewar, *Moral Theology in the Modern World* (London: A. R. Mowbray & Co., Ltd., 1964), pp. 51 ff.

8. Even this is an oversimplification, for because of our creaturely rootedness in social, economic, and political institutions, changes in the latter structures do influence readiness for ideational growth.

9. Roger Mehl, *Society and Love,* trans. James H. Farley (Philadelphia: Westminster Press, 1964), p. 211.

3 Scriptural Primacy

by Donald G. Bloesch

A conflict that had already emerged in biblical times concerns the relation between the written Scriptures and the rabbinical and ecclesiastical traditions. Jesus himself made the Scriptures the ruling norm.[1] The Pharisees on the other hand added their traditions to the Scriptures while the Sadducees subtracted the supernatural from Scripture. Jesus accused the Pharisees of making the word of God void (Mark 7:13; Matt. 15:6) and reprimanded the Sadducees for being ignorant of it (Mark 12:18-27).

For the most part both the patristic fathers and the medieval theologians before the fourteenth century taught that the Bible is the unique and sole source of revelation.[2] To be sure, it was generally assumed that the Scriptures need to be supplemented and interpreted by the church tradition. In the Eastern church it was believed that the *Philokalia,* an anthology of patristic texts on prayer, clarifies and illumines what the Bible holds in secret and which cannot be easily grasped by our limited understanding. Yet the traditions of men cannot add anything new to what is already contained in the Scriptures, either explicitly or implicitly. The priority of Scripture over tradition was clearly enunciated by Thomas Aquinas: "Arguments from Scripture are used properly and carry necessity in matters of faith; arguments from other doctors of the Church are proper, but carry only probability; for our faith is based on the revelation given to the apostles and prophets who wrote the canonical books of the Scriptures and not on revelation that could have been made to other doctors."[3]

In the fourteenth and fifteenth centuries, with the rise of nominalism and the flowering of mysticism, an appeal was made not only to Scripture but also to mystical experience and the church tradition. Roman Catholic theologians came to speak of a parallel source of truth—the

Donald G. Bloesch is Professor of Systematic Theology at Dubuque Theological Seminary and a minister of the United Church of Christ. This chapter is from his book *Essentials of Evangelical Theology,* Vol. 1 (Harper & Row, Publishers, 1978).

oral tradition which continues in the history of the church. According to Gabriel Biel, Scripture and tradition should be held in equal esteem. Heiko Oberman contends that this was also the view of the Council of Trent, though some contemporary Catholic theologians are of the mind that Trent made no decision on this matter.[4] In late medieval theology it was also assumed that the church authenticates Scripture and therefore has a certain primacy over Scripture. In the words of Duns Scotus: "The books of the holy canon are not to be believed except insofar as one must first believe the church which approves and authorizes those books and their content."[5]

Many Catholic scholars today (including Karl Rahner, Hans Küng, Yves Congar, and George Tavard) speak of only one source of revelation, sacred Scripture. While contending, however, that all the truth of salvation is contained in Scripture, they affirm that the teaching office of the church gives the authoritative interpretation of Scripture. Yet although the church tradition interprets the truth of revelation, it does not create this truth. Congar goes so far as to declare, "Scripture has an absolute sovereignty."[6]

Against the prevailing view in their time that church tradition is on a par with Scripture, the Reformers resolutely maintained that there is only one source of revelation, Holy Scripture. Scripture, moreover, contains not only the revealed, divine truth but the *whole* revealed truth. For the Reformers the church is under the Word and simply attests and proclaims it but does not authorize it. "The church of God," said Luther, "has no power to establish any article of faith, and it neither has established nor ever will establish one."[7] Augustine had declared: "I should not believe the gospel except as moved by the authority of the Catholic Church."[8] Calvin explains that when this remark is seen in its proper context it is clearly understood that Augustine was not maintaining that Scripture is authenticated by the church but only that Scripture has its most potent appeal when reverence is given to the church as well.[9] Luther also seeks to interpret Augustine's statement in an evangelical sense, but in the "papist" sense, he says, it is "false and un-Christian. Everyone must believe only because it is the word of God, and because he is convinced in his heart that it is true."[10]

Luther gave poignant expression to the newly emerging consensus of the Reformation when he referred to the Word as the judge and creator of the church. At one place he pointed to Scripture as the light and the church tradition as the lantern. He spoke approvingly of Bernard of Clairvaux who said that he would rather drink from the spring itself (the Scriptures) than from the brook (the fathers of the church). For Luther and other Reformers, as well as for Bernard, the brook is helpful mainly in leading us back to the spring.

The Reformers intended not to denigrate the church, but to make clear that the church must be a servant of the Word, not its master. They were even willing to affirm that the true church, the church which subordinates itself to the Word, is infallible, though this infallibility is derivative and relative. Zwingli declared that the true church "depends and rests only upon the word and will of God. . . . That Church cannot err. . . . That is the right Church, the spotless bride of Jesus Christ governed and refreshed by the Spirit of God."[11] And as Luther put it: "The church cannot err for the Word of God which it teaches cannot err."[12]

Against their Catholic opponents the Reformers contended that Scripture authenticates itself and interprets itself. It gains its credence neither from the church nor from reason but from the One to whom it testifies and who is himself its living center, Jesus Christ.[13] By the power of his Spirit it is able to impress upon the minds of its readers and hearers the trustworthiness of its doctrine and the urgency of its message (cf. Luke 24:32; 2 Tim. 3:15, 16). It is not Scripture in and of itself but Scripture ruled and imbued by the Spirit of God that convicts people of their sins and convinces them of the truth.

The Reformers also staunchly affirmed the perspicuity of Scripture, its inherent clarity. They meant by this that its basic message is clear even to the unsophisticated layman, and therefore every person can go to the Bible directly to search and find the truth. The doctrinal mysteries need to be expounded by theologians so that one can perceive them rightly, but everything necessary for salvation is plainly attested in the Scriptures. The language in certain parts of Scripture will also prove difficult to the layman, but God's truth shines through even obscure terminology. Luther maintained that the clearness of Scripture is twofold: the one kind is external, referring to the objective testimony in Scripture and the other internal, referring to the illumination of the Spirit.

> If you speak of the *internal* clearness, no man understands a single iota in the Scriptures by the natural powers of his own mind, unless he have the Spirit of God; all have obscure hearts. The Holy Spirit is required for the understanding of the whole of Scripture and of all its parts. If you allude to the *external* clearness, there is nothing left obscure and ambiguous, but all things brought to light by the Word are perfectly clear.[14]

In neo-Protestantism the consciousness of the ecclesial community again came to take precedence over the Scriptures. For Schleiermacher the Holy Scripture as the witness to Christ is subject to the judgment of "the corporate spirit." It is the result of faith, not the basis of faith. Culture came to be seen as a source or norm of theology in addition to Scripture.

Modern neo-Catholicism reflects a similar orientation. Karl Rahner, for example, refers to the church's "awareness of faith" as "a theological supreme court."[15] Avery Dulles holds that the living magisterium is endowed with authority from Christ to interpret rightly the Word for the community.[16] In some neo-Catholic circles reference is made to the infallibility of the people of God, which takes precedence over the infallibility of the Word.

Against both Roman Catholicism and neo-Protestantism the dialectical theology vigorously asserted the primacy of Scripture over the church as well as over religious experience. Karl Barth declared: "Scripture is in the hands but not in the power of the Church."[17] It was his conviction that

> the Church is most faithful to its tradition, and realizes its unity with the Church of every age, when, linked but not tied by its past, it today searches the Scriptures and orientates its life by them as though this had to happen today for the first time. And, on the other hand, it sickens and dies when it is enslaved by its past instead of being disciplined by the new beginning which it must always make in the Scriptures.[18]

Dietrich Bonhoeffer, who shared with Barth a dynamic view of revelation, also subordinated the church to the criterion of the divine Word in Scripture:

> The Word of God seeks a *Church* to take unto itself. It has its being *in* the Church. It enters the Church by its own self-initiated movement. It is wrong to suppose that there is so to speak a Word on the one hand and a Church on the other, and that it is the task of the preacher to take that Word into his hands and move it so as to bring it into the Church and apply it to the Church's needs. On the contrary, the Word moves of its own accord, and all the preacher has to do is to assist that movement and try to put no obstacles in its path.[19]

In identifying ourselves with the theology of crises over neo-Protestantism and Roman Catholicism we do not mean to deprecate the role of the church or deny the movement of the Holy Spirit in the church. Yet while Scripture is inspired by the Spirit, the church is assisted by the Spirit (Max Thurian). The role of the Spirit is to awaken the church to the truth contained in the Scriptures and then to empower the church to proclaim this truth. With the Reformers and the dialectical theologians, we contend that Scripture when illumined by the Spirit authenticates itself. The church simply recognizes the truth that Scripture upholds and then applies this truth to the world.

Our position is that the Spirit both indwells the church and judges the church by the Word. The Word functions normatively over the church as the Sword of the Spirit. With Berkouwer we have definite reservations concerning the contention of Roman Catholic scholars that the Spirit is the church's immanent life principle, since this seems to deny the transcending, judging role of the Spirit. An American Benedictine Kilian McDonnell reflects Reformation motifs when he declares: "The Word always calls the church and constitutes it. And having constituted it, warns, judges, purifies, strengthens, nourishes, edifies it."[20]

Evangelical theology holds that Scripture has primacy not only over the church but also over religious experience. The Word, said Luther, must be believed "against all sight and feeling and understanding." The Word must indeed be experienced, but this is the experience of faith itself, which transcends the reach of man's perception as well as the power of man's conception. Moreover, the experience of faith is forever critical of itself as an experience and always points beyond itself to the Word. Luther averred that our theology is certain because "it snatches us away from ourselves and places us outside ourselves, so that we do not depend on our own strength, conscience, experience, person, or works. . . ."[21]

This brings us to the perennial misconception that Reformation theology elevates the individual conscience as the ultimate authority. In the words of Forsyth: "The Reformation . . . stood not for the supremacy of conscience, but for the rescue of the conscience by the supremacy of Christ in it."[22] Luther averred that his conscience was bound to the Word of God, and this is why he could not go against conscience. In evangelical theology the authority for faith is nothing in us but something within history (Forsyth). It is the voice of the living God speaking to us in the sacred history mirrored in the Scriptures. This voice to be sure also speaks to us in our conscience, but its basis and origin are beyond man's conscience and imagination. Conscience, like experience, can be a trustworthy guide only when it is anchored in the divine revelation given in Holy Scripture.

In addition we affirm the primacy of Scripture over dreams, signs, and wonders. Also to be included in this connection are proofs and evidences of the faith. In the book of Deuteronomy we read that a prophet or dreamer of dreams who gives a sign that comes to pass must not be listened to if what he says contradicts the word of God (13:1-5). Forsyth gives a timely warning on seeking after proofs and empirical evidences for faith:

> They are tests of nature and not of faith, tests of feeling rather than insight, tests of empirical experience instead of soul experience, of success rather than of devotion. We withhold full committal till we have tested things in life. We make no inspired venture of faith, but we put Christ on His mettle to see if He is effective in thought or practice. We turn pragmatists and trust Christ because He works; which may come suspiciously near to trusting Him because it spiritually pays and enhances our spiritual egoism.[23]

Signs and wonders have a place in the life of faith, but they are to be seen not as the basis for faith but as illuminations of the truth of faith for those who already believe (cf. Rom. 15:19; II Cor. 12:11-13; Heb. 2:4). We are not to seek after signs or put God to the test, but we should be open to the signs which he is already working for his people. The most authentic signs are those that form part of the message of faith itself, such as the resurrection of Jesus Christ from the grave. In this light we can understand these words of our Lord: "This generation is an evil generation; it seeks a sign, but no sign shall be given to it except the sign of Jonah" (Luke 11:29).

Likewise we must resist any claim to a new revelation, one that completes or even supersedes Scripture and does not merely illumine or clarify Scripture. Various cults and sects have arisen in the modern age which in effect deny Scripture as the original and fundamental vehicle of divine revelation, the sole and unique source of saving truth. We can here mention Mormonism, Christian Science, Anglo-Israelism, the Unification Church of Sun Myung Moon, the Church of the Living Word, Bahaism, and to a lesser degree Seventh Day Adventism and the Community of True Inspiration.[24] Against these new religions we affirm with Luther: "No one is bound to believe more than what is based on Scripture."[25] We also concur with Watchman Nee's timely word of wisdom: "All the revelation today is but the light regained from the word of the past."[26]

Again, we must assert the primacy of Scripture over culture. Too often in the past theologians have drawn upon the creative thought of their culture as well as the Bible in constructing their theology. Although Albrecht Ritschl believed that theology should derive its content from the New Testament and from no other source, he in fact unwittingly accepted the guiding principles of the then current philosophy (Kantianism) including the conflict of man with nature and the need to gain mastery over nature. Schleiermacher, in his *Speeches on Religion,* upheld not the biblical Christ, the divine Savior from sin, but a cultural Christ, the principle of mediation between infinite and finite. Karl Barth on the contrary was strident in his criticisms of what he termed culture-Protestantism and contended that the basic content of our faith must be derived from Scripture alone (*sola Scriptura*). For him culture is not a norm or source for theology but the field in which theology functions and addresses itself.

In concluding this section on Scriptural primacy, we must bear in mind that the ultimate, final authority is not Scripture but the living God himself as we find him in Jesus Christ. Jesus Christ and the message about him constitute the material norm for our faith just as the Bible is the formal norm. The Bible is authoritative because it points beyond itself to the absolute authority, the living and transcendent

Word of God. Against both fundamentalism and the old Catholicism we do not conceive of the authority of Christian faith in heteronomous terms. Our authority is not an external standard that impresses itself upon the soul, but a Word from God that enters into the depths of the soul and creates its own response. As Forsyth put it:

> The authority in theology is not external to the matter it works in. It is spiritual. It is inherent in the fontal fact, and connate to the soul. It belongs to the revelation as such, and not to any voucher which the revelation created, like a book or a church. It is an authority objective to us in its source, but subjective in its nature and appeal.[27]

We must go on to affirm, however, that the absolute authority of faith, the living Christ himself, has so bound himself to the historical attestation concerning his self-revelation, namely, the sacred Scripture, that the latter necessarily participates in the authority of its Lord. The Bible must be distinguished from its ground and goal, but it cannot be separated from them. This is why Forsyth could also say: *"The Bible is not merely a record of the revelation; it is part of the revelation.* It is not a quarry for the historian, but a fountain for the soul."[28]

Jesus Christ is the one who speaks, the message of the Bible is the word that he speaks within history, and the church is the mouth through which he speaks. Just as the church is subordinated to the Bible, so the Bible in turn is subordinated to Jesus Christ, who embodies the mind and counsel of God. To put it another way, the church is the phonograph by which we hear the voice of Christ on the record, the Scriptures.[29] To carry the illustration further, it is the Holy Spirit who sets the phonograph in motion. The authority of the Bible is operative within the context of the church by the action of the Spirit. Where these analogies fall down is that Christ is free to speak his Word in a slightly different way for every age and culture, though he remains faithful to the Word that he uttered once for all in the history of the biblical revelation.

Forsyth points to this higher criterion within the Bible, the canon within the canon, when he says: "The gospel of God's historic act of grace is the infallible power and authority over both church and Bible. It produced them both. They both exist for its sake, and must be construed in its service."[30] The ruling criterion of the Gospel, however, must not be construed as referring only to particular sections of Scripture, but it is either implicit or explicit in the whole of Scripture.

The authority and infallibility* of the Bible as well as of the church are derivative, having their basis in Christ and his Gospel. We must listen to the dictates of the Bible and also to the counsel of the universal church because they have their ultimate sanction in God himself. When these authorities seem to disagree, this means that we have not really made contact with the real Word of Scripture or the true head of the church, who are one and the same. We must subject the discordant voices that we hear to Christ's self-witness within the Scriptures thereby bringing a transcendent norm to bear upon the point of contention. Yet this transcendent norm is not within our possession: to hear the voice of the living Christ is a miracle of grace which we can hope and pray for but cannot take for granted.[31]

*In the next section of his book Dr. Bloesch says that infallibility refers to "the doctrine or message of Scripture," to "Scripture illumined by the Spirit." He advises, "this does not mean that they [the biblical writers] were faultless in their recording of historical data or in their world view. . . ." (Vol. 1, p. 65).

NOTES

1. It should be recognized that Jesus' ultimate criterion was not Scripture by itself but the Scripture and the Spirit together. He said that the Sadducees erred because they knew "neither the scriptures nor the power of God" (Mark 12:24; cf. Jn. 5:39, 40; 14:15-17).

2. See George Tavard, *Holy Writ or Holy Church* (New York: Harper & Row, 1959), p. 22 f.

3. Thomas Aquinas, *Summa Theologica* I, 1, 8.

4. See Heiko Oberman, *The Harvest of Medieval Theology* (Grand Rapids: Eerdmans, 1967), p. 406 f. Also see his "The Tridentine Decree on Justification in the Light of Late Medieval Theology" in Robert W. Funk, ed., *Journal for Theology and Church,* vol. 3 (New York: Harper & Row, 1967), pp. 28-54.

R. J. Geiselmann argues that Trent really did not have anything to say about the relationship between Scripture and tradition. He says that Trent did not mean to teach a theory of two sources of revelation. The final report of Trent read: "Scripture *and* tradition"; the original reading was "partly Scripture . . . partly tradition." See Geiselmann, *Die Heilige Schrift und die Tradition* (Freiburg: Herder, 1962).

Lennerz argues against Geiselmann that the alteration did not represent a material revision of the original report. But many Catholic scholars including Karl Rahner and Hans Küng are now speaking of only one source of revelation, sacred Scripture.

For an illuminating account of the recent discussion in Catholic theology see G. C. Berkouwer, *The Second Vatican Council and the New Catholicism,* trans. Lewis B. Smedes (Grand Rapids: Eerdmans, 1965), p. 89 f.

5. Quoted in Lev Shestov, *Athens and Jerusalem,* trans. Bernard Martin (Athens, Ohio: Ohio University Press, 1966), p. 298.

6. Yves Congar, *La Tradition et les traditions* II (Paris: Artheme Fayard, 1963), p. 176.

7. Luther, *Werke,* W.A., 30, II, p. 420.

8. Augustine, "St. Augustin: The Writings Against the Manichaeans and Against the Donatists" in *A Select Library of the Nicene and Post-Nicene Fathers,* ed. Philip Schaff, vol. 4 (Grand Rapids: Eerdmans, 1956), p. 131.

9. John Calvin, *Institutes of the Christian Religion,* ed. John T. McNeill, trans. Ford Lewis Battles (Philadelphia: Westminster Press, 1960), I, 7, 3, pp. 76-78.

10. *Luther's Works,* ed. E. Theodore Bachman, vol. 35 (Philadelphia: Muhlenberg Press, 1960), p. 151.

11. S. M. Jackson, ed., *Selected Works of Huldreich Zwingli* (Philadelphia: University of Pennsylvania, 1901), pp. 85-86.

12. Luther, *Werke* W.A. 51, p. 518.

13. The Christocentric orientation of the Reformation doctrine of Scripture is ably delineated in J. K. S. Reid, *The Authority of Scripture* (New York: Harper & Row, 1957), pp. 29-72.

14. In Heinrich Schmid, ed., *Doctrinal Theology of the Evangelical Lutheran Church,* 3d ed. rev. (Minneapolis: Augsburg Publishing House, 1961), p. 73.

15. In L. Bruce Van Voorst, "Follow-up on the Küng-Rahner Feud," *The Christian Century* (Aug. 25, 1971), [pp. 997-1000] , p. 999.

16. Avery Dulles, *Models of the Church* (Garden City, N.Y.: Doubleday, 1974), p. 81.

17. Karl Barth, *Church Dogmatics* I, 2, p. 682.

18. Karl Barth, *Church Dogmatics* II, 2, p. 647.

19. Dietrich Bonhoeffer, *The Cost of Discipleship,* rev. and unabridged ed. trans. R. H. Fuller (London: SCM Press Ltd., 1959), p. 225.

20. Kilian McDonnell, *John Calvin, the Church, and the Eucharist* (Princeton, N.J.: Princeton University Press, 1967), p. 358.

21. Martin Luther, *Luther's Works,* vol. 26 ed. Jaroslav Pelikan (St. Louis: Condordia Publishing House, 1963), p. 387.

22. P. T. Forsyth, *The Gospel and Authority* ed. Marvin Anderson (Minneapolis: Augsburg Publishing House, 1971), p. 172.

23. P. T. Forsyth, *The Principle of Authority* (London: Independent Press Ltd., 1952), p. 335.

24. Though some of these groups uphold the infallibility of Scripture they regard continuing revelation through the gift of prophecy as on a par with Scripture if not superseding Scripture.

25. *Luther's Works,* vol. 32 ed. George W. Forell (Philadelphia: Muhlenberg Press, 1958), p. 96.

26. Watchman Nee, *The Ministry of God's Word* (New York: Christian Fellowship Publishers, 1971), p. 67.

27. P. T. Forsyth, *The Principle of Authority,* p. 396.

28. P. T. Forsyth, *The Gospel and Authority,* p. 25.

29. Another pertinent illustration is the church as the lamp, the Bible as the light bulb, and Christ as the light. The light comes to us only through the vehicles of the light bulb and lamp, but apart from the light these have little value.

30. *Ibid.,* p. 17.

31. It should be borne in mind that the voice of the living Christ cannot be divorced from either the Scriptures or the church. This voice is none other than the Word of God in the Scriptures which speaks to and through the church in every age.

4 Questions On Exegesis and Hermeneutics

by Gerald M. Sanders

The purpose of this essay is to raise some questions about the exegetical conclusions and hermeneutical principles used in the study on human sexuality produced by the Board for Homeland Ministries of the United Church of Christ as it addresses the issue of homosexuality in the Old Testament. The essay hopefully will lead to a real dialogue about certain assertions made in the work *Human Sexuality: A Preliminary Study* and its handling of relevant Old Testament materials. This essay intends to raise questions about the viewpoint in the *Study* which seeks to debunk the traditional approach to the Sodom and Gomorrah stories. The essay will offer a critique of the hermeneutical approach taken by the *Study* as it deals with the Levitical Codes and raise additional questions to assist an on-going dialogue on this topic. The examination will conclude with a comment on the hermeneutical basis offered for the abandonment of the traditional exegesis of the Sodom and Gomorrah stories.

In *Human Sexuality: A Preliminary Study,* the account of Sodom and Gomorrah in Genesis undergoes a critical exegetical examination to determine the transgressions which brought about the destruction of the two cities. The general thesis of the *Study* is that inhospitality is possibly the real sin and that homosexuality was probably not involved. Whether homosexuality was or was not involved, a violation of hospitality was involved, a serious offense in Middle Eastern culture even today and the biblical student should take note of this fact. It is not unlikely that homosexuality was also part of the story of Sodom and Gomorrah even though the *Study* devotes some length to the refutation of homosexuality as a factor.

According to the *Study,* "The ancient and traditional interpretation is well known but merits repetition even for those who believe it is a valid interpretation" (p. 69). The *Study* repeats what the basic

Gerald M. Sanders is the Pastor of the Church Of The Master U.C.C. in Hickory, North Carolina, Vice-President of the United Church People for Biblical Witness, and has an M.A. in Philosophy.

claims of the traditional interpretations are but fails to give the rational for the traditional interpretation. This means that an apologetic for the traditional viewpoint is absent from the *Study*.

Considerable length is devoted in the *Study* for an apologetic of a new interpretation of the Sodom and Gomorrah story. This apologetic merits consideration to determine if the new mode of interpreting this story has adequately dealt with the older mode of interpretation.

The basic claims of the *Study* regarding the account of the Sodom and Gomorrah story are based upon a word study of the Hebrew *yadha* and the absence of homosexuality in the list of Sodom's sins when the city is mentioned in other parts of the Scriptures.

The following is a quotation from the *Study* as it deals with the aforementioned word study.

> In the Hebrew-English lexicon of the Old Testament the word *yadha* is used 943 times and ordinarily means "to know" in the common sense of that word. Apart from this disputed Genesis 19:5 text (and its derivative in Judges 19:22), *yadha* is used without qualification to mean engage in coitus only ten times out of 943. And in such cases, aside from the two exceptions just mentioned, it refers to heterosexual intercourse. The verb used in those instances where the Old Testament refers to either homosexual intercourse or bestiality is *shakabh* (not found in this passage). Linguistically, it is only a rare and singular chance that the verb means homosexual intercourse in this story. Probably it simply means to know, to identify the strangers, to find out who they are (pp. 69-70).

There are several problems in the above quotation which demand to be addressed. The comparison of the Hebrew verbs *yadha* and *shakabh* by this contributor to the *Human Sexuality Study* is very inadequate. The material used by the *Study* does not call attention to the complete way in which the word *shakabh* is used throughout the Old Testament. The literal meaning of *shakabh* is to lie with or lay down. Incidentally, this is the most common use of the word and its use to denote sexual intercourse is limited. The *Study* leads one to conclude that *shakabh* is used exclusively to denote homosexual intercourse or bestality when it states, "The verb used in those instances where the Old Testament refers to either homosexual intercourse or bestiality is *shakabh* (not found in this passage)" (pp. 69-70). Although the contributor to the *Study* does not footnote where in the Old Testament the term *shakabh* is so used, this writer will assume that the contributor to the *Study* has in mind Leviticus 20:13 and 20:15. In both of these passages the term used is *shakabh*. It is true that this is the term used to describe homosexual intercourse and bestality; however, it should be noted that in the same pericope *shakabh* is used to describe heterosexual intercourse. *Shakabh* is a verb that is used to describe intercourse and not just homosexuality or bestality. Its use is not selective in reference to gender relationships but is used to describe both heterosexual and homosexual intercourse and as such has no linguistic bearing to discount the traditional mode of interpreting the Sodom and Gomorrah story. The fact that the same verb is used to describe intercourse between heterosexuals or homosexuals could lend credibility to the traditional interpretation of Sodom and Gomorrah since it implies that *yadha* could also mean either heterosexual or homosexual intercourse.

In the consideration of the use of *yadha* in the pericope on Sodom and Gomorrah in Genesis 19, the following should be noted, which is in contrast to the apologetic offered in the *Study*. First, it can be seen in the above paragraphs that there is no specialized term for homosexual intercourse in the Levitical codes; hence the citing of the absence of the word *shakabh* has no bearing upon this text. Second, in verse eight of Genesis 19 *yadha* is used with obvious and specific sexual connotation in the description of the virginity of Lot's daughters, "Behold, I have two daughters who have not know man." Considering these facts, what is the basis for the claim that linguistically the traditional mode of interpretation is incorrect? If *yadha* is to be understood with sexual connotation in verse eight of Genesis 19 then why is it not to be so understood in verse five, "and they called to Lot, 'Where are the men who came to you tonight? Bring them out to us, that we may know them.' " The linguistic argument presented in the *Study* has not answered these questions and, in this writer's thinking, the linguistic argument of the *Study* does not seem to be as sound as the traditional mode of interpretation. The traditional mode can build a linguistic case for giving sexual connotation to *yadha* and apply the term to both homosexual and heterosexual intercourse just as the term *shakabh* has been demonstrated to apply to both types of intercourse.

The *Study* turns from the linguistic concern to consider why homosexuality is not mentioned among the sins of Sodom when that city is mentioned elsewhere in the Old Testament and in the pericope where Sodom and Gomorrah are mentioned in Luke 10. The implication of the *Study*, while never specifically stated, is that the sins of Sodom and Gomorrah did not include homosexuality. The proof-texts for the inference that homosexuality was not involved in Sodom and Gomorrah are four from the prophetic writings (see Ezk. 16:49-50; Isa. 13:19; and Jer. 49:18; 50:40), one from the Apocrypha wisdom literature (Ecclesiasticus 16:8) and the aforementioned pericope in Luke.

It can be contended that the absence of homosexuality from the list of Sodom's sins does not say as much about Sodom as it says about the particular *Sitz im Leben* of the prophetic writings, Ecclesiasticus and the Gospel of Luke. The *Study* does not refer to extra-biblical texts (with the exception of Ecclesiasticus which neither Judaism nor Protestant Christianity regards as canonical) from the tradition of Judaism on the matter of homosexuality and hence the viewpoint expressed has not taken into consideration the rabbinic insights on this matter. This can lead to gross oversimplification because it allows one to read the Old Testament (and the New Testament as well) through the intellectual eyes of Europe rather than Jerusalem.

The concerns of the prophetic writers and of the Apocrypha writer of Ecclesiaticus were addressed to the situations within Judaism which were contrary to the faith of Judaism. The absence of disapproving commentary on homosexuality in later Old Testament writing does not necessarily mean that homosexuality was not regarded as an evil but that it was not the problem which the writers of Jeremiah, Isaiah, Ecclesiasticus, and Luke found themselves compelled to address. An examination of commentaries on these works indicates the issue which they sought to address was the mistake of depending upon any covenant but the Covenant of God. The story of Sodom and Gomorrah is used as symbolism of destruction and not for the purpose of providing a commentary on moral theology. At one place the *Study* advises, "we find, both in the case of scripture and human experience, a living, changing tradition and history that requires reinterpretation in the given historical moment" (p. 34). This observation has been ignored by the *Study* itself in the use of the prophets, Apocrypha, and the Gospels without clarifying the situation which each one of these works addresses in their unique moment in the history of the faith.

The failure to mention homosexuality in biblical sources outside the Pentateuch and the archaic books of the Bible (e.g. Judges) may mean that homosexuality was not a problem for later Hebrew and Judaistic culture. Immanuel Jakobovits commenting on the absence of prohibitions against homosexuality in the *Shulhan Arukh* of Rabbi Joseph Caro writes, "This ommission reflects the virtual absence of homosexuality among Jews rather than any difference of views on the criminality of these acts" (*Encyclopedia Judaica,* Vol. 8, p. 961). It is not unfeasible that the lack of association of homosexuality with Sodom's sins in the writings cited by the *Study* is a result of historical situations which did not demand that homosexuality be addressed.

This writer wishes to challenge the following statement of the *Study:*

> . . . the above critique of the customary biblical basis for the historic condemnation of homosexuality shows that the tradition is at least open to serious question and at most may be a hermeneutically untenable point of view (p. 72).

Given the failure of the *Study* to make its case linguistically and that its consideration of the prophetic texts and wisdom writings does not consider the *Sitz im Leben* of their references to Sodom and Gomorrah, it does not follow that any significant doubt has been cast upon the traditional mode of interpretation of the Sodom and Gomorrah pericope.

The hermeneutical principles of the *Study* as it addresses the Levitical Codes are often difficult to extract from polemics against views
which the *Study* obviously finds objectionable. This writer will address
the parts which deal with hermeneutical matters with attention to the
methods used to exclude the laws in Leviticus 18:22 and Leviticus
20:13 as binding upon the church.

The first principle introduced to dismiss the binding authority of
Levitical passages related to homosexuality is that the laws were established to encourage a procreative ethic. The *Study* states that "The
command of God to 'be fruitful and multiply' was the overriding
principle in the ordering of human sexuality and was clearly necessary
for survival in ancient culture. On those premises homosexuality had
to be outlawed" (pp. 72-73). It is obvious that procreation was important to ancient culture; however, it does not follow that these Levitical
Codes are based solely upon the procreative ethic. The judgement that
they are seems to be some sort of 'a priori' assumption. The Hebrews
were a people who had a theology about creation and who saw all
creatures as purposive beings. The creation of male and female was seen
as a definitive act of the Creator (Gen. 1:27). The relationship of man
and woman is a special and intentional relationship and the union of
these two genders reflect in Hebrew thought a new and unique identity
for both of them (Gen. 2:18-24). There are those who might wish to
claim that both of the first two Chapters of Genesis are mere reflections of the procreative ethic. A consideration of verses 27 of Chapter
one and 18 of Chapter two call into question the procreative ethic
as the sole basis for the understanding of human sexuality in the Old
Testament. In 1:27 the Word seems to imply that maleness and femaleness are intentional parts of the creation. In 2:18 the primary enjoin-
ing of male and female does not seem to be procreatively based but
rather is a response to human loneliness and incompleteness, "It is not
good that men should be alone." The theology of human sexuality if
founded only on "be fruitful and multiply" (Gen. 1:28) does not
address the whole of Creation Theology and human sexuality in
Hebrew thought. It seems that homosexuality could be forbidden on
the grounds that it does violence to the basic relationships of the
creation. It seems that the procreation ethic is only part of the theology
of sexuality and possibly not as important as the contributor to this
section of the *Study* thinks it to be.

Before closing commentary on the question of the procreative
ethic, this writer wishes to call attention to the following quotation
from the *Study*.

> Today the procreative ethic has been largely abandoned by Chris-
> tians in those churches in Western industrialized nations that do not
> recognize the Bishop of Rome. Indeed, our own situation may be
> more nearly the opposite, where an unbridled procreative ethic may

now be a sin.... The question naturally arises, then, about the continuing merit of the proscription of homosexuality when its original premise no longer obtains (p. 73).

This quote states in its opening lines that "the procreative ethic has been largely abandoned by Christians...in Western industrialized nations that do not recognize the Bishop of Rome." On what authority does this contributor claim that the procreative ethic 'per se' has been abandoned by the Protestant West, many of whom recognize the Bishop of Rome as a religious leader who is a witness of the Faith but simply do not regard him as infallible? It is true that Protestants, for the most part, repudiate an unbridled procreative ethic; but an unbridled procreative ethic represents irresponsibility in sexual unions in the same sense that gluttony represents irresponsible eating habits. Unbridled procreative ethic does not mean procreative ethic 'per se.' If, as has been demonstrated in the foregoing apologetic via a theology of purposive ordering of human sexuality, procreation is not the only reason why the Levitical Codes reject homosexual behavior, then the proscription regarding homosexuality may still obtain.

This writer has read and re-read the Levitical Codes and therefore has met the hermeneutical recommendation by the contributor of this part of the *Study*. This writer recommends that those who dismiss certain Levitical Codes because the church no longer judges itself bound by those Laws examine the basis for the abandonment of these Laws. The *Study* makes a point of noting the dietary Laws. In Acts 10 the Apostolic tradition deals with the Codes which regulate clean and unclean foods and of the acceptability of persons who are in Christ regardless of racial purity or lack of it. The Apostolic tradition does not make the 'Laws of Purity' binding on the New Testament Church; thus the contemporary Church also does not make these sorts of Laws binding. The New Testament tradition does not teach that we are free from Codes which regulate moral behavior but only that we are free from the penalty of lawbreaking if the lawbreaker is repentent. The New Testament is with one accord on the disapproval of homosexual behavior, for example, and is not in one accord with Laws of diet or racial purity.

The long commentary about killing (p. 75) is very difficult to understand as it is presented in the *Study*. Does this commentary wish to say that those who believe moral laws are binding are the same ones who ignore the prohibitions against murder and the slaughter of women and children? If this is what it means, then the claim is simply not true and constitutes an 'ad hominem.' Does the contributor wish to call the church into a total responsibility to those moral Laws of the Levitical Code? If this is what is intended then this writer is in agreement with this contributor to the *Study*.

Finally, this writer would ask the contributor of this article in the

Study to meet his own standard of divination. The contributor to the *Study* states, "Those who claim divine authority for certain laws and who call for current ecclesiastical enforcement of them are obliged, as a matter of simple honesty and fairness, to explicate the principles of divination being used" (pp. 75-76). The *Study* offers great praise for certain of the Laws (see page 74) and yet does not inform the reader the principles of divination being used. The Levitical Codes praised in the *Study* (and greatly appreciated by this writer) are subject to the same critique of being 'culturally bound' as are the Laws the *Study* rejects. Certain philosophic traditions would say these teachings are no more authoritative than the rest of the Code. The *Study* does not set forth why it thinks certain Levitical Codes are appropriate and others not. It fails in itself the requirement it places on others.

In closing, this writer wishes to comment on the hermeneutical principle used in the *Study* to dismiss the traditional interpretation of Sodom and Gomorrah as communities involved in homosexual practices. This writer believes that significant linguistic and exegetical questions have challenged the view put forward in the *Study;* however, laying aside these problems, consider the statement from the *Study* which implies that because Biblical scholars disagree on how the story should be interpreted the traditional interpretation is called into question (page 69 beginning with "This interpretation . . . has persisted"). Is exegetical consensus required for the teachings of the church and for its moral instruction? Consider the excellent work done by some Jewish and Christian scholars on the Messianic claims of Jesus of Nazareth and their exegesis of the relevant passages. Obviously exegetical consensus has broken down at this point. Does this imply, if we take the hermeneutical principle of consensus set forth in the *Study,* that the church's teaching on the Messiahship of Jesus is no longer binding upon Christian faith? It seems that exegetical consensus is not the determining rule for the teaching of the Church. If consensus were the format then the church today would be Arian rather than Trinitarian. It seems that the hermeneutical principle of exegetical consensus has some real defects. Exegetical accuracy is more important than exegetical consensus.

5 Foundations In Christian Ethics

by Gerald M. Sanders

The publication of the work *Human Sexuality: A Preliminary Study* has caused considerable concern within the United Church of Christ. Certain contributors to the work produced by the Board for Homeland Ministries have offered criticisms of the historical moral directives of the church. The church must address these criticisms and re-prove its historical stance or modify its teachings in light of these criticisms. To do this the church has to deal with the very foundations in Christian ethics.

The purpose of this chapter is to help clarify the issues for people involved with the questions presented in the *Human Sexuality Study* and to provide some assistance in dealing with basic issues in Christian ethics in the United Church of Christ. It seems logical to begin with a critique of certain approaches to ethics which, in this writer's opinion, represent a danger for those who are struggling with the direction of the church's moral theology. These approaches are the confusion in the work of some writers between ethical and scientific statements, the recommendation of positions of ethical relativism and the subjectivistic approach to value judgements.

First among the issues which must be clarified is the function of science and how science relates to moral theology. The *Human Sexuality Study* is not very clear in describing and defining what the relationship is between science and ethics. There are places where it is asserted that there is a difference between science and ethics but that distinction is not made clear. The reader is hit by a barrage of scientific data and the effect is bewildering. The bewilderment can be largely overcome by making clear the difference of function between assertions of science and those of ethics, secular or sacred.

A very helpful resource in understanding the function of science and how it differs from ethics is the work of Moritz Schlick, a founder of the famed Vienna Circle on philosophers. In an essay on the nature of scientific and moral law, Schlick writes that the intention of moral law is to prescribe certain forms of behavior but that the word law

43

as used by science "means something quite different. The natural law is not a *prescription* of how something should behave but a formula of how something does in fact behave."[1] Kepler's laws about orbital mechanics do not compel (*pre*scribe) the planets to follow certain orbits but *de*scribe how the planets are orbiting. The function of science is to describe what *is* and the function of ethics is to prescribe what behavior *ought* to be.

The student of ethics should be acutely aware of the difference between the *is* statement of the scientist and the *ought* statement of the ethicist. This is very important in an age such as the present one when the accomplishments of science are so impressive. The recognition of this difference will help the person attempting to make moral assertions from appealing to science as a basis of authority for the moral assertion and thus falling victim to the invalid reasoning associated with "the appeal to authority" (*Argumentum ad Verecundiam*). The advice of Immanuel Kant should prove helpful as one struggles with those who wish to substitute the authority of the scientist for that of the moral philosopher or theologian. Kant asserted that when an anthropologist begins to speak in terms of 'ought' he ceases to be an anthropologist and becomes a moral philosopher.[2]

If the functions of science and ethics differ in a basic way, is there any way that they relate to one another? The answer is that science and ethics can relate to one another. One of the clearest and most artistic descriptions of the relationship between science and ethics is in the work of John Kemeny when he quotes from Lewis Carrol's *Alice Through the Looking Glass:*

> "Would you tell me, please, which way I ought to go from here?" (asked Alice).
> "That depends a good deal on where you want to get to," said the Cat.[3]

The point is that science cannot prescribe what is moral or immoral or what the ends are that ought to be affirmed. Once the ends are prescribed then science can help obtain those ends most efficiently. Science cannot tell one that war is evil but once one decides that war is evil then science can describe a path that is most probable for the avoidance of war. Science cannot function to tell one that it is one's duty to feed the starving of the world but once one decides that the feeding of the world's starving people is one's moral duty then science can help bring about the most efficient means for accomplishing that end.

Another recent trend in ethical methodology is ethical relativism. Ethical relativism seeks to deny the existence of any universal ethical prescriptives. This theory has advocates from various fields but perhaps the best known are those anthropologists who promote the position

that all that is meant by terms such as *good, right, praiseworthy* is that
the acts assigned these terms are merely what is customary. There are
certain places in the consideration of Judaism in the *Human Sexuality
Study* that a methodology resembling that of the cultural relativists
appears. The use of "cultural conditioning" as a method of ethical
criticism in the sections of the *Human Sexuality* report dealing with
Old Testament moral prescriptives bears remarkable similarity to the
cultural relativists. This writer has already commented on that method
in his article on Old Testament hermeneutics and will not repeat
it here.

Before pointing out what the basic problem seems to be in regard
to ethical relativism and Christian ethics, this writer wishes to call
attention to a side issue which has an indirect effect upon the main
issue. That side issue is the work of Joseph Fletcher and certain statements in favor of ethical relativism. This writer is aware that another
contributor to *Issues in Sexual Ethics* is critiquing the position of
Fletcher; however, because certain comments by Fletcher seem relevant
to ethical relativism and because Fletcher seems to have exhibited
considerable influence upon parts of the *Human Sexuality Study,* this
writer feels it germane to comment upon him. Some may think that
Fletcher is advocating ethical relativism in Chapter II of *Situation
Ethics* but Fletcher is not an ethical relativist because he affirms one
unvarying norm: that one must always seek to do that which is motivated by *agape*.[4] In terms of true ethical relativism, Fletcher believes
in a universal definition of *good*. The real problem with Fletcher's
norm is that it repudiates the rules (e.g. the tradition of Torah) while
failing to see that these very rules have functioned to form a sense of
love's responsibility. It is true that love does not take advantage of the
helpless but who told Fletcher that it was unloving so to do? The point
is clear, it seems, that we do not form concepts of love apart from a
definitive tradition. This is an error in Fletcher and in the *Human
Sexuality Study;* a proclivity to too quickly dismiss the fact and value
of tradition, failing to recognize the influence of that tradition on
their own system. Those who appeal to Fletcher as a justification for
ethical relativism will, in the end, be disappointed. Situational ethics
is not a study in a new approach to ethics but a recovery of the study
of Casuistry.

Turning again to the question of ethical relativism proper, there is
one statement in the *Human Sexuality Study* which seems very near
relativism. In Chapter 2 of the *Human Sexuality Study* one encounters
the statement that "Taken as a whole, one finds in the Bible a multi-
plicity of viewpoints rather than a single perspective on human life."[5]
This quote may be understood in a number of ways. First, it may be
calling attention to the fact that the Bible does not always agree within
itself. This is obviously the case at a number of points. But does it

follow that the Bible has no single perspective, in an ultimate sense, about human life? A second way of understanding this quote is that the Bible does not define an ultimate perspective on human life. If this is so, are we not compelled to accept a position of ethical relativism, since there is no final authority within Scripture about understanding human life? If the Biblical tradition does not reflect in some final form a single perspective on human life, then it offers no basis for a final decision about how to perceive existence. The chief failure of ethical relativism is the failure to provide a basis for resolving differences in basic value judgements. This is a problem that it shares with another current ethical perspective. That perspective can be termed ethical subjectivism.

The position termed ethical subjectivism represents a danger to the very foundation of Christian ethics; yet it finds many supporters within the church. The approach of ethical subjectivism comes in both sophisticated and unsophisticated forms. The unsophisticated form is often mirrored in the expression "what is right for me is not right for others." This may be true about mundane things like one's preference for tomatoes and aversion towards oranges but it cannot be true about the final valuations in moral theology. The sophisticated form occurs in certain philosophers in such diverse traditions as Linguistic Analysis, existentialism, and theology. Some philosophers of language hold that the only thing one means when one says "X is good" is that one likes X. Some existentialists assert that the only statements which have authority are those which elicit an authoritative response in the realm of the subjective. The critiques of these two positions are so numerous as to prevent consideration in this essay. C.S. Lewis in the *Abolition of Man* has presented real difficulties for the emotivist theory of values[6] and Helmut Thielicke has presented some of the problems with the subjectivistic approach of certain existentialist writers and their criteria of value.[7]

The central problem with the ethical subjectivists and the ethical relativists is that both find it impossible to provide a basis for preferring one value judgement over another since they implicitly deny any universal basis for moral judgement. If there is no ultimate value that is true for all times and places and is true regardless of one's consent to that value, then there is really no compelling reason for a person to behave in one manner over another. If there is no ultimate value that has authority over all, then there is no logical reason why one should not say "to hell with your moral imperatives" anytime those imperatives conflict with one's own desires. If there is no value before which all people and all acts are judged, then the only logical rule is "that might makes right" and whoever has sufficient power has a right to accomplish whatever they desire. All talk of duty to neighbor and love for neighbor is, given relativism or subjectivism, no more than sentimental jargon of people who are too weak to defend themselves from the powerful.

The Christian tradition has rejected the basic concepts behind both subjectivism and relativism. The Christian tradition has confessed that there is an ultimate value before whom all stand and are called to obedience. This is the foundation in Christian Ethics. All talk of 'right', 'good' and 'responsible' always comes back, in the end, to this foundation. The foundation of all Christian ethics rests ultimately in the Person of Jesus Christ. *All Christian ethics are Christocentric.* Jesus is confessed as "the Way, the Truth, and the Life"[8] and He and His Personhood has been the norm throughout the history of the Christian faith, though not always have those who professed His Lordship been faithfully obedient.

Seemingly, with Christ as the foundation of all Christian ethics, the ethical task for the church should be relatively simple. It would seem that all that would be required would be a simple referring to the Scriptures for the answer of every difficulty. However, it is not that simple.

Beginning with the publication of A. Schweitzer's *Quest for the Historical Jesus* and continuing through the work of R. Bultmann and those in the Bultmannian tradition, there has been considerable hesitancy to make any assertion about the Person of Jesus. It has come to be regarded as naive to think that the church can know anything about the Person of Jesus and of any concrete historical fact (*Historie*). The testimony of the Gosples and Epistles have as their intention, not the recording of historical (*Historie*) facts, but the proclamation of a *kerygma* whose basic intent focuses upon the Risen Christ and is historic (*Geschichte*) in concern. The focus of the historic (*Geschichte*) is upon existential truth and not upon historical (*Historie*) fact. The Gospels and Epistles, in this tradition, give witness to the faith of the early Church. The whole fabric of the Gospel narrative and the instructions of the Epistles consists of the witness of the existential situation and experience of the early church. The function and meaning is existential and not historical (*Historie*) and is intended to beget an existential decision and not to inform the hearer about factual content.

Among the endorsers of the Bultmannian tradition, Fritz Buri, Professor at Basel, has noted that Bultmann is inconsistant. Buri believes, with the Bultmannians, that the essence of the Christian tradition is concerned with the existential approach to existence and is concerned with subjective truth rather than historical fact. Buri presses the question, if the essence of the New Testament is concerned with calling attention to one's own existential situation, why do Christians arrogantly give extra reverence to their tradition over any other philosophy of authentic existence? If authentic existence is the definition of truth, then what would preclude any fulfilling approach to existence even though that approach is non-Christian? It seems Buri's observation, if one agrees to the purely existential basis of truth, is correct. There is no reason to approve Christian tradition over any other tradition of authentic existence. There is no basis for preferring one subjective experience of authentic existence over another if it is the experience alone which is the defining criteria of truth.[9]

At this point the reader may ask, what does this have to do with foundations in Christian ethics? This writer wishes to assert that it has something very important to do with foundations in Christian ethics. If it is true that the whole of the New Testament is subjective in intent and content, then Buri's conclusion is justified. If Buri's conclusion is justified, then it must mean the abandonment of the *kerygma* as the sole foundation, or even a necessary part of the foundation, of ethics; it must mean abandoning the whole final authoritative tradition accorded to the church's Christological claims. It means that the foundation in ethics, for the Christian, is not 'per se' Christological. The result is the dilemma inherent in subjectivism: if there is no final authority *extra nos* then there is no ground for a person recommending one set of beliefs over against another contradicting set which is also subjectively fulfilling.

Commenting on the effect of the Bultmannian rejection of a historical (*Historie*) approach to Jesus, W. D. Davies writes,

> Lives of Jesus became scarce, and such as did appear were treated as neglible, because it had become a commonplace in many theological classrooms that Form criticism in its various emphasis made the writing of a life of Jesus a scientific impossibility. Either from an unconscious urge to make a virtue out of a necessity (because in any case, the Jesus of History could not be known), or from genuine theological conviction, the *kerygma* of the Church came to be regarded as alone significant and determinative for Christian faith. This lead to the further claim that the Church itself was from the first uninterested in the Jesus of History as such. With this decline in the seriousness with which the historicity of the detailed Gospel tradition was treated, it is not surprising that the door was opened for what, with all due deference, we must be allowed to characterize as an extremely subjective, typological and patternistic interpretation of the Gospel tradition. . . .[10]

At many points in the *Human Sexuality Study* one encounters a low view of history and interpretation which must be characterized as "extremely subjective, typological and patternistic" as it deals with the Gospel tradition. Consider the following statements of R. L. Scheef, Jr.:

> In other words, in its present task the church should seek to be free from any righteousness based upon mere history or dogma and should be open to any new righteousness that may come through faith in God (Romans 9:30-10:4).[11]

or

> the church needs to deal anew with the problem of scriptural authority. On the one side, this means to reexamine, redefine, and redevelop the "canon within the canon" . . . the church today needs to reexamine its own canon and find ways of separating "strawy" statements embedded in casuistry from essential theological principles related to God's faithfulness and love. On the other side, the church needs . . . to take into consideration whatever truth God may reveal from whatever source. . . .[12]

In terms of the foundations in Christian ethics, Scheef's contribution should have been the most important of all since in the study of the New Testament the Christological message is focused upon directly. But Scheef has not proved to be of much help. He calls for a new understanding of the canonical message but does little to give the church a criteria for coming to terms with such a judgement. How does one recognize righteousness without some kind of reference to *mere history?* The assertions about the fundamental principle of neighbor love do not help much because he does not adequately deal with the meaning of *love.* Scheef provides very little help in coming to terms with the real foundations in Christian ethics.

It seems imperative, if the Church is to be free from the problems imposed by subjectivism, to ground her claims in historical revelation. It must recognize that the non-historical approach to the New Testament has forced us to the situation described by Davies when he wrote,

> the kerygma increasingly came to be interpreted as an event hanging in mid-air, as it were, a phenomenon in a vacuum, the necessity to give it meaning became urgent. It is dangerously easy to be facile at this point, and I am fully aware that I may here be guilty of theological naivete, but I venture to suggest that as long as the Jesus of History was a significant factor in the interpretation of the Faith of the New Testament, the works and words of Jesus themselves provide a context for the kerygma which was religiously and ethically enriching. But once the kerygma was materially divorced from these, it could not but become to some an empty shell, or as I have expressed it, a skeleton with no flesh. And it is a part of the nature of skeletons that they call for explanation. . . . Exegesis, no less than nature, abhors a vacuum.[13]

The *Human Sexuality Study* fails to come to terms with the meaning of the *kerygma,* the content of the Gospel tradition, as it addresses the person of Jesus Christ. The position presented as the Christian tradition does not address the task of interpretation except in a most subjectivistic fashion. This manner of doing theology has serious defects.

This writer believes that if the church is to witness for any ethical stance in the world it cannot be based upon purely subjectivistic criterias of value but must rest in the claim that God came into history in the Jesus of History and in Him spoke definitively and authoritatively. This witness of and to the Jesus of History has been the source of ethical and religious enrichment for the Faith.

Reviewing the problems with the Bultmannian position, it seems necessary that Christians come to terms with the meaning of the Faith in a manner which differs both with Bultmann and the Old Liberal School of New Testament Interpretation. The most logical choice is the tradition of such scholars as T. W. Manson and W. D. Davies. They are able to deal with the observations of the Form critics and yet are able to avoid the traps into which Form criticism's purely existentialistic theology must eventually fall. This means a recovery of some sense of the historical (*Historie*) approach to Christology.

It seems to this writer that the down-grading of traditional ethical judgements, often exhibited in the *Human Sexuality Study,* is based upon an inadequate approach to Jesus Christ as the foundation in Christian ethics. When one wishes to depose the traditions, termed mere history and dogma by the *Human Sexuality Study,* one should approach this task with utmost hesitancy lest one saw off the very limb upon which oneself is sitting.

W. D. Davies wrote that it would probably be the great ethical issues in the 20th Century which would force the church to seriously address the Historical Jesus. It seems he is both a scholar and a prophet for such is now the demand. Against the viewpoint expressed in the *Human Sexuality Study,* this writer would point to a serious examination of the ethical traditions from the Old Testament and Judaism which find much currency in the Gospels and Epistles. The understanding of these traditions may lead us into a more adequate understanding of Jesus, the foundation in Christian ethics. Davies wrote that one of the sources which may lead us into a new and vital understanding of Jesus and His message could be the Pharisees.[14] It may well be as we consider the teachings of the great rabbinic scholars and the New Testament, we shall understand who we are as Christians and from where we came and the direction of our pilgrimage. Assistance for beginning such an understanding will be supplied in *Issues in Sexual Ethics* by another writer more knowledgeable in rabbinic literature than this writer.

In conclusion, this writer would like to set before the student of Christian ethics the following propositions which seem important in coming to terms with the foundations in Christian ethics.

1) That scientific assertions differ in kind from ethical assertions in that scientific assertions seek to *describe* behavior and moral assertions seek to *prescribe* behavior.

2) That the relationship of science to ethics can be understood as a method to provide for ethics the most efficient means of the attain-

ment of the ends which ethics desires.

3) That ethical relativism fails to provide an ultimate foundation in ethics because by definition it denies the existence of ultimate foundations.

4) The position of ethical relativism must be rejected by the Christian ethicist because it, by definition, rejects the Christ-event as the ultimate definition of existence, moral or otherwise.

5) Ethical subjectivism fails to provide an ultimate foundation in ethics because if all criteria for critical judgement outside the subject (*extra nos*) are denied, there is no criteria for preferring one ethical assertion by one subject over contradicting assertions by another subject.

6) The position of ethical subjectivism must be rejected by Christian ethicists because it reduces all Christological assertions to a criteria of judgment based on purely personal preference. It lacks any compelling authority outside the self and hence means one is free to chose in terms of their own preference what can be said about Christ.

7) Christian ethics can avoid the problems inherent in both relativism and subjectivism by seeking to ground its revelation in the Personhood of Jesus Christ as the definitive historical (*Historie*) event which is true ultimately and is non-dependent on the approval of the subject for its authority.

8) That the *kerygma* of the New Testament incorporates not only the occurence historic (*Geschichte*) but that the historical (*Historie*) is the source of the historic (*Geschichte*).

9) All Christian ethics are necessarily Christological and Jesus Christ is the foundation in all Christian ethics.

10) Any attempt to understand Jesus apart from the Old Testament is irresponsible to the basic categories of understanding inherent in the thought of the New Testament.

11) Among the sources which serve to attain a more helpful understanding of the historical Jesus are the Rabbinic sources in Judaism.

12) The division of the historical Jesus from the Risen Christ is foreign to the New Testament.

13) There are tendencies in the *Human Sexuality Study* which entail the problematic positions of subjectivism and relativism. That the "love" ethic proposed by the *Study* is vague and lacks adequate consideration of those texts of Scripture which have given content to the term "love."

14) The radical separation from the Law (Torah) as revelation and the revelation in the New Testament is not faithful to either Law or Gospel since both function to complement and elaborate the under-

standing of God's Will.

15) Jesus Christ as the foundation in Christian Ethics entails a real coming to terms with the relatedness of Law and Gospel.

NOTES

1. Moritz Schlick, "When Is a Man Responsible" in *Free Will And Determinism,* ed. Bernard Berofsky (New York: Harper & Row, 1966), p. 57.

2. Immanuel Kant, *Foundations of the Metaphysics of Morals* (New York: Bobs-Merrill Co., 1959), p. 5.

3. John G. Kemeny, *A Philosopher Looks At Science* (New York: D. Van Nostrand Company, Inc., 1966), p. 230.

4. Joseph Fletcher, *Situation Ethics* (Philadelphia: Westminster Press, 1966), p. 57.

5. *Human Sexuality: A Preliminary Study* (New York and Philadelphia: United Church Press, 1977), p. 31.

6. C. S. Lewis, *The Abolition of Man* (New York: MacMillan Publishing Co., 1947).

7. Helmut Thielicke, "The Restatement of New Testament Theology" in *Kerygma and Myth* Vol. I, ed. H. W. Bartsch, trans. R. H. Fuller (London: S.P.C.K., 1953).

8. John 14:6

9. John Macquarrie, *20th Century Religious Thought* (London: SCM Press, 1976), pp. 365-367.

10. W. D. Davies, *Christian Origins and Judaism* (Philadelphia: Westminster Press, 1962), pp. 8-9.

11. R. L. Scheef, Jr., "New Testament Perspectives on Human Sexuality" in *Human Sexuality: A Preliminary Study* (New York and Philadelphia: United Church Press, 1977), p. 85.

12. *Ibid.,* p. 86.

13. W. D. Davies, *op. cit.,* p. 9.

14. W. D. Davies, *Introduction to Pharisaism* (Philadelphia: Fortress Press, 1967), p. 28.

6   Jesus and the Law

by Martin Duffy

Our denomination's preliminary study *Human Sexuality* contains a number of provocative statements about Jesus and the Law, the Bible and how we interpret it, the position of women in the Old Testament, the Leviticus Holiness Code and the Christian sexual ethic. Taken singly, statements that Jesus had authority to contradict and disobey the ancient scriptures, that he broke laws (either Scripture or the oral tradition), that one does not find in the Bible a single, unifying perspective on human life, deserve profound exploration. Taken together, the statements to which I refer suggest a great antinomian departure from historical Christianity (a rejection of the Law of God); they imply a gulf between Jesus and the Hebrew Bible, between the Christian and the Judaic ethic, between God's Justice and his Love. This thematic complex of statements likewise deserves a profound and searching examination by Christian people.

RÉSUMÉ

The statements about Jesus and the Law occur on pages 32 and 78 of our United Church of Christ study. They deny a venerable Christian tradition that of all persons only Jesus perfectly kept God's Law. Jesus' teachings on sexual morality are appraised on pages 78-79, where they are reduced to the sole motif of neighbor love. That, taken as a whole, the Bible does not provide a single perspective on human life is stated on page 31. On page 32 contradiction within Scripture is raised to a principle of interpretation (hermeneutics); this principle is reaffirmed on page 35 where we read, "scripture rises up angrily to contradict and correct scripture." On page 36 the report asserts a gnostic distinction between Biblical faith and Biblical religion. On page 86 the report recommends that we "redevelop the 'canon within the canon.' " In plain language this means getting rid of Scripture we do not like as Luther did when he declared the epistle of James an epistle of straw.

Martin Duffy, who lives in Susquehanna, Pennsylvania, is a minister of the United Church of Christ and a writer; his field of study is the relationship between Judaism and Christianity.

However, in contrast to its first statement about the Bible, on page 34 the report suggests that God's revelation of the holy in the covenant history of Israel and the person of Jesus Christ, providing redemption for humanity, *is* the Bible's unifying theme.

Comments upon the low position of women in the Old Testament are found on pages 14 and 35-40. The Leviticus Holiness Code is treated on pages 72-77. Both subjects are handled pretty roughly. Sexual prohibitions relate to women as property in a male dominated society and may not be universally valid. In the Holiness Code we find ethical pearls scattered among "superstitious remnants of primitive religion." Paul's condemnation of homosexuality is discounted on pages 83-85. Recommendations for shaping a responsible sexual ethic are made on pages 92-102. In this latter treatment, beginning with Paul, the authors of the report cannot find it in themselves to use negative canons. Their key words are freedom, sensuousness, love and sensitivity. Obedience to God is merely one among several options. The authors say little or nothing about self-control, discipline and personal holiness. In their summary of principles for sexual morality on pages 103-105, they omit the need for Christians to search out God's will and simply conclude, "God is present and at work in all sexual loving."

Nowhere in the report do the statements I have reviewed receive the searching examination their importance demands. The central factor in this complex of ideas is the report's conception of Jesus' relationship to the Law. From this center flows the report's tendency to set aside the "Thou shalts" and "Thou shalt nots" of Scripture. A low valuation of the Holiness Code follows. So does the report's unwillingness to grapple with the judgements of a Just and Holy God. And its failure to understand that obedience is founded in love. That there can be no grace without commandment, no mercy without judgement, no Gospel without Law. That revelation, including the Incarnation of the Son of God, came in and through Hebrew culture, not despite it. That the transcendent came near to us precisely in historical, particular and accidental forms (cf. p. 36). That human sexuality is defined not only by fidelity to neighbor love but also by fidelity to the creative purpose and will of God. This chapter therefore is primarily concerned with Jesus and the Law.

As an illustration of the kind of resources the report might have used to explore a vital question, I refer to Appendix I of W. D. Davies' recent book, *The Gospel and the Land.* The appendix is entitled, "Reflections on Judaism and Christianity: Their Mutual Dependence."[1] Dr. Davies summarizes certain results of modern Judaic-Christian studies:

> First, the old distinction between priestly, legalistic, Judaism and prophetic Judaism has broken down.
> Secondly, there has been a rejection of any sharp distinction

between Apocalyptic and Pharisaism.

Thirdly, a deeper Jewish and Christian understanding of the first century, often informed by the agony of our time, has made it easier to do justice to the legal tradition in Judaism.[2]

He mentions the work of Christian scholars such as Dalman, Schurer, Bousset, Jeremias, Moore, Bonsirven and Herford; of Jewish scholars such as Abrahams, Loewe, Daube, Schechter, Montefiore, Finkelstein and Lieberman. To these I would add important studies by Finkel, Baeck and Buber. To my knowledge, none of the findings quoted above, none of the Christian or Jewish scholars mentioned by Dr. Davies or myself, and none of their works or insights were utilized in our *Human Sexuality* report to probe the vital question of Jesus' relationship to the Law and its bearing upon our sexual ethic.

THE GREAT COMMANDMENT

Mark 12:28-34 reads: *And one of the scribes came up and heard them disputing with one another, and seeing that he answered them well, asked him, "Which commandment is the first of all?" Jesus answered, "The first is, 'Hear O Israel: The Lord our God, the Lord is one; and you shall love the Lord your God with all your heart, and with all your soul, and with all your mind, and with all your strength.' The second is this, 'You shall love your neighbor as yourself.' There is no other commandment greater than these." And the scribe said to him, "You are right, Teacher; you have truly said that he is one, and that there is no other than he; and to love him with all the heart, and with all the understanding, and with all the strength, and to love one's neighbor as oneself, is much more than all whole burnt offerings and sacrifices." And when Jesus saw that he answered wisely, he said to him, "You are not far from the kingdom of God."*

We are fortunate that Mark preserved this friendly exchange between a scribe and Jesus during the almost unbearable stress and conflict of Passion Week. Luke either omitted the exchange or adapted it for the preface to his story of the Good Samaritan (Lk. 10:25-28). His lawyer is a less attractive figure than Mark's scribe. Matthew turned the scribe's question into a test and omitted his friendly agreement with Jesus (Mt. 22:34-40). But in Mark, the original account, Jesus' fundamental agreement with Judaism and with the best in rabbinic teaching shines forth. Jesus answers the question, "Which commandment is the first of all?" with the *Shema* from Deuteronomy 6:4—the central tenet of Jewish faith—at once the heart of the Temple and synagogue liturgy and the daily confession of every Jew, combining the profound conception of monotheism with intimate faith and wholehearted love.[3] R. H. Lightfoot says of this passage in *The Gospel Message of St. Mark:*

Nor was the Lord hostile to the law of Moses; when He was asked to state the foremost commandment in the law, His answer, though perfectly adapted to express His own deepest convictions, is none the less orthodoxy itself; Israel's great confession with respect to God, combined with the kindred precept of love to a neighbor. . . . St. Mark seeks to prove that the Lord met His death, not because His thought or His life ran counter to the law, but because He claimed to be the Messiah.[4]

I would like to make the following observations about our Lord's summary of the Law in the Great Commandment to love God and neighbor.

(1) The commandment to love God precedes the commandment to love our neighbor. All other Biblical commandments are valid if God is confessed and loved; else none are valid. Why? The Rabbis answer in *Sanhedrin* 106b, "The Merciful One desires the heart."[5] The person who loves God desires to please him and obeys his will as a child who loves his parents obeys and pleases them. We refrain from adultery and other sexual sins not simply because they do violence to neighbor love, as our *Human Sexuality* report says (pp. 78-79), but because we love God who gave us his commandments for our good and his Son for our redemption. For some reason our preliminary study never connects the second with the first commandment.

(2) Jesus accepted God's teaching in commandment form. He repeated the Old Testament commandments with great forcefulness. The Gospels are full of his own commandments (cf. Mt. 4:17; Mk. 1:17; Mt. 7:21-27; Mt. 28:18-20; Jn. 15:12-17) which became the turning point in his hearers' lives. But a number of Christian theologians, especially Protestants, have been troubled by teaching in the form of commandment. For them the imperative detracts from the grace and freedom of the Spirit (but compare their attitude with John chapters 14 and 15). A glaring example is contained in the *Theological Wordbook of the New Testament.* Noting the commandments to love God and neighbor in Dt. 6:5 and Lv. 19:18, the authors see a paradox; what "is prescribed as law really lies outside the province of legal regulation." They suggest that in Deuteronomy the idea of love has hardened into dogma; that putting love in terms of legal significance retreats from ultimate reality.[6]

Evidently Jesus ignored the paradox just as he ignores it in John 15:31, "but I do as the Father has commanded me, so that the world may know that I love the Father." And 15:14, "You are my friends if you do what I command you." The answer to the paradox is simple. Only love can command love. And God is Love.

(3) Jesus' words, "There is no other commandment greater than these" (vs. 31b), validate all the commandments. Each commandment has its greatness, more or less, but none exceed the two quoted. In Matthew's version of the saying, the two commandments quoted are

the ground of all Scripture, "On these two commandments depend all the law and the prophets" (22:40). All other Biblical commandments and teachings derive from the Great Commandment but are not reduced to it.

(4) The scribe's reply to Jesus is a great statement of religion in its own right. The scribe adds to Jesus' words an implicit and at times explicit teaching of the Hebrew Bible—that love for God and neighbor far exceed the ritual of sacrifice. Without this prophetic teaching Judaism could not have survived the destruction of the Temple in 70 A.D. The scribe's answer implies another point: when he used the word commandment or Law he was referring to the whole Hebrew Bible—Pentateuch, Prophets, Writings—and to the normative Pharisaic or rabbinic interpretation of the Bible, the oral tradition. Jesus enjoyed this scribal interpretation, for he told the man, "You are near God's kingdom."[7]

LAW AND SCRIPTURE

Matthew 23:23 reads: *Woe to you, scribes and Pharisees, hypocrites! for you tithe mint and dill and cummin, and have neglected the weightier matters of the law, justice and mercy and faith; these you ought to have done, without neglecting the others.*

Christian interpreters have focused on the "hypocrites" and have themselves "neglected the weightier matters of the law." This passage does not admit the Pauline distinction between law and grace. Mercy and faith form the Law's substance together with justice. The entire Biblical word is Law: here Jesus views Law through Micah's dictum, "He has showed you, O man, what is good; and what does the LORD require of you but to do justice, and to love kindness, and to walk humbly with your God?"[8] The prophets clarify the meaning of Torah; the substance was given at Sinai. Neither does this passage support the idea that Jesus opposed *Halachah,* the binding rules and customs of rabbinic Judaism. Tithing the smallest matters should be practiced; but all religious practice must press to fulfill the Law's purpose. If God does not have the heart, observance is false. What is the practice of religion worth, asks Jesus, without justice, mercy and faith?

Although all religions have their hypocrites, Christians have made the word synonymous with Pharisee. Did Jesus mean to stigmatize the entire sect? Historical studies tell us that the Pharisees were a high minded party devoted to the will of God and that most of Jesus' teachings fall within the Pharisaic orbit.[9] Whether Jesus' criticism was unfair, or directed against one type of Pharisee, or whether the gospel editors have altered the record are matters for debate.[10] Another strain of evidence in the New Testament shows friendly relations between Pharisees and Jesus or his followers. Mark 12:28-34, as noted above, states scribal agreement with Jesus on the main point of Jewish faith. In Luke 13:31 Pharisees warn Jesus, "Get away from here, for Herod wants to kill you." Mark 15:42-46 says that "Joseph of Arimathea, a respected member of the council, who was himself look- ing for the kingdom of God, took courage and went to Pilate, and asked for the body of Jesus," which he wrapped and laid in a tomb.[11] Acts 5:33-39 has Paul's teacher Gamaliel save the lives of Peter and the apostles before the Sanhedrin. Acts 15:5 says that Pharisees were members of the primitive church. In Acts 23:1-10 Paul is brought before the council and he cries, "Brethren, I am a Pharisee, a son of Pharisees," and scribes of the Pharisaic party respond, "We find nothing wrong in this man." The account demonstrates that Pharisees could at that time imagine a Christian leader one of themselves.

In Great Ages and Ideas of the Jewish People, Ralph Marcus writes: "It is to the Pharisees that we owe the preservation of Prophetic Judaism with its stress upon the primacy of social justice and its messianic belief in the ultimate conversion of all mankind. . . . "[12] In the same book Gerson D. Cohen describes how the Pharisees restricted the priesthood to Temple ritual, arguing that it was the function of laymen, the disciples of Moses and heirs of the prophets, to judge behavior and apply the Law to the daily life of the people. The opening lines of *Pirke Abot (Chapters of the Fathers),* a renowned tractate of the Mishnah, give classic form to this tradition: "Moses received the Law from Sinai and committed it to Joshua, and Joshua to the elders, and the elders to the Prophets; and the Prophets committed it to the men of the Great Synagogue." Dr. Cohen comments, "Clearly, the tradition was not a priestly but a *prophetic* one handed over to the men of the Great Assembly, whom the Pharisees identified with Ezra and other 'Men of the Book.' "[13]

The finest illustration of the prophetic character of Pharisaism I have found is contained in *The Fathers According to Rabbi Nathan,* an earlier and amplified version of *Pirke Abot.*[14] In the passage below the text is commenting upon a saying of Simon the Righteous (a survivor of the Great Assembly): "ON THREE THINGS THE WORLD STANDS—ON THE TORAH, ON THE TEMPLE SERVICE, AND ON ACTS OF LOVING-KINDNESS." The extended comment reads:

> ON ACTS OF LOVING-KINDNESS: how so? Lo, it says, *For I desire mercy and not sacrifice* (Hos. 6:6). From the very first the world was created only with mercy, as it is said, *For I have said, The world is built with mercy; in the very heavens Thou dost es- tablish Thy faithfulness* (Ps. 89:3).
>
> Once as Rabban Johanan ben Zakkai was coming forth from Jerusalem, Rabbi Joshua followed after him and beheld the Temple in ruins.
>
> "Woe unto us!" Rabbi Joshua cried, "that this, the place where the iniquities of Israel were atoned for, is laid waste!"

"My son," Rabban Johanan said to him, "be not grieved; we have another atonement as effective as this. And what is it? It is acts of loving-kindness, as it is said, *For I desire mercy and not sacrifice"* (Hos. 6:6).[15]

Johanan ben Zakkai, a contemporary of Jesus, survived the destruction of the Temple in 70 A.D. He was the leading disciple of the great Pharisee Hillel and is credited with securing the future of Judaism by establishing an Academy at Jabneh after the Roman-Jewish war.[16] It is notable that he based his daring interpretation on the same verse from Hosea that Jesus used to justify his ministry to sinners (Mt. 9:10-13). Note too the agreement between Johanan ben Zakkai's interpretation and the scribe's answer to Jesus in Mark 12. But there is a further significance to this account. In defining atonement, Johanan ben Zakkai places the Prophets on a par with the Pentateuch, which established the ritual of sacrifice. (The commentator reasons that "the world was created only with mercy" from a text in the Psalms. Thus the entire account relies equally upon the three divisions of the Hebrew Bible—Law, Prophets and Writings.) With Hosea in mind, Johanan ben Zakkai decided the future of Judaism, a decision that has been fully incorporated into Jewish life and liturgy. It follows that for Johanan ben Zakkai the Law meant the Hebrew Bible creatively interpreted according to the prophetic and scribal tradition. We need to pause for a closer look at the term Law.

In the Old Testament the Hebrew word for law is *torah.* In English the term is frequently transliterated as Torah and from this point I will use Torah interchangeably with Law. Nahum Glatzer points out that the Septuagint, the Greek translation of the Hebrew Bible, renders the word Torah by *nomos* (this is also the Greek term used in the New Testament). Dr. Glatzer says that in the ancient Greek-speaking world *nomos* had a wider meaning analagous to the range of meaning conveyed by Torah, but that in translating *nomos* by law we considerably narrow down that range of meaning. "To later users," he says, " 'Law' suggested a collection of statutes, commandments and injunctions."[17] I believe that most Christians interpret the Law in this sense. Law becomes equivalent to commandment. But for Jews raised with the Hebrew Bible Torah means far more. Jesus was an observant Jew, not a Greek-speaking or English-speaking Christian. What did the word Torah mean to him?

According to the *Universal Jewish Encyclopedia* the normative meaning of the Hebrew word is teaching, instruction, doctrine or guidance. Within Judaism it has been used to designate (1) the Law of Moses; (2) the Pentateuch; (3) the Hebrew Scriptures; (4) the Bible plus the Oral Tradition; and (5) Divine Revelation: the Word of God. "As the most comprehensive name for divine revelation, the Torah represents both 'the heritage of the congregation of Jacob' (*Deut.*

33:4) and the vitalizing and regulative principle and standard of Judaism."[18] G. F. Moore in his great work *Judaism* agrees: "The comprehensive name for the divine revelation, written and oral, in which the Jews possessed the sole standard and norm of their religion is *Torah.* . . . 'Law' must, however, not be understood in the restricted sense of legislation, but must be taken to include the whole of revelation—all that God has made known of his nature, character, and purpose, and of what he would have man be and do."[19]

I suggest that the above is what Torah meant to Jesus. Commandment is an important part of Torah but by no means the whole of it. The Law is Creation in Genesis, God's love for Abraham and the Fathers, his self-disclosure at the burning bush, Jonah's preaching of repentance, the strong, tender promises of the Prophets and Psalms.[20] Torah is the Presence of the Living God ("he is not God of the dead, but of the living") calling his children into fullness of life. The Presence is witnessed and reflected in the Hebrew Bible, which Jesus continually quotes as the authoritative Word of God. Matthew 23:23 gives his view of "the weightier matters of the law, justice and mercy and faith." In Mark 7:13 he calls the commandment to honor father and mother "the word of God." He uses the standard Rabbinic formula "it is written" when citing Scripture in a definitive sense. He tells Satan (from Deuteronomy), "It is written, 'Man shall not live by bread alone, but by every word that proceeds from the mouth of God' " (Mt. 4:4). He quotes the great promise from Isaiah as he cleanses the Temple, "Is it not written, 'My house shall be called a house of prayer for all the nations?' " (Mk. 11:17). In the Psalms he finds testimony to the Messiah, saying, "David himself, inspired by the Holy Spirit, declared. . . . " (Mk. 12:36). How ironic that our human sexuality document speaks of Jesus violating Scripture, citing Matthew 23:23, the very place Jesus supports tithing the smallest matters while pressing to fulfill the Law's greatest purpose.

THE ETERNITY OF THE LAW

Luke 16:17 reads: *But it is easier for heaven and earth to pass away, than for one dot of the law to become void.*

Luke's saying has a parallel in Matthew 5:18, "For truly, I say to you, till heaven and earth pass away, not an iota, not a dot, will pass from the law until all is accomplished." We may judge that Luke has preserved the saying in its original form for these reasons: (1) Luke's version is simpler and clearer; Matthew's "until all is accomplished" adds an ambiguous note; (2) Luke's version is less palatable to Christian theology, evidence that it has not been edited; (3) Luke's version has almost the exact grammatical structure of Mark 10:25, "It is easier for a camel to go through the eye of a needle than for a rich man to enter the kingdom of God." It has a close parallel in Mark 13:31, "Heaven and earth will pass away, but my words will not pass away." All three of these sayings have Jesus' simple, penetrating style; (4) Matthew's version has the symmetry of the original by adding "not an iota" and by using two "untils."

The second until brings the thought of 5:17 (Jesus came to fulfill the Law and the Prophets, not abolish them) into verse 18. Like all of Matthew's extensive teaching discourses, this part of the Sermon on the Mount is a careful construction, preparing the way for the exposition of 5:21-48 where Matthew shows how Jesus fulfills and transcends the Law. The Hebrew-Aramaic scholar Gustaf Dalman in *The Words of Jesus* agrees that "the original spoke, as in Luke 16:17, only of a single hook" (the point or hook of a Hebrew letter), and that "the mention of the *iota* in Matthew would be intended for Greek readers" for whom "iota was actually the smallest letter."[21]

Despite Matthew's shading, the two versions are close enough to strongly support each other. Comparing them, *The International Critical Commentary* says, "It is therefore a well-authenticated traditional utterance of Christ."[22] The great Reformer Calvin remarks, "In both places Christ intended to teach that in all the structure of the universe there is nothing so stable as the truth of the Law, which stands firm, and that in every part."[23]

Luke's version consists of a double hyperbole which clearly means: *The Law in all its parts is permanently valid.* The saying therefore represents a classic doctrine of Judaism known as the eternity of the Law. Many parallels to Jesus' saying occur in rabbinic literature. The following examples illustrate the scope and meaning of the saying. Cited in *The International Critical Commentary:*

> Everything has its end, the heaven and the earth have their end, only one thing is excepted which has no end, and that is the law (*Bereshith Rabba* x.1).[24]

Cited in the *Universal Jewish Encyclopedia:*

> Berechiah says, "The whole world is not equal to a single word of the Torah" (*Yer. Peah* 1:1, 15d).[25]

Cited in the *Jewish Encyclopedia:*

> Every letter of it is a living creature. When Solomon took many wives, Deuteronomy threw himself before God and complained that Solomon wished to remove from the Pentateuch the yod of the word . . . (Deut. xvii. 17), with which the prohibition of polygamy was spoken; and God replied: "Solomon and a thousand like him shall perish, but not one letter of the Torah shall be destroyed" (*Lev. Rabba* xix.; *Yer. Sanhedrin* 20c; *Cant. Rabba* 5, 11).[26]

Cited by Israel Frankel:

> The Rabbis say: "It is written, 'Hear O Israel the Lord our God

the Lord is One' . . . if you make (the letter) . . . 'daleth' into (the letter) . . . 'resh' you cause the destruction of the whole Universe . . . . " (*Lev. Rabba* 19,2).[27]

The Hebrew word for One ends with the letter *daleth,* nearly identical with the letter *resh,* except for a small projection. If *resh* were substituted for *daleth* the meaning of the word would change to "other" or "strange" and the confession would become blasphemous. To summarize the ideas contained in these sayings: Torah is permanently valid; it is the most valuable thing in creation; the closest attention must be paid to the letter since the letter carries the meaning.

In Mark 12:24-27 Jesus supports the doctrine of resurrection with a single word from Exodus 3:6, "have you not read in the book of Moses, in the passage about the bush, how God said to him, 'I am (*anokiy*) the God of Abraham, and the God of Isaac, and the God of Jacob'?" Jesus read the Scriptures closely and creatively to discern the deep meaning carried by the letter. He did not, however, separate that meaning from the letter, which goes far to explain why the church took the Hebrew Bible into its canon, why the church followed Judaism's example in having a canon. Given Jesus' immense respect for Torah, an argument from silence (that he does not mention homosexuality) carries no weight. The presumption of favor lies with Biblical teaching. Only actual statements and actions of Christ should be used to indicate new directions of thought. Any position which seeks to eliminate doctrines, books, or moral teachings from the Bible has first to answer Jesus of Nazareth.

BUT I SAY TO YOU

The doctrine of the eternity of the Law could lead to a static, inflexible concept of Scripture. The Sadducees, according to Israel Frankel, "in fanatically adhering to the 'letter' in the strictest sense of the word, sought to destroy the 'spirit' of the Torah."[28] The Sadducees used the Bible to buttress their priestly authority but refused to apply its principles to contemporary issues. The Pharisees, like Jesus, sought to bring the Word of God to bear on every area of human life. No one who reads the Gospels or rabbinic literature with care can fail to appreciate how both Jesus and the rabbis interpreted Scripture in a dynamic and creative manner. We have seen that Johanan ben Zakkai found comfort and instruction in Hosea for the loss of Temple sacrifice. Through *Midrash* (the Hebrew word for interpretation) the rabbis sought to penetrate to the bed rock principles of Scripture to guide their reading of the text. The *Jewish Encyclopedia* says, "the term 'Midrash' designates an exegesis, which, going more deeply than the mere literal sense, attempts to penetrate into the spirit of the Scriptures."[29] Israel Frankel writes:

the Rabbis take the words "he shall live by them," to mean that

God's commandments are to be a means of life and not of destruction. With the exception of three prohibitions—murder, idolatry and adultery—all commandments of the Law are, therefore, in abeyance whenever life is endangered.[30]

This is the rabbinic principle (that God's commandments are to be a means of life and not of destruction) Jesus appealed to when he pointedly asked, "Is it lawful on the sabbath to do good or to do harm, to save life or to kill?" (Mk. 3:4).

In Matthew 5:21-48 Jesus explains Scripture with a series of midrashic comments, using the formula, "You have heard that it was said . . . But I say to you. . . ." Our *Human Sexuality* report cites this formula as evidence of Jesus' authority "to reinterpret, contradict, and even disobey the ancient scriptures" (p. 32). Is that what Jesus was doing?

First, that Jesus' formula applies to the Old Testament is obvious from the quotations that follow it: "You shall not kill," "You shall not commit adultery," et. al. Solomon Schechter in *Aspects of Rabbinic Theology* quotes Talmudic and Midrashic passages with an expository formula and style very close to Jesus in Matthew 5.

> "We have heard that it is written, 'Thou shalt not kill'. . . . We should then think that the prohibition is confined to actual murder. But there are also other kinds of shedding blood, as, for instance, to put a man to shame in public, which causes his blood to leave his face. Hence to cause this feeling is as bad as murder, whence he who is guilty of it loses his share in the world to come." (*T.Z. Baba Mezia*, 59a).

> "Again, we have heard that it is written, 'Thou shalt not commit adultery'. . . . But the phrase in Job (24:15), 'The *eye* also of the adulterer waiteth for twilight,' teaches us that an unchaste look is also to be considered as adultery." (*Lev. Rabba* 23, 11).[31]

Second, given the parallels cited, it is not so clear that Jesus intended "to disobey and contradict ancient scripture." Leo Baeck examines this section of Matthew in *Judaism and Christianity* and concludes, "All that is said here is meant not as a contradiction of the Torah but as a commentary: it is 'oral Torah,' and there are manifold parallels to these sayings in the Talmudic writings."[32]

Jesus' formula covers six cases: murder, adultery, divorce, oaths, retaliation and love of neighbor. On the commandments against murder and adultery, Jesus extends and deepens their meaning; he does not contradict them. There is nothing in the passage on adultery to indicate a revision of the Jewish sexual ethic. I will consider the divorce question below in my review of Mark 10:2-9, where Jesus gives the reasoning behind his decision. On the question of oath-taking, the rabbis were moving in Jesus' direction to combat superstitious and frivolous oaths common among the people. Moses Luzzato quotes these Rabbinic dictums in his spiritual classic *The Path of the Just:*

As has been stated (*Shevuoth* 36a), "R. Eleazer said, 'No' is an oath and 'Yes' is an oath." . . . And, (*Bava Metzia* 49a), " 'A righteous measure' (*Leviticus* 19:36)—your 'No' should be righteous and your 'Yes' should be righteous."[33]

Jesus does not cancel the law on oaths but gives its true intent against popular practice: people should speak truth from the heart.

The question of retaliation is more difficult. The difficulty is not so much with the *lex talionis,* "an eye for an eye, and a tooth for a tooth." The original law in context (Exodus 21:23-32) suggests monetary compensation, not the cruel loss of a member. Dr. J. H. Hertz says that this can be seen from parallel passages Lev. 24:18 and Num. 35:31; the latter *forbids* taking ransom for murder. Murder was the only injury which literally demanded "a life for a life." Dr. Hertz says of Exodus, "The Rabbis ruled that since no homocide was here intended, it was a case for monetary compensation." He adds, "there is no instance in Jewish history of its literal application ever having been carried out."[34]

The problem is Jesus' interpretation which appears to present an extreme doctrine of non-retaliation. But if the *lex talionis* is not a literal law, neither is "do not resist one who is evil." Jesus himself resisted evil to the death. Within its context, the phrase has to mean, "do not resist violently; do not seek vengeance and strike back." Some of Jesus' following words may employ hyperbole to underline his point. Leo Baeck remarks, "The meaning of this saying . . . can be understood only when it is recognized that [it is] directed against the Zealots."[35] The burning question of violent revolt against Rome provides an excellent historical background for the saying. If Dr. Baeck is right, Jesus meant something like this: The *lex talionis* requires justice, not savage vengeance. You will have to overcome evil with good. The majority of the rabbis would have agreed with this interpretation.

The final section (5:43-48) contains the most distinctive saying of Jesus in the New Testament. "But I say to you, Love your enemies and pray for those who persecute you, so that you may be sons of your Father who is in heaven; for he makes his sun rise on the evil and on the good, and sends rain on the just and on the unjust." Those who love their enemies have become children of God and imitate his ways. In his brilliant study of Jesus, *Two Types of Faith,* Martin Buber addresses this, saying, "nowhere else is love to man precisely made the presupposition of the realized sonship to God as here, and that in the unheard of simple form of this 'so that', in the form . . . of open entrance for everyone who really loves. . . . the most daring arc has been described, and yet a circle has thereby been completed."[36] Buber means that Jesus has supplemented Judaism; yet has completed the circle of Hebrew revelation begun with the commands to love our neighbor, the stranger and the alien.

God forbid that I should detract from the uniqueness and beauty of Jesus' word! But a question must be raised about its counterpart, "You shall love your neighbor and hate your enemy." Does this sentence do justice to the Hebrew Bible? Leo Baeck thinks that the words "hate your enemy," which he calls "alien and opposed to the Bible," are an editorial addition. They "deprive this saying of its evident tendency: its concern with the meaning of the love of the neighbor."[37] In some sense we have to agree with Dr. Baeck. Jesus may have directed these words against people who so interpreted the Bible.[38] Or they may indeed be an editorial addition. Hatred for one's enemy is not absent from the Old Testament but is far removed from its central teaching. To give a single example: receiving the Law on Mount Sinai, Moses discovered "a God merciful and gracious, slow to anger, and abounding in steadfast love and faithfulness" (Ex. 34:6). The Psalmist makes this phrase universal (145:8-9): "The LORD is gracious and merciful, slow to anger and abounding in steadfast love. The LORD is good to all, and his compassion is over all that he has made." The prophet Jonah, sent to convert Israel's worst enemy, reminds God (4:2b): "That is why I made haste to flee to Tarshish; for I knew that thou art a gracious God and merciful, slow to anger, and abounding in steadfast love, and repentest of evil." The book of Jonah ends with God's reply, "And should I not pity Ninevah, that great city . . .?"

There is no great gulf between Judaism and Christianity over loving one's enemy. *The Fathers According to Rabbi Nathan* contains the aphorism, "Mighty is he who makes of his enemy a friend."[39] More important, the great *Aleynu* prayer from the Jewish liturgy, a prayer from before the time of Jesus and still central in the synagogue service, invokes the day

> When Thou wilt establish the world under Thy rule omnipotent,
> And all mankind shall invoke Thy name,
> And all the wicked on earth Thou wilt turn to Thee.[40]

Observant Jews literally fulfill Jesus' admonition to love their enemies and pray for those who persecute them.

Finally, the words "But I say to you" tell us something quite special about Jesus. The great rabbis spoke in the name of their teachers and expounded the received tradition. No one but Jesus used the exact formula, "But *I* say to you." In the same vein Christ said, "Heaven and earth will pass away, but my words will not pass away" (Mk. 13:31), placing his own words on the level of Torah. Jesus claimed authority not only to interpret and expound Torah—the revelation of God—but also to announce and declare it. He himself is the living Word of God.

IS IT LAWFUL

Just before interpreting our Lord's teachings about human sexuality, the preliminary *Study* says, "Jesus actually broke some laws . . . in order to reveal their inadequacy or harmful effects. For example, he apparently disregarded laws pertaining to fasting . . . working in the grainfields . . . healing on the sabbath . . . ." Jesus broke these laws to illustrate the basic principle "that laws exist to serve human welfare and enhance life" (p. 78).

That laws exist to serve human welfare and enhance life *was* a basic principle of both Jesus and the rabbis; it was complemented by the teaching that the laws of God *define* human welfare. Twice in the Gospels Jesus was asked what a person must do to inherit eternal life (Mk. 10:17; Lk. 10:25). In the first instance he replied, "You know the commandments;" in the second, speaking of the inquirer's summary of the Law, Jesus said, "You have answered right; do this, and you will live." The early church knew that infanticide did not serve human welfare or enhance life because it accepted Jesus' exposition of Torah (cf. *The Didache* 2, 2); the ancient Greeks and Romans, without that standard of revelation, practiced infanticide believing that it did serve human welfare.

If the laws of God (including the customary, ethical and theological norms derived from Scripture) *define* human welfare, we need to examine any statement that Jesus broke such laws with great care. The *Human Sexuality Study* cites several Gospel references and quickly passes on to the next subject. These references generally represent "conflict stories"—brief accounts of sharp exchanges between scribes and/or Pharisees and Jesus. The Gospels group these conflict stories in sections without much historical or contextual background. Careful study is necessary to determine the issues, people and movements involved and whether Jesus was commenting upon Scripture, upon settled rabbinic tradition or upon an isolated opinion. When Jesus, for example, condemns a *Corban* ruling in Mark 7:9-13, we cannot find such a ruling in rabbinic sources; in fact the Talmud agrees with Jesus that honoring one's father and mother takes precedence over a *Corban* vow. If the Gospel account is accurate, Jesus condemned either an isolated opinion or a ruling which the rabbis themselves later rejected.[41]

It should also be noted that the conflict stories refer to live, unsettled issues. At the time of Jesus, questions such as divorce, sabbath rules, the resurrection and paying taxes to Rome were in dispute among various sects, parties and schools; classical Judaism did not clearly emerge until after the destruction of the Temple in 70 A.D. when Sadducees, Zealots and Essenes had been eliminated from leadership. In many cases a violation of rabbinic law under consolidated Judaism would have been a difference of opinion or interpretation under earlier conditions. If we keep these factors in mind, a careful examination of the conflict stories reveals much about Jesus' attitude toward the

Law and his method of interpreting Scripture.

First, the preliminary *Study* says that Jesus disregarded laws pertaining to fasting, citing Mark 2:18-22 and the parallel passages from Matthew and Luke. Mark has the people ask Christ why John's disciples and the Pharisees fast but his disciples do not fast. In Matthew it is John's disciples who put the question to Christ (9:14); in Luke the Pharisees and scribes ask the question, adding prayers to fasting (5:30, 33). If we agree with the theory of source criticism, we will follow Mark. Strictly speaking this pericope is not a conflict story but an inquiry by the people into a custom distinguishing the *haberim* or religious brotherhoods from Jesus' disciples.

Contrary to the claim of the *Human Sexuality* report, *no question of the laws on fasting is involved.* According to *The Interpreter's Bible,* "Fasting was obligatory only on the day of atonement—Yom Kippur—and publicly proclaimed fast days. The reference is to private, voluntary fasting, which was not characteristic of Jesus' followers."[42] G. F. Moore writes, "a man might impose upon himself by a vow the obligation to fast every Monday and Thursday throughout the year," although his vow had to give way on feast days when fasting was not permissible.[43] This evidently was the custom of the Pharisees (cf. Lk. 18:12). Jesus gives the reason for the different custom of his disciples, "Can the wedding guests fast while the bridegroom is with them?" (Mk. 2:19). His disciples were celebrating the good news of the kingdom of God and preparing for the Messianic feast.

Despite the difference in custom, Jesus did not reject fasting, a vital religious practice among pious Jews. Jesus himself fasted "forty days and forty nights" in preparation for his temptation (Mt. 4:2). In the Sermon on the Mount (Mt. 6:1-18), he gives his disciples instructions for almsgiving, prayer and fasting—three closely connected Jewish practices believed to cleanse the heart from sin and establish communion with God. The Apocryphal book of *Tobit* acclaims, "Good is prayer with fasting and alms and righteousness, . . . for alms rescues from death and it will cleanse from all sin" (12:8-9).[44] In his instructions for observing these customs, our Lord enjoins purity of heart and warns against outward show. As we shall see throughout this section, the intention of the heart vivifies religious law, custom and practice. A good heart reveres God and keeps his Law. A bad heart may or may not profess to keep the Law. When it does it creates a terrible gap between the purpose and practice of the Law, between the Spirit and the letter. We find no such gap in the life and teaching of Jesus.

Second, the *Human Sexuality Study* says that Jesus broke the sabbath law regarding working in the grainfields, citing Mark 2:23-28 and parallel passages. Again, the issue is not discussed. The report ignores the fact that Jesus' disciples, *not Jesus,* plucked ears of grain on their way through a grainfield on a Sabbath. I believe that a majority of scholars would agree in this case that Jesus' disciples are guilty of a minor infraction of Jewish Law. Supposing the majority opinion to be correct, does it justify the conclusion reached in the *Study?* At most we have a minor infraction of a secondary rabbinic construction not committed by Jesus himself but defended by him on grounds of human need. In such a case I cannot see that Jesus disregarded the Sabbath law. But there is evidence to support a view opposed to the majority opinion.

An opposing view is suggested in *The Interpreter's One-Volume Commentary On The Bible:*

> The action is not clear (in the Greek); the manuscripts have many different scribal "corrections," or "improvements." Matt. (12:1) makes the offense plucking and eating; Luke (6:1) makes it a kind of crude threshing ("rubbing them in their hands"). The Pharisees permitted "plucking and eating" in case of need, but not harvesting or threshing.[45]

Joseph Klausner compares Jesus' argument in defense of his disciples with the rabbinic mode of reasoning from Scripture:

> When he allowed his disciples to pluck ears of corn on the Sabbath, he defends it by proofs drawn from David's eating of the altar-bread, and from the offering of sacrifices in the Temple on the Sabbath, and said that "the Sabbath was given for man and not man for the Sabbath" . . . ; and in exactly the same way the Pharisees also proved by this *a fortiori* argument, from the Temple and David's eating of the altar-bread (in *Y'lamm'denu,* Yalkut II §130), that the needs of life override the Sabbath restrictions . . . : and they also said (the early Tanna R. Shimeon ben Menassia, in *Mechilta* on Exodus 31, 14, beginning of §1): "The Sabbath was given for you: ye were not given for the Sabbath" (p. 92).[46]

The Talmud lists and discusses 39 labors forbidden on the Sabbath in the tractate *Shabbath* (73a-75b).[47] First the Talmud gives the text of the *Mishna,* the authoritative collection of oral traditions codified toward the end of the second century; it then adds *Gemara,* the discussions of the Mishna by later rabbis, also containing earlier traditions. The 39 labors listed in the Mishna begin with *sewing, ploughing, reaping, binding sheaves* and *threshing.*[48] It is usually said that the Pharisees, by constructive reasoning, condemned Jesus' disciples for either reaping or threshing when they plucked the ears of grain. In my opinion, a careful reading of *Shabbath* 73a-75b does not support the purported construction.

The Gemara (73b), relying upon an early tradition, groups reaping with gathering and collecting agricultural produce. But the disciples were not gathering; they were satisfying their immediate hunger. The Gemara contains a disagreement over whether a person is liable for throwing a clod of earth at a palm tree and dislodging dates. One rabbi says yes; another says no. This seems to be a more purposive activity than plucking some grain while passing through a field. The Gemara on threshing is very brief and groups threshing with beating out fibre plants.[49]

Just before the Gemara on reaping, we find the Gemara on ploughing.[50] Ploughing includes digging or trenching. It is said that if one digs a pit on the Sabbath to obtain the earth, not to create a pit, he is not culpable for the pit. He is not liable because the labor was not required on its own account (i.e. for the pit). He would be liable if the pit represented an improvement. But since it has damaged the ground, not improved it, he is not liable. This case seems parallel to that of Jesus' disciples. Their labor was not required for reaping the field. They merely took some ears of grain to satisfy their hunger. Their labor did not affect an improvement but caused damage.

The footnotes to the Soncino Press edition of the Talmud at this point refer the reader to *Shabbath* 12a and 31b, where the same line of reasoning is applied to collecting water and extinguishing lamps. Lamps may be extinguished in cases of danger or need, but not to spare the lamp, oil or wick (29b).[51] A footnote to 31b says that culpability depends upon the *intention* of the person extinguishing the wick.[52] The intention is determined by whether the person extinguishing the wick prepares it for future use. If we apply this principle to the case of the disciples, they had no intention of reaping and they prepared nothing for future use.

Jesus defended his disciples with the famous dictum, "The sabbath was made for man, not man for the sabbath" (Mk. 2:27). Our Lord perceived both the objective facts and the intention of his followers. They had not worked on the Sabbath and had no intention of working on the Sabbath. Had they intended to break the Sabbath, Jesus would not have defended them for the Sabbath was given to enhance man's relationship with God while easing his burden of labor. Therefore "the sabbath was made for man." Only when human intention is aligned with Divine intention is life enhanced. Because God is love no law of God denies human need. But it is God's will not human will which determines the nature of human need. Our Savior taught us to pray, "Thy kingdom come. Thy will be done, on earth as it is in heaven," and in his hour of deepest agony he prayed, "not what I will, but what thou wilt." In the discipline of obedience and suffering for the sake of Christ, we too discover that "his will is our peace."

Reviewing the Talmudic passages bearing upon the case, it is doubtful that the disciples were guilty of breaking the law since they had no intention of either reaping or threshing. That certain Pharisees believed the disciples had broken the law need not be questioned. Obviously Jesus did not agree with these Pharisees and challenged their view with arguments from Scripture in the rabbinic mode. Whether the view of the Pharisees in question had *halachic* or legal force at that moment of Jewish history is impossible to say from the available evidence. But Jesus' understanding of the intention of his disciples and of the Law of God is definitive.

Third, the preliminary *Study* says that Jesus broke the law forbidding healing on the sabbath, citing Mark 3:1-6 and parallel passages. On this point the *Study* is substantially correct. Joseph Klausner in *Jesus of Nazareth* maintains that Sabbath healing was a major cause of the breach between Jesus and the Pharisees. He writes:

> The *Talmud,* it is true, concludes that not only "the saving of human life sets aside the laws of the Sabbath," but that the same applied in cases where doubt arises as to imminent danger to life. . . . But it is wholly forbidden to heal an illness which is in no sense dangerous.[53]

The Gospels confirm the Talmudic material. Conflict stories over healing are numerous; we find them for example in Mark 3:1-6; Luke 13:10-17; 14:1-5; and John 7:21-24. Two questions should be asked. (1) What law did Jesus break? (2) Did Jesus believe he was breaking the Law of God?

The first question has a simple answer. Jesus did not break any law of Scripture in his Sabbath healings. He broke the scribal ruling which, by constructive reasoning, equated healing with work, bringing it under the prohibition of Exodus 20:10. This can be seen in Luke 13:14, "But the ruler of the synagogue, indignant because Jesus had healed on the sabbath, said to the people, 'There are six days on which work ought to be done; come on those days and be healed, and not on the sabbath day.' " Jesus' healings were a breach of *halachah* or oral law, an extremely serious matter in Judaism. The grounds for the breach may be found in the answer to the next question.

Did Jesus believe he was breaking the Law of God? The answer clearly is no. In Mark 3:4 he asks, "Is it lawful on the sabbath to do good or to do harm, to save life or to kill?" This question is echoed in Luke 14:3. His accusers remain silent. Jesus appeals to the great principle of the Law that God's commandments are a means of life and not of destruction, a principle fully recognized by the rabbis.[54] From this principle he reasons constructively that healing on the Sabbath is lawful. His conclusion is implicit in his question, "Is it lawful . . . ?" Jesus did not believe he was breaking the Law of Scripture or halachah. He announced his own halachic ruling, something fully within the power of the living Word. A brief examination of the arguments used by Jesus to support his decision sheds light on his hermeneutical method.

In Matthew 12:11-12 Jesus says:

> What man of you, if he has one sheep and it falls into a pit on the

sabbath, will not lay hold of it and lift it out? Of how much more value is a man than a sheep! So it is lawful to do good on the sabbath.

In Luke 13:15-16:

You hypocrites! Does not each of you on the sabbath untie his ox or his ass from the manger, and lead it away to water it? And ought not this woman, a daughter of Abraham whom Satan bound for eighteen years, be loosed from this bond on the sabbath day?

In John 7:22-24:

Moses gave you circumcision (not that it was from Moses, but from the fathers), and you circumcise a man upon the sabbath. If on the sabbath a man receives circumcision, so that the law of Moses may not be broken, are you angry with me because on the sabbath I made a man's whole body well?

These arguments conform to the rabbinic rule of interpretation known as *Kal va-homer. Kal va-homer* is the first of seven rules attributed to the great Hillel but almost certainly used before his time. The classic formula for *Kal va-homer* is, "If x is true, how much more must y be true."[55] It is a rule of inference. John Bowker defines it, "what applies in a less important case will certainly apply in a more important case." He tells how Hillel used *Kal va-homer* with other arguments to prove that the Passover offering could be slaughtered on the Sabbath. In essence Hillel argued, if the *tamid* (the daily sacrifice) takes precedence over the Sabbath, how much more must the Passover sacrifice take precedence over the Sabbath.[56]

This is exactly the kind of argument Jesus uses to justify Sabbath healing. He adds another thought in Luke 13 and John 7. A sick person is like a trapped or bound animal. To fully enjoy the Sabbath blessing they ought to be released from bondage and stand before God *whole.* Christ's major premise is inferred from the minor premises of Scripture and rabbinic rulings on (1) kindness to animals; and (2) circumcision.

The Pharisees believed that Jesus broke the Law. But Jesus, reasoning from Scripture and using the Pharisaic hermeneutic, believed that he fulfilled the true intent of the Law. Solomon Schechter in his *Aspects of Rabbinic Theology* calls this characteristic saintliness. The saint, he says, "like a good son studies his father's will, inferring from the explicit wishes of the father the direction in which he is likely to give him joy."[57] I would add that the saintliness or loving-kindness of Jesus does not distinguish between Law and compassion. Compassion is inferred from the text of the Law.

WHAT GOD HAS JOINED

After remarking that Jesus broke certain laws, the preliminary *Study* reviews his teachings on human sexuality. The review runs about a page and a half (pp. 78-79). It begins, "Jesus' teachings contain few explicit statements regarding human sexuality." It points out that Jesus crossed sexual and customary barriers to be close to women and affirm their worth, an excellent observation. It mentions the teachings of Jesus on divorce, adultery and lust, citing several Gospel passages. The *Study* interprets all of these teachings in the context of neighbor love. "Divorce is wrong because it violates and destroys love between persons. . . . ." In the paragraph on adultery, we read that sexual relationships "are wrong only when they do violence to neighbor love. . . ."

It is surprising that this section of the *Study* does not examine all of Jesus' explicit statements on human sexuality since they are few in number. Three important passages are not considered. The first is John 8:2-11, the case of the woman taken in adultery. When challenged, Jesus does not repudiate the Law of Moses but comments, "Let him who is without sin among you be the first to throw a stone at her." This illustrates his teaching, "and should not you have had mercy on your fellow servant, as I had mercy on you?" (Mt. 18:33). At the end of the pericope Jesus says to the adulterous woman, "Neither do I condemn you; go, and do not sin again." This saying combines our Lord's compassion for sinners with his righteous judgement upon sin.

A second passage the *Study* omits at this point is Mark 7:21-23:

> For from within, out of the heart of man, come evil thoughts, fornication, theft, murder, adultery, coveting, wickedness, deceit, licentiousness, envy, slander, pride, foolishness. All of these evil things come from within, and they defile a man.

Sexual immorality is prominent among the evils of the heart in Jesus' list. "All these evil things come from within, *and they defile a man.*" Fornication, adultery and licentiousness are not defined by context or situation; they are inherently evil just as theft, murder, coveting, deceit, slander and pride are inherently evil. The two passages cited above place Jesus at the center of the Judaic sexual ethic, his great compassion notwithstanding.

A third passage ignored in this review is Matthew 19:10-12. There Jesus says, "For there are eunuchs who have been so from birth, and there are eunuchs who have been made eunuchs by men, and there are eunuchs who have made themselves eunuchs for the sake of the kingdom of heaven," implying that people are able to give up their sexual proclivity for the sake of Christian service.

More remarkable than the *Study's* omission of the three passages above is its failure to explore the pericope on divorce in Mark 10:2-9. Here Jesus makes a definitive statement on human sexuality and explains his alternation of the Mosaic command. Certain Pharisees asked Jesus if it was lawful for a man to divorce his wife. This was not an abstract question. The School of Hillel allowed divorce; the

School of Shammai admitted divorce only on the grounds of unchasity.[58] After listening to the Mosaic ordinance (allowing a man to write a certificate of divorce), Jesus commented:

> For your hardness of heart he wrote you this commandment. But from the beginning of creation, 'God made them male and female.' 'For this reason a man shall leave his father and mother and be joined to his wife, and the two shall become one.' So they are no longer two but one. What therefore God has joined together, let not man put asunder.

Two salient points stand out in Jesus' comment. First, he quotes twice from the creation accounts (Gen. 5:1-2; 2:24). Remembering our definition of Torah earlier in this chapter, the words of creation in Genesis were just as much Law to Jesus as the words of Moses in Deuteronomy. Jesus recalls his hearers to God's original intention for humanity, an indissoluable union of male and female; by comparison Moses gave a permissive ruling adapted to the hardness of the human heart. Second, Jesus uses Hillel's second hermeneutical rule to interpret the Biblical material. This rule is known as *Gezerah shavah* and is a rule of comparison or verbal analogy. If the same word or phrase appears in two Pentateuchal passages, then the law applying in the first should be applied to the second.[59] Asher Finkel in his study of Jesus and the Pharisees says this is how Jesus arrived at the Great Commandment. By verbal analogy he applied the full force of "Thou shalt love thy God" in Deut. 6:5 to the love of neighbor in Lev. 19:18, so that he could say, "On these two commandments rest all the Law and Prophets."[60]

In the two passages from Genesis Jesus quotes, we do not have identical words but very similar words: (1) "male and female;" and (2) "man . . . wife" (also "father and mother"). The law or rule applying to Genesis, God creating mankind male and female (two being one), is applied to marriage: God joining male and female (two becoming one). In the intention of God the unity of male and female in marriage can no more be broken than their unity in creation, an irrevocable act of God determining the essential nature of man. The rule for creation is applied to marriage. God irrevocably joins male and female in one. Jesus' rationale against divorce is his Scriptural exposition of the creative purpose and will of God. True love of neighbor is bound up in the will of God in Jesus' teaching on divorce just as it is bound up in the love of God in his Great Commandment.

NOTES

1. W. D. Davies, *The Gospel And The Land* (Berkeley: University of California Press, 1974), pp. 377-389.

2. *Ibid.,* p. 378.

3. Harry Gersh, *The Sacred Books of the Jews* (New York: Stein and Day, 1972), pp. 218, 222. *Shema,* meaning 'Hear,' is the first word of Deut. 6:4 in the Hebrew text.

4. R. H. Lightfoot, *The Gospel Message of St. Mark* (London: Oxford University Press, 1962), pp. 46-47.

5. *Sanhedrin* is a tractate from the Talmud.

6. G. Quell & E. Stauffer, *Love,* Bible Key Words From Gerhard Kittel's *Theologisches Worterbuch Zum Neuen Testament,* trans. J. R. Coates (London: Adam And Charles Black, 1949), pp. 14, 23.

7. A free translation.

8. Micah 6:8.

9. Nahum N. Glatzer describes the major studies of the Pharisees in his forward to R. Travers Herford's *The Pharisees* (Boston: Beacon Press, 1962). Among other works he lists: Leo Baeck, *The Pharisees* (New York, 1947); Louis Finkelstein, *The Pharisees,* 2 vol. (Philadelphia, 1938); Jacob Z. Lauterbach, *Rabbinic Essays* (Cincinnati, 1951); I. Abrahams, *Pharisaism and the Gospels,* First and Second Series (Cambridge, 1917 and 1924); David Daube, *The New Testament and Rabbinic Judaism* (London, 1956). Dr. Glatzer himself has written a brief, illuminating work: *Hillel the Elder: The Emergence of Classical Judaism* (New York: Schocken Books, 1966).

Lauterbach's opinion is typical: "And while Jesus may have expressed some teachings different from those of the Pharisees, or on some questions may have argued against the Pharisaic interpretation of the Law, in most of his teachings he is in full accord with the Pharisees and his sayings echo the teachings of the Pharisees" (*Rabbinic Essays,* p. 89).

10. Matthew's version of the Great Commandment gives evidence of editing unfavorable to the Pharisees (cp. Mt. 22:34-40 with Mk. 12:28-34). Asher Finkel in *The Pharisees And The Teacher Of Nazareth* (Leiden/Köln: E. J. Brill, 1964) presents a strong case for his opinion: "The polemics with the Pharisees . . . were, in fact, directed at the zealous Pharisees, the disciples of Shammai's academy. On the other hand, the Pharisaic approach adopted by the disciples of Hillel's school—their humbleness, restraint, clear argumentative reasoning and liberal stand—was close in spirit to that of the teacher of Nazareth" (p. 134f.).

11. Joseph of Arimathea's Messianic belief indicates that he was probably a Pharisee.

12. *Great Ages And Ideas of the Jewish People,* ed. Leo W. Schwarz (New York: The Modern Library, 1956), p. 109.

13. *Ibid.,* pp. 156-157. Dr. Cohen quotes from the amplified version of *Pirke Abot* known as *The Fathers According to Rabbi Nathan;* but I have preferred to use *Pirke Abot* from *The Mishna,* trans. H. Danby (Oxford: Clarendon Press, 1933), p. 446.

14. *The Fathers According to Rabbi Nathan,* trans. Judah Goldin (New York: Schocken Books, 1974). My descriptions of this book and of *Pirke Abot* have been taken from Judah Goldin's introduction.

15. *Ibid.,* p. 34.

16. Nahum N. Glatzer, *Hillel the Elder: The Emergence of Classical Judaism,* revised ed. (New York: Schocken Books, 1966), p. 85. I am indebted to this work for introducing me to Johanan ben Zakkai's statement on atonement.

17. *Ibid.,* pp. 51-52.

18. *The Universal Jewish Encyclopedia,* ed. Isaac Landman (New York: The Universal Jewish Encyclopedia, Inc., 1943), Vol. 10, "Torah," p. 267f.

19. G. F. Moore, *Judaism In The First Centuries Of The Christian Era,* Vol. I (Cambridge: Harvard University Press, 1927), p. 263.

20. In contrast to Jesus, Paul uses the term Torah or Law in a narrower sense. The Law came 430 years after the promise to Abraham (Gal. 3:17); it is to be distinguished from grace and faith (Rom. 6:15; Gal. 3:23). The Law is God's standard of righteousness or *commandment* which defines transgression and sin (Rom. 4:15; 7:7-12). If we take Paul's concepts of Law and Grace together (and each requires the other), we have approximately what Jesus meant by Torah.

I would also call the reader's attention to Paul's statements, "So the law is holy, and the commandment is holy and just and good" (Rom. 7:12); "Do we then overthrow the law by this faith? By no means! On the contrary, we uphold the law" (Rom. 3:31). Finally, Paul names the ultimate expression of human pride and rebellion against God *ho anomos,* "the lawless one" (II Thess. 2:8).

21. Gustaf Dalman, *The Words Of Jesus,* trans. D. M. Kay (Edinburgh: T. & T. Clark, 1902), pp. 5-6.

22. *The International Critical Commentary, Matthew* by W. C. Allen (New York: Charles Scribners Sons, 1907), p. 46.

23. *Calvin's Commentaries, Matthew, Mark and Luke,* Vol. I (Grand Rapids: Wm. B. Eerdmans Publishing Co., 1972), p. 180.

24. *The International Critical Commentary, op. cit.,* p. 45.

25. *The Universal Jewish Encyclopedia, op. cit.,* p. 268.

26. *The Jewish Encyclopedia* (New York & London: Funk & Wagnalls, 1906), Vol. XII, "Torah," p. 196.

27. Israel Frankel, *Peshat in Talmudic And Midrashic Literature* (Toronto: La Salle Press, 1956), p. 108.

28. *Ibid.,* pp. 27-28.

29. Cited by Frankel, *op. cit.,* p. 48.

30. Frankel, *op. cit.,* p. 30.

31. Solomon Schecter, *Aspects Of Rabbinic Theology* (New York: Schocken Books, 1961), pp. 213-214.

32. Leo Baeck, *Judaism And Christianity,* trans. Walter Kaufmann (New York: Ahteneum, 1970), p. 126, n. 54.

33. Moshe Chayim Luzzatto, *The Path of the Just,* Second Revised Ed., trans. Shraga Silverstein (Jerusalem—New York: Feldheim Publishers, 1966), p. 143.

34. *Pentateuch And Haftorahs,* Second Edition, ed. Dr. J. H. Hertz (London, Soncino Press, 1975), pp. 309, 405.

35. Leo Baeck, *op. cit.,* p. 130, n. 64.

36. Martin Buber, *Two Types of Faith,* trans. Norman P. Goldhawk, Harper Torchbooks (New York: Harper & Row, Publishers, 1961), p. 76.

37. Leo Baeck, *op. cit.,* p. 128, n. 57.

38. This is Martin Buber's opinion, *op. cit.,* pp. 72-73.

39. *The Fathers According to Rabbi Nathan, op. cit.,* p. 101.

40. Harry Gersh, *The Sacred Books of the Jews, op. cit.,* p. 228.

41. The evidence is summarized by Joseph Klausner, *Jesus of Nazareth* (New York: The MacMillan Co., 1925), pp. 289-290.

42. *The Interpreter's Bible* (New York: Abingdon Press, 1951), Vol. VII, p. 354.

43. G. F. Moore, *op. cit.,* Vol. II, p. 261.

44. Cited in *The Interpreter's Bible, op. cit.,* p. 306.

45. *The Interpreter's One-Volume Commentary On The Bible* (New York: Abingdon Press, 1971), p. 650.

46. Joseph Klausner, *op. cit.,* p. 122.

47. *The Babylonian Talmud, Seder Mo'ed In Four Volumes,* Vol. I, ed. I. Epstein, *Shabbath,* trans. H. Freedman (London: The Soncino Press, 1938), pp. 348-359.

48. *Ibid.,* pp. 348-349.

49. *Ibid.,* pp. 350-351.

50. *Ibid.,* p. 350.

51. *Ibid.,* p. 131.

52. *Ibid.,* p. 144, n. 7.

53. Joseph Klausner, *op. cit.,* pp. 278-279. For Mishnaic references see *Shabbath* 109b & 111a, *op. cit.,* pp. 532, 539.

54. See page 62 above.

55. *Encyclopaedia Judaica* (Jerusalem: The MacMillan Co., 1971), "Hermeneutics," Vol. 8, p. 367. The article says that in symbolic logic the formula is: If A has X, then B certainly has X.

56. John Bowker, *The Targums And Rabbinic Literature* (Cambridge: The University Press, 1969), pp. 315, 317.

57. Solomon Schecter, *op. cit.,* p. 209.

58. G. F. Moore, *op. cit.,* Vol. II, pp. 123-124.

59. *Encyclopaedia Judaica, op. cit.,* pp. 367-368.

60. Asher Finkel, *The Pharisees And The Teacher Of Nazareth* (Leiden/Köln: E. J. Brill, 1964), p. 174.

7 Ordination In the United Church of Christ

by John C. Shetler

What is ordination in the United Church of Christ? Since this is a denomination that permits diversity one at first may think there are as many answers as there are pastors and congregations. However, by looking at the documents of the church one discovers there is a doctrinal and ecclesiastical standard that runs back to the Reformation in Switzerland and England. These documents include the Constitutions of the United Church of Christ and the antecedent bodies, published doctrinal statements, confessions and catechisms. They are set against the background of tradition and the Holy Scripture. An exhaustive study would result in a book. Therefore, we consider this chapter to be a summary statement.

Ordination is a rite of the church—a sacred act of worship whereby a person is set aside for the full time ministry of Jesus Christ, the Lord and Head of the Church. The participants in the rite of ordination are (1) God, (2) the ordinand and (3) the church. The Constitution of the United Church of Christ speaks as follows:

Ordination is the rite whereby the United Church of Christ through an Association, in co-operation with the local church, sets apart by prayer and the laying on of hands those of its members God has called to the Christian ministry. By this rite ministerial standing is conferred and authorization is given to perform all the duties and to exercise all the prerogatives of the ministry.

An *Ordained Minister* of the United Church of Christ is one of its members who has been called of God and ordained to preach and teach the gospel, to administer the sacraments and rites of the Church, and to exercise pastoral care and leadership.

Ministerial Standing in the United Church of Christ is held in an Association.

The Call of a minister to a pastorate establishes a covenant relation-

John C. Shetler is the Conference Minister of the Pennsylvania Southeast Conference.

ship between the minister and the local church. This relationship is also a concern of the Church at large as represented by an Association and a Conference.

A rite is distinguished from a sacrament by Biblical interpretation. The sacraments are traditionally based on evidence that Jesus performed the act, made it central to ministry and worship and commanded the church to follow His example. Thus the sacraments of Baptism and the Eucharist are the central acts of the Protestant Church. The rites take a lesser position among the sacred acts of worship. At times they are called occasional services. Traditionally in the Reformed family of churches they include ordination, marriage, confirmation and burial.

Ordination or the laying on of hands with prayer is first mentioned in the New Testament in Acts 6:6. This reference, the occasion of the ordaining of deacons, is the beginning of the practice of Holy Orders where the deacon is the first step to pastoral ministry. As the congregations were established beyond Jerusalem, the apostles found it necessary to ordain not only deacons but also elders who were the overseers for one or more congregations. The New Testament uses the words elder and bishop interchangeably in this function of overseer. There is clear evidence that all these offices were filled by the act of prayer and laying on of hands.

The selection of persons to serve as deacons and elders was important; Luke is careful to make clear that Stephen was called because he was a man *"full of faith and of the Holy Spirit."*[1] Of the seven Luke says *"Pick out from among you seven men of good repute, full of the Spirit and of wisdom"* (Acts 6:3). Paul in speaking of Timothy clearly indicates Timothy's Christian preparation by his mother and grandmother, Eunice and Lois, both women of faith. The apostle says *"I am reminded of your sincere faith, a faith that dwelt first in your grandmother Lois and your mother Eunice and now, I am sure, dwells in you."*[2] Notice the requirements (1) wisdom (which comes after knowledge), (2) good reputation, (3) spirit filled and (4) men of faith.

The laying on of hands was the indication of appointment or call by God and by the church. The church was in some instances the apostles and in others the congregation until the formation of the councils and presbyteries which gathered together the representatives of the congregations of the region.

St. Paul believed that God participated in the laying on of hands. As the hands were laid on the head so God's blessing was bestowed on the ordinand. To Timothy Paul said, *"I remind you to rekindle the gift of God that is within you through the laying on of my hands."*[3] What was the gift? The generally accepted understanding is that the Holy Spirit was the gift. *"God did not give us a spirit of timidity but a spirit of power and love and self control."*[4] Power, love and self control are among the gifts of the Spirit. However, the apostle understands God's gift to be greater than the blessing of His Spirit. God gave of Himself as the gift. The gift was of the wholeness and completeness of Himself. The salutation to Timothy (as in Paul's other letters) indicates clearly when we keep the phrases of his letter in context that God's blessing included the grace, mercy and peace of the Father and of the Son, Christ Jesus our Lord. For Paul, then, ordination was no partial, weak or limited ordination but involved the blessing of Father, Son and Holy Spirit.

By the giving of Himself to the ordained one, God makes it possible to live a holy life, a life that reflects the wholeness of God. A lifestyle is described for Timothy by Paul. Certainly the dedicated life was evident before the call, but Paul sees the gift of God at ordination resulting in a new dimension and further development of the person. The apostle in the First Letter to Timothy makes general statements regarding the quality of life to be lived by elders and deacons who are ordained to preach the Gospel. Paul sets forth at least sixteen character manifestations for elders and five for deacons, but, of course, does not limit the gifts of God. These manifestations reflect the gifts of God, but are also indicative of the character of the person at the time of the call. Luke in Acts 6:3 says, *"Pick out from among you seven men of good repute."*

Having considered our Biblical roots, it is important to look at our Reformation roots. In one brief chapter, we cannot look at all strains of our Reformation history but we can look at the chief Reformed theologian who stands behind the United Church of Christ.

Ordination by prayer and laying on of hands is a prerequisite to ministry for Calvin. Prior to the ordination, education and careful preparation for ministry were required. This preparation was tested by a rigorous examination which also determined the genuine condition of the call to the ministry.[5] The exercise of the rite with its prerequisite requirements was the initiatory means of maintaining order among the clergy and thereby in the church. The extreme importance of order in Calvin's system can be seen in his statement, *"No society, no house can be preserved in proper condition without discipline. The Church ought to be the most orderly society of all. As the saving doctrine of Christ is the soul of the Church, so discipline forms the nerves and ligaments which connect the members and keep each in its proper place."*[6]

The church through ordination bestowed authority on the pastor *"to preach the Word of God, to instruct, to admonish, to exhort and reprove in public and private, to administer the sacraments and jointly, with the elders, to exercise discipline."*[7] The other offices (teacher, elder and deacon) as defined by Calvin did not include the authority to administer the sacraments. The authority which accompanies ordination has as its central function the protection of the purity of the doctrine preached, the correct administration of the sacraments and the veracity of the historical Biblical discipline of the ministry and of the church. This protection rested on very careful selection and preparation of the candidates for ordination. *"In the examination, the candidate must give satisfactory evidence of his knowledge of the Scriptures, his soundness in doctrines, purity of motives and integrity of character."*[8]

Calvin saw in the act of ordination more than the conferring of authority by the church. It was for him an act of worship in which both man and God were the participants. The life of the ordinand was offered to God and the gifts of the Holy Spirit were conferred by the laying on of hands and by prayer. The reformer further spoke of ordination as *"highly useful both to recommend to the people the dignity of the ministry and to admonish the person ordained that he is no longer his own master, but devoted to the service of God and the Church."*[9]

The examination of candidates was conducted by the pastors of the district and they as the members of the *Venerable Company* approved the candidate as well as ordained him. The consent of the council and the congregation were also necessary.

These concepts of Calvin and the Genevan Church have generally prevailed in the Reformed and Presbyterian Churches of the continent, Great Britain and the United States. In particular in the Reformed Church in the United States licensure and ordination were lodged with the district unit called "classis" which was composed of pastors and elders.

Other strains than the Calvinistic are present in the United Church of Christ and they were reflected in the antecedent bodies. While Calvinistic in theology early New England Congregationalism never accepted the connectional polity of Geneva and placed the actions involved in ordination in the authority of the congregation. The evolution of the Associations in the Congregational Churches included the development of the practice of examination for licensure as a prerequisite for ordination. An early development in this direction in England and which affected New England may be seen in the "Heads of agreement, Assented to by the United Ministers in and about London, 1691"–"In so great and weighty matter as the calling and chusing a Pastor, we judge it ordinarily requisite, that every such Church consult and advise with the Pastors of Neighbouring Congregations."[10]

The Evangelical Synod of North America, one of the bodies forming the Evangelical and Reformed Church, had its roots in both the Lutheran and Reformed Churches in Prussia. When the Prussian Union of these Churches occurred in 1817 a reaction to the Reformed Consistories and the influence of Lutheran pietism from Basel and Barmen missionaries led to the acceptance of Luther's idea of the Pastorenkirche and the formation of the Kirchenverein. The Pastorenkirche can be interpreted to indicate that *"the essential element of the Church is the pastoral office."* The Kirchenverein was a *"kind of pastoral Conference with only pastors holding full membership."*[11] Licensure and ordination were in the hands of the pastors of the Kirchenverein and its district organizations. The Evangelical and Reformed Church which united the Evangelical Synod of North America and the Reformed Church in the United States placed the authority for licensure and ordination in the regional synod which included pastors and lay delegates.

The United Church of Christ continues the spirit of the Reformed Church of Geneva, Switzerland, and the Palatinate. The bylaws of the national church assign the responsibility for student care, licensure and examination for ordination to the Association and the Conference. The initiator of all action related to examination and ordination is the home church of the student. Only after careful examination the Consistory or Council recommends the student to be taken under care of the Association. The first point of control is the congregation. Later a similar request is made for ordination. The bylaws do not recommend to the congregation what characteristics and qualities must be present in the student for such recommendation. However, the Association and Conference Committees on the Ministry are to examine for fitness, aptitudes, Christian experience and commitment.[12] Certainly the congregation would not expect less. It would be well for the Consistory, Council, Association and Conference Committees to examine each candidate for "in care" status by using the questions which later are used in the United Church of Christ service for ordination. There is no reason why these questions should be left for the ordination examination.

"Before God and this congregation we ask you:

Are you persuaded that God has called you to be ordained a minister in the church of the Lord Jesus Christ, and are you ready to enter this ministry and faithfully to serve in it?

Do you, with the church throughout the world, hear the Word of God in the scriptures of the Old and New Testaments, and do you accept it as the rule of Christian faith and practice?

Do you promise to be diligent in your private prayers and reading of the scriptures, as well as in the public duties of your office?

Will you be zealous in maintaining both the truth of the gospel and the peace of the church, speaking the truth in love?

Do you accept the faith and order of the United Church of Christ; and will you, as a minister in this communion, show brotherly affection toward all who are in Christ?"[13]

These ordination questions, when summarized as follows, show a very direct relationship to the ordination doctrines of the Genevan Church:

Called by God into the ministry of Christ.
Recognition of the Word of God and acceptance of it as the rule.
Faithfulness in communication with God.
Faithfulness in communication of the Gospel in word and deed.
Loyalty to the Church as the body of Christ.
Demonstration of Christian love to others.

Regular meetings and counselling sessions should take place among the pastor, committees and each student during each year of the preparation for the pastorate. Each year the fitness, development, academic preparation and sense of calling should be examined. It is important that the student know and experience the development for ministry in the corporate life of the church. The development of the student can not be left for any independent seminary which is not fully incorporated into the life of the church. It is the church's prerogative to prepare young people for lifetime ministry. The Constitution and Bylaws of the United Church of Christ make it clear that ministry and the preparation for it are not individualistic, solitary, humanistic, nonecclesiastical matters of life and practice. The sections pertaining to ministry and ordination are to be considered in the complete context of the document. It is very important to consider preparation for licensure and ordination in the light of the preamble which emphasizes the centrality and headship of Christ, the Word of God in the Scriptures, the presence and power of the Holy Spirit, the historic faith of the church and common witness in Him (Christ) to serve His kingdom in the world.

A manifestation of the fact that ordination is one of the principle keys to order in the church can be seen in its relationship to the sacrament of the Eucharist. Since the days of the New Testament the church has restricted the administration of the sacraments to ordained persons. By such action it has attempted to assure the proper celebration of the Eucharist with the use of the words of Jesus and the Pauline narrative which is incorporated in the Eucharistic prayer. This emphasis on right celebration by New Testament standards has been one of the chief marks of the Reformed tradition.

As the preparation and the examination of the ordinand are the business of the church, so also is the act of ordination. One individual does not ordain another for personalistic and individualistic reasons. Rather the corporate body in the service of ordination recognizes, celebrates and witnesses that (A) God acts: (1) a call from God does prevail, (2) the gifts of God are evident; (B) that the ordinand acts: (1) by the acceptance of the call through commitment, education and service, (2) the making of the vows and (3) the acceptance of laying on of hands; (C) the church acts: (1) a congregation has called, (2) members have come to witness and participate in worship. These requisites now fulfilled in the ordination of the person have inherent in them a certain authority and outwardly vest the ordained with rights, privileges and authority. In consequence of this the church says, *"committing unto him (her) authority to preach your Word, to administer the sacraments, and to exercise the responsibilities of pastor and teacher."*[14] John W. Nevin, professor of theology at Mercersburg and Lancaster taught that God through the apostles and the church conveyed an objective authority through the laying on of hands.

"The selection and recognition of ministers were prerogatives of the eldership, so that an unbroken line of ministers extended from the Apostles to his (Nevin's) day as a self perpetuating corporation within the Church."[15] *"The Rev. Joseph Lathrop, . . . pastor in West Springfield, Massachusetts in the last generation of the eighteenth century . . . wrote to warn the congregations of the state church against irregular lay preachers and itinerant revivalists. He followed President Ezra Stiles of Yale in contending that in the Congregational church there was an unbroken succession of presbyterially ordained clergy since the apostles. There was divine authority, he argued, not for any particular polity but for an uninterrupted ministerial order in the church. New ministers, consequently, were to be received only if approved and recommended by Elders of churches."*[16] To this we add another statement of Nevin, *"Ordination does convey in this sense, objective virtue or force, such as no man in the ordinary course of things, can be allowed to possess without it."*[17]

Included in the authority of ordination is the "power of the keys" or the loosing or binding the sins of people on earth. The Reformed concept is that God through the grace of Christ frees from sin through the individual having heard the Gospel preached. The preaching of the Word and the administration of the Word through the sacraments then is for the ordained pastor the power of the keys. This concept is carried further to include the discipline of the church which involves the receiving of members, the fencing of the table for communion and the disciplining of members prior to erasure from the rolls of the church. The ordained pastor with ordained elders (lay persons) form a council in common to administer these functions.

There is an expected life style for the ministry and it does not automatically settle down upon the ordinand when the hand is laid on the head and the robe is laid over the body. There is also an expected life style for a Christian and it is out of this life of the corporate body that style of life for the ordained pastor develops during the long years of preparation. One of the reasons for any weakness in the church in any age is the adoption by the pastors and members of the ways of the world. One may call this reverse leavening where the world permeates the church with its materialistic paganness rather than the church permeating the world with the spirit of the Christ and the Gospel. It is important that very early in the period of preparation the person becomes aware of the exhortations of Paul—*"A bishop (elder) must be above reproach, married only once, temperate, sensible, dignified, hospitable, an apt teacher, no drunkard, not violent but gentle, not quarrelsome, and no lover of money. He must manage his own household well . . . He must not be a recent convert, or he may be puffed up with conceit"* (I Timothy 3:2-6).

These injunctions with regard to life style are most serious. Because the ordained has been called of God they rest heavily on mind and heart with an understanding that people learn from the pastor by word and deed. At this point it is important to emphasize again the pastor has been called from the Christian community which is also under the injunctions of Jesus and the Apostle Paul. There are to be no double standards. Jesus in speaking to the disciples about the Kingdom and children said, *"Whoever causes one of these little ones who believe in me to sin, it would be better for him to have a great millstone fastened round his neck and to be drowned in the depth of the sea"* (Matthew 18:5-6). Paul in writing to the Christians in Rome about their relationship to one another said, *"Decide never to put a stumbling block or hindrance in the way of a brother . . . It is right not to eat meat or drink wine or do anything that makes your brother stumble"* (Romans 14:13, 21).

It is important that the pastor not consider the disciplined life a burden, but know that the Spirit of God at the laying on of hands both blesses and sanctifies. As the risen Christ drew near to the disciples on the way to Emmaus and broke bread with them, so He draws near to His pastors. Joy is one of the gifts of the Spirit and this too is imparted. As one assumes the mantle of servanthood under Christ, the mystical union with Christ the Savior and Lord is deepened and strengthened. The pastor is the minister of the risen Christ—a herald of the resurrection! This in itself brings the blessing of deep inner peace and joy.

It is appropriate to close this brief summary of the doctrine and practice of ordination with the prayer of ordination from the service of the United Church of Christ.

"O Lord our God, in wisdom you govern all things, and from the beginning you have chosen men to serve you in the ministry of reconciliation, calling some apostles, some prophets, some evangelists, some pastors and teachers, to equip the saints for the work of ministry, and for building up the body of Christ; now bless and sanctify by your Holy Spirit this your servant, whom we, in your name and in obedience to your will, by prayer with the laying on of hands, do ordain to the ministry of the Church, committing to him authority to preach your Word, to administer the sacraments, and to exercise the responsibilities of pastor and teacher. Bestow upon him the power of your Holy Spirit, confirming what we do. Let the same mind be in him which was also in Christ Jesus. Enable him to nourish your people in the faith of the

Gospel. Fill his speech with truth and his life with purity. Increase his faith in you, strengthen him in the day of trouble, and prosper his words and works, that your name may be glorified and your truth exalted; through Jesus Christ our Lord. Amen."

NOTES

1. Acts 6:5.
2. II Timothy 1:5.
3. *Ibid.,* 1:6.
4. *Ibid.,* 1:7.
5. Schaff, *History of the Christian Church,* Vol. VII, p. 477.
6. Calvin, *Institutes of the Christian Religion,* Book 4, Chapter 5.
7. Schaff, *History of the Christian Church,* Vol. VII, p. 477.
8. *Ibid.*
9. Calvin, *Institutes of the Christian Religion,* Book 4, Chapter 5, para. 16.
10. Walker, *The Creeds and Platforms of Congregationalism,* p. 548.
11. Gunnemann, *The Shape of the United Church of Christ,* p. 187, 186.
12. *The Constitution and Bylaws of the United Church of Christ,* para. 102.
13. *The Order for Ordination to the Ministry, United Church of Christ.*
14. *The Order for Ordination to the Ministry, United Church of Christ,* p. 4.
15. Nichols, *Romanticism in American Theology,* p. 264.
16. *Ibid.,* p. 25, 26.
17. *Ibid.,* p. 265.

BIBLIOGRAPHY

A Book of Worship for Free Churches, prepared under the Direction of the General Council of the Congregational Churches in the U.S. (Oxford University Press, New York, 1948).

A Manual on the Ministry, Office for Church Life and Leadership, United Church of Christ (New York, 1977).

Ainsle, J.E., *The Doctrine of Ministerial Order in the Reformed Churches of the Sixteenth and Seventeenth Centuries* (Edinburgh, T. & T. Clark, 1940).

Book of Order, edited for Pennsylvania Southeast Conference, United Church of Christ (Collegeville, Pa. 1978).

Book of Worship, Approved by the General Synod of the Evangelical and Reformed Church (Eden Publishing House, St. Louis, Mo. 1947).

Calvin, John, *Institutes of the Christian Religion,* J. Allen, B.B. Warfield and T.C. Pears, Vols. I & II (Presbyterian Board of Christian Education, Phila.).

Erb, W.H., *Dr. Nevin's Theology* (I.M. Beaver, Publisher, Reading, Pa. 1913).

Gans, Daniel, *"The Office of Bishop," The Mercersburg Review,* Vol. XI, 1859, Chambersburg, Pa. 1859.

Gunnemann, L.H., *The Shaping of the United Church of Christ* (United Church Press, New York, 1977).

New Testament, Quotations are from the Revised Standard Version (Thomas Nelson Sons, New York, 1946).

Nichols, J.H., *Romanticism in American Theology* (University of Chicago Press, 1961, Chicago, Ill.).

Order of Worship, for the Reformed Church in the U.S. (S.R. Fisher, Co., 1866).

Schaff, P., *History of the Christian Church, Vol. VII, The Swiss Reformation* (Charles Scribner's Sons, New York 1894).

Services of the Church, the Order for Ordination to the Ministry, United Church of Christ (United Church Press, Philadelphia, Pa. 1969).

Schneider, C.E., *The German Church on the North American Frontier* (Eden Publishing House, St. Louis, Mo., 1939).

The Constitution and Bylaws of the United Church of Christ (New York, 1977).

Walker, W., *The Creeds and Platforms of Congregationalism* (The Pilgrim Press, Boston, 1960).

8 Christian Marriage and the Christian Family
The Challenge to the Church

by Robert L. Stogner

When a Christian man marries a Christian woman, this is a "Christian marriage." When this couple has children this becomes a "Christian family." At least this is often our traditional and simplistic concept of Christian marriage and Christian family. In a society that is basically traditional and simplistic this seems to be an acceptable concept. However, in a society that is searching, experiencing, and pluralistic, this is indeed an inadequate concept. At this point many of us who are very involved with and committed to the concepts of Christian marriage and family begin to defend the traditional concept in fear of losing it. The awesome and urgent challenge before the church today is not so much to "defend" but to "define" and to "deliver." The challenge is to discover and to rediscover the meaning of married spirituality and the mystical union of man, woman, and God. Then, to make these discoveries so "meaningful" and so available that every Christian couple can experience them. The church is called to provide a ministry wherein the Christian couple is constantly learning and experiencing more satisfying levels of spiritual union and emotional and physical intimacy. Christian marriage is not simply the marriage of two Christians, but rather a known process that can be taught by the church and experienced by the couple. A Christian marriage that is fulfilling and beautiful does not need to be defended. Its existence is its own defense. The challenge before the church is not to spend its energies in defending Christian marriage but rather to explore, to discover, to reveal, and to deliver to its people the beauty, joy, and fulfillment that is uniquely Christian in a marriage of two Christians. For some of us this means "losing" our static, traditional concept to "find" something dynamic and more valuable.

Usually the experience of loss is painful and difficult. In the case of traditions and institutions, loss (which is experienced as change) is slow in addition to being painful and difficult. But for many Christian

Robert L. Stogner is Director of Family Life Services for the Elon Home For Children U.C.C., Elon College.

couples their loss compared to their gain, will make that loss not a pain, but a joy. In the book *Mirages of Marriage*, psychiatrist Don Jackson, after an intensive investigation of many marriages, estimated that not more than five to ten percent of all married couples in our culture enjoy a really good relationship. Dr. David Mace developed a test that couples could use in finding out how much of their potential they had already reached in the marriage. It was discovered

> that most of them had hidden wealth in their relationships . . . they had settled for a comparatively superficial relationship. These couples had stable marriages and considered themselves to be free from specific problems. But the true state of their relationship . . . was one of dull, dreary mediocrity.[1]

After ten years of work in churches and with families, it is my conviction that many marriages within the church function far below their potential. These marriages are often "stable," especially in terms of longevity and support of the church. However, in the areas of relationships, joy, fulfillment, intimacy, and growth there is a great void. There is a level of "life," but certainly not "life more abundant." For the church to call these couples to a more dynamic experience of Christian marriage is to ask them to undergo a loss. They must lose the only experience or concept of Christian marriage they have ever known.

Many times the young people raised in these "stable" but unfulfilled marriage-families want "more" out of their relationships. Since this something "more" was not present within their traditional Christian family, they reason that they must go outside of the church and outside of the traditional marriage model. Their relationships emphasize pleasure, fulfillment, intimacy, and satisfaction of their desires and needs. "Stability," commitment, tradition, and rules are seen as blocking or even denying these relationship goals. The same experience is sometimes true for the husband or wife. After years of marriage, one or both partners want out. It is one of those situations where everyone says, "I just can't understand it." Yet within us is a haunting voice that says, "I think I can understand it."

It seems that our view of marriage is divided into two "camps" or concepts. The one stresses the stability needs of marriage, which include some of the traditional physical and social functions. The other stresses the relationship needs which include the emotional, the "feeling" and the satisfaction of needs. If a Christian couple holds to either view, then this particular concept is labeled "Christian marriage." This is obviously very dangerous for we have built our concept of Christian marriage from our images of ourselves. Here again the challenge is to let go of where we "are" and to sincerely search for God's best intentions for a man and woman's relationship together. Difficulty in a marriage often springs from an emphasis on one of these viewpoints while ignoring the other. In either situation the marriage is left with a void. As we allow the focus of a marriage relationship to be rooted in the Christian experience, we realize that all needs are important. The cause of Christian witness is hurt when either point of view is championed as "the Christian" one. So often I have met Christians who are very sincere and vocal in their Christian witness but who are locked into stable but empty and painful marriages. Frequently these people are unaware of the source of their discomfort. The ministry of the church has not touched their pain.

THE CHALLENGE TO DEFINE

The challenge before the church is to "lay hold upon" the essence of Christian marriage and family life, which is a goal far beyond the reach of this paper. Our hope is to bring forth some of the issues that are a part of this rediscovery process. The central theme of the Christian experience is a spiritual experience. In referring to married spirituality Father Gordon Lester, Director of the Marriage-Family Center at Picture Rock Retreat Center in Arizona, states that

> the human reality of marriage is a sign of Christ's presence . . . the reality is that by the choice of God, marriage has been marked to bring God present in and through the realities of married life.[2]

Married spirituality is not seeking God as an escape from the troubles of marriage or for strength only to bear it or as a source of divisiveness.

> Rather one's personal relationship with God is a treasure to be shared with the other patiently, reverently, and delicately. It is a showing that one watches for the right moment, strives to set the right conditions.[3]

Father Gordon makes two other points concerning married spirituality. One is

> that marriage is a vocation which chooses to pursue together the full potential of human love . . . Marriage lived out in its fullness is a human sign of the fulfillment a person can find only in the union of love with God.[4]

Married spirituality is a sexual spiritual life.

> Married spirituality resists and rejects the idea that nonsexual love is somehow better than sexual love. Married spirituality is a reaffirmation that human holiness means integrating the whole human being as designed by God, not eliminating part of his design as unworthy.[5]

Gabriel Calvo, founder of Marriage Encounter, writes about marriage spirituality and the value of mutual confiding.

> Marriage Spirituality has its special characteristics which are presented and assimilated only gradually. Mutual Confiding—An opening

of minds and hearts between husband and wife in the areas of the human and supernatural—is the fundamental first step. The path which the couple should pursue together to reach the goal which God proposes has spiritual aspects whose value is basic . . . No one should lose his or her personality in marriage. Instead there must be an attempt to bind the two human beings into a new and common personality . . . The confrontation and conjunction of ways of thinking and feeling are necessary so that the marriage will have a definite personality rather than just a hodgepodge of opinions and emotions. Beyond simple trust which is basic, there is mutual confiding which is opening one's life to the other.[6]

In a more poetic way, Temple Gairdner, whose life was spent as a missionary to Egypt, writes of marriage and spiritual life as he prepared for his wedding day.

That I may come near to her,
draw me nearer to thee than to her;
That I may love her with the perfect love of a perfect heart,
cause me to love thee more than her and most of all.
That nothing may be between me and her,
be thou between us every moment.
That we may be constantly together, draw us into separate
     loneliness with thyself.
And when we meet breast to breast, O God, let it be upon thine own.

In an article for *Marriage and Family Living* Magazine, David Mace talks about the spiritual aspects of marriage that have been part of the experience and belief of him and his wife Vera. He feels it was God who brought them together in the first place.

Further, it is unthinkable that God should have a plan for other aspects of my life, but not one for the very special relationship with the person whom I share life at the closest and most intimate level . . . we both believe it was in the providence of God that we were brought together. We were very sure of this on our wedding day, and we have never questioned it since.[7]

The Mace's also see their continuing life together as a part of the divine purpose.

When we married, we both held the view that, while we looked for deep and enduring happiness together that was not of itself a sufficient goal. We agreed we were being united in order to serve others, and it was only in this context that we could achieve lasting happiness. This belief has been abundantly fulfilled.[8]

Just as the issues of Christian marriage are far greater than the marriage of two Christians, so are the issues of service and purpose. It is not only the question of what can I do or what can you do, but what can "we do," what is "our" calling. As a Christian couple, how can we find a mutual purpose in our lives, a mutual calling for the service of God?

The exploration of Christian marriage will lead to an exploration of prayer in the life of the couple. "A vital marital spirituality will be rooted in prayer," states Dr. David M. Thomas, an Associate Professor of Theology at St. Meinrad School of Theology.

> The many moments of marital life become content for prayer. The excitement of new birth and first steps, the confusion of honeymoon and overdrawn bank accounts, the fear of new experiences and locations, the anxiety of separations and illness, the innumerable surprises and setbacks contribute to the mosaic of conjugal prayer . . . it remains the privileged responsibility of each family to formulate their prayer which expresses their uniqueness and individuality. Prayer is a matter of personal expression and it should therefore express the special qualities which are unique to you and your family.[9]

Father Armand Nigro of Spokane, Washington directs retreats for married couples, with the purpose of helping them experience God together, especially by praying together as a couple. The experience of these couples is usually mixed with many emotions from hesitation, fear, and embarrassment to hope and longing. The retreat usually results in the couple experiencing deep peace and joy. In relation to this he comments:

> Isn't it strange, even tragic that so few couples pray together? They share meals and conversation, words and play; they share their own bodies and hopes and plans. But they do not openly share God together. Yet God is their deepest reality, their deepest source of unity, joy, and fulfillment.[10]

Certainly Christian marriage is a call to prayer and the church is called and challenged to minister to this need in lives of its couples and families.

In an article about the spiritual awareness and needs of women by Dolores Curran, an educator and author, she expresses her concern that more be written about spirituality among couples. She states that

> many women are lonely in prayer and disappointed that their husbands are not even minimally prayerful . . . The phenomenal success of marriage enrichment weekends shows that when the husband's spirituality becomes a viable part of his life, the wife's spirituality soars.[11]

Often when the woman alone embraces a new spiritual awareness, the husband tends to withdraw even more. In referring to Dr. William McCready's research indicating that the parents religious behavior, particularly the father's, is the major prediction of a child's lifelong faith, Ms. Curran comments that this "tells us clearly the importance of a family spirituality."

A further look at spirituality in marriage and the family challenges the church to address the issues of gender. Is there a spirituality that is specially feminine or masculine? To the question, "Is there a feminine spirituality today?" Ms. Curran responds,

> Yes, many; I propose that we become more accepting of the plurality of women in our church with a corresponding plurality of spiritual modes to serve them and if there is a spirituality that is distinctly feminine, we must allow it to operate in our lives. It is a gift of God, to be sure but a gift that must be cherished, nurtured, and shared.[12]

In an article entitled "Reflections on the Spiritual Life and Fatherhood," Dr. William C. McCready, Senior Study Director of the National Opinion Research Center in Chicago, writes about the implication of the biological and sociological factors of being male or female.

> The biosocial perspective is not intended as an absolute to determine our behavior, rather it sets limits and establishes parameters within which we grow, learn, and live out our lives. If biosocial differences are important for the sociology of the family ... then it is also sensible that there are biosocial differences which influence our spiritual lives as well.[13]

Perhaps some of the differences are most clearly seen in the specific barriers that men and women must overcome in order to enter an intimate and trusting relationship with each other in which they grow as individuals and as a couple. Dr. McCready refers to Herbert Hendrin, a psychiatrist at Columbia University who has written a book, *Age of Sensations,* in which he explores a modern-day battlefield; relations between men and women.

> Hendrin finds, particularly among young people, that men and women engage in psychic battles which greatly reduce their ability to create satisfying intimate relationships. The causes of such conflicts are only speculated upon, but one possibility is that many of these people never received from their parents the image of an intimate relationship which worked its problems through to a mutually satisfactory solution. These were children who received many material things from their parents, but who did not receive any of the parents personality ... Though undocumented, it is also a likely consequence of this state of affairs that the parents themselves suffer because of their inability to share themselves with their children and therefore, with each other ... More important, for the discussion at hand is the idea that males are less well prepared to take the risks of intimacy because they have been taught that they ought to be self-reliant and independent of others. This constrains

men to adopt a non-sharing posture regarding women, particularly their wives.

Too often men come to believe that if they turn to their wives for emotional aid, or if they 'confess' their fears to their loved ones, they are less masculine. On the other hand, if they harbor everything inside they are more masculine. Ideally, both men and women should be able to develop self-reliance as well as the ability to turn to and depend upon others. . . .[14]

In this article, Dr. McCready shares several other issues with spiritual implications that men must deal with. I will briefly mention two of these. One is the "Apex-of-the-Career" Crisis.

This particular life-cycle issue is getting much more attention these days because there are so many men going through it now. In general, it strikes between 40 and 55 years of age when we finally realize that we are not going to move any higher up the 'success ladder' than we are right now . . . What I see happening also is that with the occupational and psychological problems which beset us at this time, there is also a spiritual one which is frequently the one that is the hardest to deal with because we never expected it. The spiritual issue is whether we are worth anything anymore. The 'Apex-of-the-Career' Crisis is a fruitful, spiritual time and ought not to be buried in the worries and the fears, but rather ought to be used to help us calm them and re-orient ourselves to that deeper spiritual reality for which we are intended.[15]

The other issue I would like to look at is that of male friends.

The fact is that most of us don't make friends with other men very easily. Many men get along on the friends that they made while in high school or college. Seldom do they make any more as mature adults . . . many of us figure it's just as well. 'After all my family and job take all the emotional energy I have; what I don't need are more deep relationships.'

Unfortunately, that's wrong. We could really benefit from having other men with whom we could share our ideas, our disappointments and our victories . . . Why is it that men seldom get together to talk about their own lives? I think it is another major spiritual issue. We are afraid to appear as though we might not be able to handle life by ourselves.

Sharing ourselves is risky . . . But not doing so is even riskier. Men do have experiences, ideas, and inspirations that should be shared with each other. And until that begins to happen, the sexes will be truly divided. Many men will feel a gnawing at their spiritual gut which cannot be calmed. If we should begin to share with each other our lives and our own thoughts, if we begin to talk with our friends about something besides jobs, jocks, and jokes, we will find that our spiritual awareness will grow and begin to fill the void that has been there for so long a time.[16]

As we look at the differences of the challenges encountered by men and women we are faced with one of the most significant issues of Christian marriage—the mystical and often misunderstood issue of "two becoming one." We are permitted to see this as a mystery which helps us to realize we will never fully understand it. But the misunderstanding that often and boldly blocks an intimate and fulfilling relationship must be addressed in our attempts to better grasp the experience of Christian marriage. A quote by Teilhard de Chardin states that "Love is the only force that can make things one without destroying them." This statement seems to embody a key understanding of this "union" process. The "one" comes from a growing together of the two individuals, rather than from a tearing apart of the individuals in order to rebuild a "one." Abraham and Dorothy Schmitt, who are marriage counselors, speak to this issue in an article entitled, "Conflict and Ecstacy."

> The error in the use of the words 'And the two shall become one flesh,' is that we fail to see the words 'shall become.' It is not an instantaneous happening; it is a becoming process. It is in fact, only begun at the altar and the remaining years of marital life are the fulfillment of this promise.
>
> It is our opinion that one of the greatest causes of unhappiness, even extreme tension and needless suffering, is a failure to understand the 'becoming one' process . . . For too many marriages are contracted on the 'fairy tale' model: 'and they lived happily ever after.' Then when this does not in fact result in timeless bliss that surely is implied in ceremonial promises, they begin to wonder whether they were 'meant' for each other.
>
> It has been our repeated observation in marriage retreats that married pairs have complementary personalities regardless of how intensely they may be at odds with each other. The problem is not an error in selection, but rather an inability to let that complementation process proceed after marriage.[17]

This "union" of two is not the losing of one's identity, but finding it more fully in a complementing, intimate relationship. There must be change. Anytime there is "process" there is change; the "becoming one" process means that each individual is undergoing a change. Growing in one's self-identity, growing in capacity to care and share, better understanding one's needs—these are all changes. So the critical point between growing together and growing apart is in one's conscious and free choice to change. This process of change is not free floating and undirected. It is focused in the teaching of Christ our Lord so that as

individuals and as a couple we can grow toward the full stature of
Christ. Many marriages begin to erode when one or both partners
decide that the other partner must make changes and with great de-
termination they set out to change the other partner. Other marriages
are also destined to difficulty because they choose to ignore the differences and hide from conflict because this is "bad" and they want
a "good" marriage. They drift apart because there is no interaction to
bring about the "becoming one" process. There is no oneness without
sharing. John Powell writes of this in his book, *The Secret of Staying
in Love.*

> Sometimes this unity involves things that are painful: honesty
> when you would rather lie a little, talking out when you would
> rather pout, admitting embarrassing feelings when you would rather
> pretend certainty and confronting when you would rather settle
> for peace at any price. None of these things, which are among the
> just demands of love, brings immediate peace and happiness, they
> bring immediate pain and struggle. Yes love works if we work at it.
> The work of love is to achieve a total honesty and transparency, and
> these are very difficult attainments . . . Unity not happiness is the
> stern condition of success of love.[18]

The calling by the church of a couple into "holy matrimony" is a
calling into the process of "becoming one." Simply telling the couple
the "what" of this call and not the "how" is akin to a cruel joke. The
ministry of the church must say "how" and it must do it in a way that
is so loving and caring, so understandable and relevant that the couple
cannot help but respond.

The teaching of the "how" will at some point confront one of the
greatest barriers that is faced by the typical church couple—the difference between the images or "myths" of marriage and the reality
of marriage, in particular the reality of Christian marriage. This was
referred to earlier as the "fairy tale" model of marriage. Many young
people have images of marriage that faintly resemble the reality of
it. In "The Myth of Marriage," Dr. Richard Ittner and Sister Ann Marie
Gardiner vividly portray this awareness, "I now pronounce you husband and wife. . . . " The organ music swells or the rock group grooves.
Amid the sighs, tears, and faint whiff of corsages and cologne, the myth
that a marriage has begun continues.

> The meaning and purpose of the marriage has probably not
> entered the mind of the couple, nor of many in attendance at the
> ceremony. There is a felt sense with the man and woman that they
> delight in being together, there is a glow and a vague expectation
> that they will live 'happily ever after' . . . Deeply rooted psychologi-
> cal needs and the individual and social expectations and assumptions
> have probably not surfaced in the consciousness of the couple.
> Romance and social myth have well dispelled (and repressed) those

forces which must be dealt with before two mature individuals will be able to struggle for a relationship.[19]

As these needs, expectations and assumptions become real in their day to day lives, they must assume that they are no longer "in love." If they have not been taught, or have not had parents who modeled the process of building a marriage, they have no way of knowing how to get a handle on their marriage. Their "last hope" might be their attendance or involvement in a local church. If the church can bring them into their fellowship and provide a ministry where they can explore their "myths" and face the realities, then there is great hope.

In their book, *Marriage Enrichment in the Church,* David and Vera Mace explore the impact of these myths.

> But who told our young people to expect marriage to be a heaven of romantic bliss? We did. This was just what our culture has been very busy saying for at least a couple of generations. That's what we said—and they believed us.

> Can we then not promise happiness in marriage? Of course we can. But *not without effort.* Not without understanding the nature of the tasks . . . What we ought to have told our children is that marriage is just like everything else in human life—you get out of it in proportion to what you put into it. The dream of a happy marriage is not a cruel deception. It can come true—but it's your responsibility to make it come true.

> What the couple have on their wedding day is not the key to a beautiful garden, but just a vacant lot and a few gardening tools. The tools we have been giving them, alas, have been pretty inadequate. Now, fortunately for them we can do much better.[20]

THE CHALLENGE TO DELIVER

The "doing much better" is indeed the challenge before the church to deliver to its people "these more adequate tools" with which couples can build more effective Christian marriages and Christian families. As we begin to better define that which makes a Christian marriage Christian, we must then discover ways of delivering this within the framework of the church. This may take energy and ingenuity that will stretch our minds and even traditions. It will call us out of the shadows for it is something that cannot be born of lukewarm interest or vagueness.

In the article I mentioned earlier, Delores Curran also shares her awareness and concern as to the priorities of the church.

> Yet, family spirituality seems to come at the end of a long list of priorities in our church, after religious education, school support, social action and so on.[21]

This is no doubt true for many churches, both as local churches and as denominations. It is truly an issue of priorities. Howard J. Clinebell Jr. in his book *Growth Counseling For Marriage Enrichment* makes a similar observation.

> Many church activities are irrevelant to the deep needs of people in our society. They involve people but are essentially a waste of time, a waste of valuable opportunities to help people utilize their God given potentialities. In contrast, churches which become centers for personal growth and social change are lively and exciting places.[22]

The church's ministry to the needs of marriages and Christian families is more than involving people in activities and projects. The church is to some degree already involved in marriage and family ministry. However, this involvement is usually after-the-fact and problem focused. Most pastors spend many hours counseling and dealing with problems. Most churches and denominations support agencies and institutions that meet critical needs, such as our Elon Home for Children. Yet, this is all after the fact. Many marriages and families will never need this "Crisis" care if they are nurtured and supported through the normal stresses of life. In speaking to pastors, Dr. Clinebell looks at these two issues:

> The distinction between deficiency and growth needs provides a guideline for keeping balance in one's helping activities. The distinction points to the two sides of the counseling and pastoral care coin—counseling/healing and nurture/prevention. As every parish minister knows, marriage counseling is both unavoidable and a vital form of human help. But the church is also called to be a growth-nurture-training center for the vast majority of a congregation, who do not need counseling at any given time. Unfortunately, in recent decades, counseling has tended to be the tail that wagged the pastoral care dog. It is more productive to make the nurturing of normal people throughout the life cycle normative. For me, this means investing at least three times as much caring time and leadership (ministerial and lay) in person-building, human enrichment activities (including short-term growth-oriented counseling) as in helping those with deep deficiency needs through longer-term pastoral counseling.[23]

At a time when so many families and marriages are experiencing such great discomfort and when much is known and many resources are available, it is ironical that the church is so reluctant to get involved with the needs of Christian families. In addition to some of the factors that usually effect the ministries of the church such as time, expense and priorities, there are some factors which are uniquely related to family life issues that create special barriers.

It is my strong belief that the most significant factor is that family life issues are so intensely personal. As I write this chapter I am not dealing with issues that are far off and detached—I am speaking of issues that touch on the most personal, intimate aspects of my life. When I write "marriage" I am experiencing my awareness of my relationship with Rodema. When I write "family" I am experiencing the network of relationships among us and William and Suzanne. It is so intensely personal and that is scary! I have often longed for the detachment that would come from working with nuts and bolts, machines, boards and nails—anything that is not so personal. Even in counseling there is a certain "objectivity," a certain detachment. But ministering to the nurturing and growth needs is where "we are all at." No matter how much you know, you are not an "expert," you are always a member of a marriage or a family, confronting the issues of intimacy, fulfillment and spirituality just like everyone else. How scary! How vulnerable!

I have often wondered what gives me the idea that I can help others through these growth and change processes as I am so vividly aware of my own struggles. I have had to deal with that very issue in writing this chapter. The strength to be involved does not come from being an "expert" or from "having arrived." It comes from a sense of awareness and commitment to what I deeply value and believe. It comes from the realization that I have made progress in becoming a husband, a father, a person—a Christian. But definitely, it is not something that is detached and objective.

This is a crucial issue for the pastor and his family. Ministers spend hours giving of themselves and their time ministering and being "drained" by the needs of marriages and families. What their own family gets is usually that which is left. Often there is little "left over." So to ask them to plunge themselves into activities and programs of family life education, marriage enrichment, family clusters, is to ask the impossible. This is especially true if they see themselves as having to be the "expert" with all the answers. As I read and as I listen I am becoming acutely aware that "parsonage families" have not escaped the stresses and frustrations that other families are experiencing. The added dimension is that there is often no one they can turn to with this pain. Certainly not to their parishioners. Fellow pastors may see them as inadequate or ineffective. To share these conflicts with the conference ministers or other church leaders would run the risk of being seen as "having problems" and maybe not suitable for more significant pastoral assignments. There is often difficulty in spouses turning to each other, especially for the wife as she is aware of the burdens her husband already carries for "his people."

It is here we get the hint that the beginning point in the church's ministry to family needs *may well start with the pastor and his family.*

One of the most loving things a pastor can do for his congregation is to nurture and care for his family (and to be nurtured and cared for by them). Then reach out to others. Truly we serve best when we serve out of the fullness of our lives not from the "scrapings from the bottom of the barrel." Anyway you look at it, family life issues are intensely personal. We who are involved in these issues need to identify ourselves and find ways of giving support to each other.

Another factor that has impeded the development of family life ministries is related to what we just mentioned. It is what John Powell calls the "myth of privacy." With our culture's strong background of "rugged individualism" and philosophies such as "my home is my castle," the idea is entrenched that people just don't talk about family issues. No matter how severe the pain, how common the struggle or how appropriate the setting—the rule stays the same, you don't talk about family. ". . . we can reach a point at which an obsession with privacy could become a menace to our health and happiness," states Dr. Mace.

> Is there really any good reason why we shouldn't be able to help couples to keep out of trouble, instead of waiting until they are in trouble and then telling them what they should have known before? . . . We think there is plenty of evidence that many of them would, with a little encouragement, be glad to accept preventive help offered in the right way. The concept of prevention, in such forms as insurance policies, medical and dental check-ups, and automobile inspections is now widely accepted. As Clark Vincent once put it, are our marriages as valuable to us as our teeth?[24]

Another factor that is involved in family life ministries—"these ministries of prevention"—is that of leadership. Many people who are church leaders in other areas—music, youth, teaching, visiting— do not wish and are not qualified to lead these ministries. This often throws the total burden back on the pastor who may not feel qualified or have the time. So in addition to breaking down the barriers of the extreme "personalness" of the task and the myths and taboos around talking about it, we have to find and/or train special leaders. While this may not be the awesome task it seems, it certainly means that special time, commitment and expense is involved.

There are several other factors that I would like to mention briefly. One is that most church activities and programs are structured so that couples and families do not meet together. The men go one way, the women the other; children, the singles, the elderly, go to their own group. This has purpose and meaning. However, there needs to be opportunities for marriages and families (nuclear, extended, and created) to be together.

For some churches to have effective ministries, it may be necessary to join with other churches and "pool" resources—space, leadership, expenses. Regional, conference and denominational bodies must become more involved to help provide exchanges of information, support, coordination, training, and financial help. One of the greatest "robbers" of family time together may be the church. Family members are pulled in many directions, fulfilling many commitments and staying very busy—while the family simply falls apart. For a church to minister to the real life needs of its families, it may have to re-evaluate its demands on its members.

Herbert Otto, a pioneer and outstanding leader in the areas of prevention and enrichment programs, shares some of his understanding of the reluctance of people to be involved in these ministries. One of these factors he calls the "let the sleeping dog lie" syndrome.

> It is my observation that even in 'good marriages' where the partners love each other, like being together and wish to continue the union, affective residues from the past are often so strong that the partners have difficulty being aware of the range of struggles, positive factors and possibilities present in the relationship . . . Conformity pressures ("We can't be different from the Smith's next door") are very much operative. Many people still believe that attending a marriage or family enrichment program will be interpreted by others to mean that their relationship is beset by problems and difficulties.[25]

For those of us who actively work in these ministries, we are aware of another factor that is very complicated and a difficult one on which to get a handle. I shall call it "recruitment." To some degree this involves all the issues at which we have looked. In a practical way, it simply means, "how do we get them there?" Once a pastor or several church leaders become aware of needs and are ready to take the risk, they organize some specific ministry. Then, few if any show up. Many of us know the feeling of putting months of planning and hours of work and preparation into an event, to anxiously wait in an empty room, then unplug the coffee, cut out the lights and go home. It is not easy, but soon we will try again. There are those times when the people do come; the thrill and joy of seeing relationships strengthened, new patterns of behavior emerge and the relief and pure pleasure of sharing gives us strength to keep going. To some degree this compassion and "passion" will draw people. But there must be more: qualified leadership, intelligent planning, positive promotion, involvement of others and a sensitive evaluation of needs. It is difficult to overcome these "recruitment" or involvement factors. It is important to "connect" with someone that has experience and can give assistance and support.

Dr. Otto makes a distinction that is very crucial in the recruitment and promotion of these ministries.

This touches on one of the key issues facing this new field. The presentation of family enrichment programs in an educational context, so that first and foremost they are perceived by the public as operating from a health centered rather than a pathology—centered model.[26]

He provides some advice and a challenge to the church in this area of recruitment.

Enrollment in an enrichment program is most productively facilitated through a couple's relationship with a trusted person who recommends, sponsors, or leads such a program. From the writer's point of view, the church and the minister are in the best position to help couples take advantage of their opportunity to 'make a good marriage even better.' Primary consideration needs therefore to be given to encouraging more extensive denominational involvement in this movement on a national and a local level. Such involvement needs to be both the seminary training and the clergy training level. Next, growth centers could be encouraged to include more offerings of marriage and family enrichment programs in their catalogs.

Making the public aware of the concept of marriage enrichment and of the fact that such classes and programs are available remains a paramount issue.[27]

Truly, the church is challenged to provide ministries to couples and families that will touch the very depths of their needs and bring forth the joy and fulfillment of all their potentials. The purpose and ministry of the church is so interlaced with the needs for growth and intimacy in the marriages and families of its members, it must not ignore this challenge. Howard and Charlotte H. Clinebell relate the ministry to the spiritual and to the marriage.

A shared spiritual life strengthens a marriage: conversely, a good marriage strengths the spiritual life of the couple. Spiritual growth takes place best in a relationship in which religious values are experienced. A growing marriage provides just such a relationship.

The 'good news' is that love is supreme and is available in relationships, including our relationship with God. Our discussion of intimacy in marriage is an effort to explore the ways in which the good news can come alive in a vital human relationship—marriage . . . Fortunate is the couple in whose relationship there is something which allows them both to experience grace—the accepting love which one does not need to earn because it is present as a spontaneous expression of the relationship.[28]

THE CHALLENGE TO BEGIN

"Where do we start?" There are many exciting and creative approaches to family life ministries. There is an abundance of programs, approaches, resources, and materials. It is beyond our purpose here to elaborate on these but they are available. After there is an awareness of the needs, the starting point seems to be learning and becoming aware of the options and resources that are available. This process means connecting with individuals and agencies that are interested and experienced in family life ministries.

There are some very practical things that need to happen in both the local church and the church organizations. First, those family life issues must be talked about, discussed, shared. Break down the myths and barriers. Money must be budgeted for resources, leadership, and training. The pastor and his family should be given prime consideration for opportunities to receive training, experience growth and to just get some "R and R." A critical issue is the development of centers and networks for training and support for leadership, both lay and clergy. The pastor cannot bear the total responsibility for these ministries anymore than he can teach the entire church school or be a choir of one. The laity must be involved. Also, there must be coordination and cooperation. No one church can constantly provide effective ministries without working with other churches, agencies, and resources.

This is a very limited discussion. Primarily I want to say that while we are charting new territory, some things have been learned and this information and understanding is available and can help.

IN CONCLUSION

The affirmation of and ministry to Christian marriages and families is greater than any one issue, point of view, program or activity. Having a sermon or starting a class on family life is not the goal of our challenge. It is so much more complex and I realize the limitations of this chapter. I do hope, however, that some doors and windows have been opened and that there are some new hills and valleys to be explored.

Also, it is important to say that any ministry or concern for family life issues must involve everyone! While it is true that everyone may not be married, *everyone* is a part of a family. After having spoken at a church on the topic of the Christian family, a dear friend of mine shared a comment that still rings in my ears to this day. Now a widow and living alone, she said, "Bob, I have a Christian family—there is no one there but me, but it is a Christian family." The challenge to family life ministry is to minister to everyone!

My hope and prayer is that all of us may hear those loving and beautiful words, first heard by Zacchaeus, "Today salvation has come to this house."

NOTES

1. David and Vera Mace, *Marriage Enrichment in the Church* (Nashville, Broadman Press, 1976), p. 37.

2. Gordon J. Lester, "Image and Reality," *Marriage and Family Living,* February 1978.

3. *Ibid.*

4. *Ibid.*

5. *Ibid.*

6. Gabriel Calvo, "Mutual Confiding," *Marriage Encounter,* September 1978.

7. David Mace, "A Personal Account," *Marriage and Family Living,* March 1978.

8. *Ibid.*

9. David M. Thomas, "Let Us Pray and Play Together," *Marriage and Family Living,* May 1978.

10. Armand Nigro, "Pray Together As A Couple," *Marriage Encounter,* August 1978.

11. Delores Curran, "Mother/Spouse/Ms: and Her Spiritualities," *Marriage and Family Living,* April 1978.

12. *Ibid.*

13. William C. McCready, "Reflections On the Spiritual Life and Fatherhood," *Marriage and Family Living,* June 1978.

14. *Ibid.*

15. *Ibid.*

16. *Ibid.*

17. Abraham and Dorothy Schmitt, "Conflict and Ecstacy," *Faith At Work,* October, 1975.

18. John Powell, *The Secret of Staying in Love* (Niles, Ill: Argus Communication, 1974), pp. 72, 73.

19. Anne Marie Gardiner and Richard Ittner "The Myth of Marriage," *Faith At Work,* October, 1975.

20. David and Vera Mace, *op. cit.*

21. Delores Curran, *op. cit.*

22. Howard J. Clinebell, Jr., *Growth Counseling For Marriage Enrichment* (Nashville: Abingdon Press, 1976), p. 16.

23. *Ibid.*

24. David and Vera Mace, *op. cit.*

25. Herbert A. Otto, *Marriage and Family Enrichment* (Nashville: Abingdon Press, 1976), p. 16.

26. *Ibid.*

27. *Ibid.*

28. Howard J. and Charlotte H. Clinebell, *The Intimate Marriage* (New York: Harper and Row, 1970), pp. 185, 186.

9 The Changing Functions of the Family

by Leslie C. Wicker

There appears to be a no more important question facing this generation than the question of the future of the family. This is evidenced by the influx of family research, the proliferation of family literature—both professional and lay, and foremost, a kind of "gut-level" feeling of anxiety about the future of traditional and Christian understandings of family life. To be sure, no modern human institution has been caught in such crossfire or been under such assault as the family. The family has been appropriately referred to as a sponge which absorbs all the wrongs, ills, and short-comings of other social institutions.[1] With all the social problems of society today, it is convenient and easy to say that when there is failure it is the family that is to blame. The family as an institution has become a catch basin, a "catch-all" for all other problems. The claim is that delinquency, crime, suicide, alcoholism, drugs, morality, etc., are all intricately related and traceable to home life. When any of these or the innumerable social problems of our day arise, we conclude that somewhere along the way there was a failure in the family setting. It is almost as if the family were the sacrificial lamb for all other institutions. Conversely, though, the family is such that when it fails, the failure is not an isolated failure, for when the family fails there is a great loss.

And again, one must think of how adaptive the family has had to become. In the "give-and-take" of the forces exerted on the family, the family has found itself more often than not on the receiving end. And because it is there it must adapt to many different times, places, and circumstances. A father and husband is employed by a large corporation. One day the manager decides that this employee would be better suited in another plant elsewhere. The family must individually and collectively adapt to a new city, new neighborhood, new schools, new places of worship, and must make new friends. Again, if the providing parent loses his or her job, it is the family that ultimately absorbs the

Leslie C. Wicker is the Pastor of Trinity United Church of Christ in Conover, North Carolina, and has a Ph.D. in Child Development and Family Relations.

pain of loss of income and the anxiety of the future. These kinds of events certainly take their toll on family members.

With so many pressures, one has to wonder how the family as an institution carries on. Some believe that many functions traditionally performed by the family have been transferred to other social institutions and that because the family has lost many functions it may be becoming unimportant and useless, a relic of the past. But we know that the family is an enduring institution and we in the church believe that it is the gift of God. There has been and always will be the human need to affiliate in close and intimate ways—ways which can only truly be known within the trust and commitment of monogamous family relationships.

There is much speculation about the future of the family especially with regards to its form and function. The church has stated that ". . . marriage is a sacred and joyous covenant, a way of life ordained from the beginning of God's creation."[2] The church believes that there are certain fruits of committed family living: loyalty, trust, love (physical and spiritual), growth, security, nurture, and warmth. It is a relationship blessed and hallowed by God himself and it is God who perfects the gift of love. It is a holy covenant. Since this is the church's faith, it appears that the church needs in a desperate way to reaffirm and recommit itself to the relationship we call the family. As the family relationship faces the ebb and flow of this era, it would seem that the right task for the church would be to offer some sense of direction and interpretation. There is a kind of need for a Christian counteroffensive which would spell out carefully the full meaning of marriage and family living from the Christian perspective. In this chapter we shall consider some of the issues and perspectives that appear important as we look at the changing functions of the family.

In family literature the term function refers to what the family does, to duties it performs or ought to perform, to what is going on when family members are interacting with one another. Historically, family researchers have isolated several functions of the family as primary: economic, educational, recreational, religious, protective, procreative, and affectional.

Some years ago William F. Ogburn, a social scientist whose major interest was the impact of technology on social change, concluded that most of the historic functions of the family were being transferred to other institutions.[3] He went on to say that increases in outside-the-home activities were only measures of decreases of traditional family functions and later carried his thesis further to speak in terms of "loss of family functions." Ogburn's pronouncement went unchallenged in the 1930's and 1940's and to the present day many accept his position as fact and believe that such a loss represents the decline and decay of the family. But we know that the family is not a corpse and is in fact very much alive. A closer examination of Ogburn's thesis will reveal that he and his disciples misread the processes of family change when they interpreted changing family functions as functional losses. We will see not only that the family has undergone structural changes, but has actually increased in its functions.

Ogburn believed that the foremost function of the family was economic as the family was a self-sufficient unity, a factory in itself. Members of the family consumed what they produced, therefore money, banks, stores, and factories were not needed. Vincent has pointed out that actually all that has happened is a structural change in that the family is now an economic consuming unit rather than a producing one.[4] And consumption can be no less important than production. From the purely economic perspective society today is almost totally dependent on the family to consume: houses, automobiles, boats, clothing, recreation, furniture, all kinds of goods and services. Families today buy almost everything readymade: food, clothing, transportation, housing. Speculation is that family economic consumption will be even greater in the future as home services will be more of a push button kind of life-style from food preparation to housecleaning. The home of the future will come furnished and chosen to suit the size of the family and particular stage of the family cycle.

Ogburn held that status-giving grew out of the economic function. A person was less of an individual and more of a member of a family. The family name took precedence over the given name. Families tended to remain in the same communities and reputations were established through the family name. It was as important to marry the right family as the right individual. The family name was a badge to be guarded. Due to the household economy the home was the locus of education from infancy through youth. This included vocational education, domestic science, and the skills necessary to cope with life. Education beyond that was either in the form of apprenticeship or employment of a live-in tutor. But these functions were lost. The religious function was also lost as evidenced by a decline in family religious activities.

But if the educational and religious functions are lost, why do children hold similar religious, political, and social views to those of their parents? And why are social attitudes and moral development of social deviants traced to the home and not to the school or church? It is the family and not the schools which is blamed for school drop-outs. Parents of the past have not prodded their children to achievement nearly to the degree of parents of today. No one can honestly say that parents who took their children from school to work on the farm had greater esteem for education than parents today who go to extreme measures and personal hardships to educate their children.

The protective function was also believed to have been transferred to other societal institutions. The husband and father was the protector of the wife and children. The aged found protection in the households of their children and children were thought of as old age insurance. An accounting of agencies and institutions which provide protection for family members today would be no small task. Law enforcement, health care, homes for the aged, social security and retirement plans, and any number of governmental programs have altered the protective function of the family. Ogburn also believed that recreation was a home activity that had mostly been lost through commercialization. Although there was some community recreation, it was often at the homestead of some family. Generally family recreation in its earlier forms had yielded to various forms of public entertainment and spectator sports.

But in reality the family continues to provide both protection and recreation for its members. The largest industry in America is the insurance industry providing various forms of family protection in the event a parent is absent or unable to provide. All forms of retirement security are means of protection for the family. Protective agencies such as law enforcement are agencies designed for the protection of the family and support for them comes through taxation of the family itself. Again, although impossible to measure, today's family spends far more time both consuming and producing its own recreation than has the family at any earlier period. Billions are spent annually on various back-yard entertainments, televisions, camping, boating, and family vacation homes. Societal values have changed in such a way that leisure and recreational pursuits have come to be accepted as valid objectives. The pursuit of time for recreation is evidenced in the increased amounts of time allotted for vacation, the increase in the number of paid holidays, and the declining age for retirement. The family is a system of interacting persons and maintains itself on the basis of underlying relational satisfaction. During times of stress or critical periods in family interactional patterns recreation may act as a shock absorber or stabilizer for the family. It is because leisure remains very much a function of the family that it sometimes is the bond that holds the family together.[5]

Ogburn's classic argument, as we have seen, was that at least six of the seven functions of the family had been lost to other agencies or institutions with only the affectional and procreative functions remaining intact. While the affectional function has emerged as paramount, we have seen that all that actually happened to the other functions is that they have been changed in structure. It is the traditional forms and content of the functions, not the functions *qua* functions that have changed. Clark Vincent, whose reasoning we have followed states: ". . . in each case of traditional function supposedly lost to the family as a social institution, the loss has in reality been but a change in *content* and *form.*"[6]

It appears that love and companionship have come forth as the primary functions of the modern family, although the other functions are no less important than in the past. Winch has stated it as follows:

It is not a logical necessity that even the relative importance of emotional gratification must increase when the others decline since it is conceivable that this too could be fulfilled in increasing degree in other relationships outside the family. But if the importance of the other functions is to continue to decrease, then it seems inescapable that if the nuclear family is to maintain its present strength, the importance of emotional gratification will have to increase absolutely as well as relatively.[7]

We believe the family today is much more than an institution. It is a relationship with many possibilities for meaning, love, and fulfillment. There is much truth in the old adage that "the family is basic to society." For we know that if we fail in families, then the society as a whole will fail. If the family is basic to society, then love and companionship must be basic to the modern family. Whereas companionship or the affectional function was least important in Ogburn's listing, it has become the most important function of the contemporary family. Perhaps love and companionship have emerged as primary functions of the modern family because there is no other relationship that can provide human emotions with the kinds of resources which are to be found in monogamous marriage and nuclear family relationships. There is no human relationship which can be as gratifying as that of love between husband and wife and parent and child. When the Apostle Paul wanted to describe this kind of love, he drew the parallel between it and Christ's love for the church. We know that such a relationship is good and was meant to be:

... from the beginning of creation, God made them male and female. "For this reason a man shall leave his father and mother and be joined to his wife, and the two shall become one." So they are no longer two but one. What therefore God has joined together, let not man put asunder (Mark 10:6-9).

It has only been in relatively recent years that we have seen the family move from an institution to a companionship basis. While World War II was in progress Burgess and Locke wrote the now influential description of the family as it changed from institution to companionship:

... the family has been in historical times in transition from an institution with family behavior controlled by mores, public opinion, and law to a companionship with family behavior arising from the mutual affection and consensus of its members. The companionship form of the family is not to be conceived as having already been realized but as emerging. . . .

The most extreme theoretical formulation of the institutional family would be one in which its unity would be determined entirely by the social pressures impinging on family members. The ideal construction of the family of companionship would focus upon the unity which develops out of mutual affection and intimate association of husband and wife and parents and children.[8]

As the industrial, and often entrepreneurial society had begun to appear, the traditional patterns of the family shifted to accommodate the new forces. Cities grew on the wake of industrialism and the new city life was one of the prevailing forces that would bring changes to the family. Industrialism and urban living meant that families left the larger groups of relatives in rural America to take up independent residence in the city. When heavy common labor was in demand men were the principal breadwinners, but increasingly women were able to handle jobs as physical strength was replaced by technology. Fewer children and the easing of some domestic burdens freed women for employment which substantially increased family incomes. As the skills, incomes, and services of women increased, their equity with men also increased.[9]

Into this urban, industrialized family came romantic love in the modern sense. If the family were not tightly tied together by the old functions, the bond of shared affection was the emerging force which would bind families together. Since affection has become the primary function, it appears that the family has a unique opportunity to fulfill the pronouncement: "It is not good for a man (or woman) to be alone." Another, for the sake of the other alone, may be singled out from all others as the only fully satisfying object in the world. Structural changes in the family functions have opened the gateway for the primacy of the affectional function. Affection, admiration, and companionship are valid objectives in themselves for the modern family. The joy of modern marriage is the possibility of companionship with time available to truly love and devote one's self to another. And with the emotional pressures of today's world, it is increasingly important that each person have someone who is loyally committed to her or him and who will provide warmth, acceptance, and understanding. Most husbands, wives, and children need someone who will bandage up a bruised ego at the end of a day.[10]

The need for love and companionship is evidenced by the fact that a higher percentage of adults are married today then ever before. When marriages are terminated for whatever reason, most persons marry again within a three year period of time. Hobart has suggested that the high divorce rate is the result of the failure of marriages to provide the needed and desired love and companionship.[11] Persons who soon remarry, remarry in the hopes of finding fulfillment through provision for this basic human need.

The church, through its wealth of resources, has an unprecedented opportunity to act on behalf of marriage and family living. And if the people of the church believe that love and marriage and family are gifts of God, then the people need to respond to the present debate on the future of the family by affirming the goodness of the relationship of marriage. The appropriate place for the church to begin such a campaign would be where the greatest need is in the family today, the enhancement of the affectional bond. If marriages make it today, they make it because of the affectional bond. If there is marital dissolution, chances are rather good that there was a "snap" somewhere in this primary function. We in the church, then, need to recommit ourselves to the thought expressed over half a century ago in Edward Carpenter's book, *Love's Coming of Age:*

> That there should exist one other person in the world toward whom all openness of interchange should establish itself, from whom there should be no concealment; whose body should be as dear to one, in every part, as one's own; with whom there should be no sense of mine or thine, in property or possession; into whose mind one's thought should naturally flow, as it were to know themselves and to receive new illumination; and between whom and oneself there should be a spontaneous rebound of sympathy in all the joys and sorrows and experiences of life; such is perhaps one of the dearest wishes of the soul.[12]

This knowledge of the joy of human love and companionship has belonged to the church all along. The church's faith is that the world is created in such a way that love and companionship are a part of the natural order. "It is not good for a person to be alone." We need that special someone in our corner, that someone with whom we are able to share the most intimate moments of life, that someone to whom we may give ourselves as to no other.

The family is a social system within a larger social system. In order for the family to carry on it must provide for replacement of its members. Hence, the function of reproduction is born out of the function of love and companionship. Children are the fruits of love and love expressed in love-making. They are the miracle of life which truly represents the oneness of a man and a woman. The oneness of a man and woman in love and in spirit become one in the gift of God in the new person born to their love. There are two purposes understood for sexual love in marriage. Sexual relations are a unique expression of neighbor love. There is no other means of human expression that brings one as close to another as this expression. It is a consummation of common-unity between husband and wife. In the plain and earthy biblical wording, "The two become one flesh." And secondly it is through sexually expressed love that marriages are blessed with children. Those who avoid having children for purely selfish reasons may be going against the divinely given order of things and may even be endangering their marriage.

Finally there is the function of socialization of children which is the process through which children gain the knowledge, skills, and dispositions which enable them to participate in life. Realistically there is no other institution or agency equipped to provide for children the function of socialization in the secure, life-affirming way as the family. We may think of monogamy graphically as father, mother, and child. The development of the child occurs best when there is the stability of one father and one mother behind him or her. Children do develop out of other life-styles than monogamous marriage, but often despite of, not because of, the kind of home behind them and very often against great odds. The proverbial wisdom, "Train up a child in the way that he should go, and when he is old he will not depart from it" (Proverbs 22:6), is trustworthy wisdom yet. The early years are the formative years, the stages in life in which children learn to love and accept themselves and others. In these years of development a child learns whether or not he can trust the world or himself; he acquires feelings of self-worth or is deficient of them. Child development is a long term process which is best accomplished in stable and secure relationships. Linton and Parsons have separately agreed that the family is needed to provide this basic function and that no other institution can provide for it as effectively and hence the family will move into the future with much stability.[13]

In conclusion, Parsons has stated: "The family is more specialized than ever before, but not in any general sense less important, because the society is more exclusively dependent on it for the performance of its certain functions."[14] John N. Edwards concludes that it is indeed questionable if family stability can be seriously effected regardless of however many or few functions the family performs.[15] Regardless of structural changes the family has a future, and in fact, few relationships are more assured of a future. Men and women will continue to want the fulfillment they find in companionship, intimacy, and the thousand and one ways husbands, wives, and children share, support, and reassure one another in family relationships. Men and women will continue to want to celebrate their love and mutuality and to experience the mystical union they find in one another. Because "It is not good for a person to be alone," and because the church believes that marriage is a way of life ordained by God, it ought to be the church's business to promote good marriages and healthy, binding family relationships.

NOTES

1. Clark E. Vincent, "Familia Spongia: The Adaptive Function," in John N. Edwards, Ed., *The Family and Change* (New York: Alfred A. Knopf, 1969).

2. "The Order of Marriage," *Services of the Church* (Philadelphia: United Church Press, 1969), p. 3.

3. William F. Ogburn, "The Changing Family," *Publications of the American Sociological Society,* Vol. 23, (1929), pp. 124-133.

4. Vincent, *op. cit.*

5. Dennis K. Orthner, "Leisure Activity Patterns and Marital Satisfaction Over the Marital Career," *Journal of Marriage and the Family,* Vol. 37 (1975), pp. 91-102.

6. Vincent, *op. cit.,* p. 30.

7. Robert R. Winch, "Permanence and Change in the History of the American Family and Some Speculations as to Its Future," *Journal of Marriage and the Family,* Vol. 32 (1970), p. 14.

8. Erness W. Burgess and H. J. Locke, *The Family from Institution to Companionship* (New York: American Book Company, 1945).

9. D. Miller and G. Swanson, *The Changing American Parent* (New York: Wiley, 1958).

10. Richard H. Klemer, *Marriage and Family Relationships* (New York: Harper and Row, 1970).

11. C. W. Hobart, "Commitment, Value Conflict, and the Future of the Family," *Marriage and Family Living,* Vol. 25 (1963), pp. 405-412.

12. Edward Carpenter, *Love's Coming of Age* (New York: Mitchell Kenerley, 1911), pp. 99-100. This quote is taken from David and Vera Mace, *We Can Have Better Marriages* (Nashville: Abingdon Press, 1974).

13. T. Parsons and R. F. Bales, *Family Socialization and Interaction Process* (New York: Free Press of Glencoe, 1955). See also R. Linton, "The Natural History of the Family," in R. N. Ashen, Ed., *The Family: Its Function and Destiny* (New York: Harper and Row, 1959).

14. Parsons and Bales, *op. cit.,* p. 10.

15. John N. Edwards, "The Future of the Family Revisited," *Journal of Marriage and the Family,* Vol. 29 (1967), pp. 505-511.

10 Alternate Life-Styles and Christian Marriage

by Leslie C. Wicker

We are hearing a great deal of talk these days regarding alternate or variant life-styles. We should expect it since we live in a heterogeneous, pluralistic society. Differing life-styles are nothing new, although many people seem to feel that they have discovered something that has not been thought of before. There is indeed, in the words of Ecclesiastes, "nothing new under the sun." Communal living, prostitution, cohabitation, homosexuality, repudiations of marriage, and the like, all have their historical precedents. What may be new is a growing acceptance of these life-styles and often an advocation of them as a solution to some problem of living.

There are two meanings implied in the term alternate. Alternate may suggest a substitute for traditional family forms or it may be taken to mean a selection of one life-style among many choices. While cross-cultural studies have indicated numerous forms of living arrangements around the world, we are increasingly becoming aware of variations within our own culture. To be sure, most of us are acquainted with any number of persons whose life-styles are quite different from our own. There are, then, both intercultural and intracultural differences.

An important question for the church is its approach to the problem of alternate life-styles. The issue has already brought much struggle and in many cases heartache to the church. What should be the right approach for the church for a host of questions which arise from the issue of alternate life-styles? Should the church be flexible and sponge-like, accepting alternatives as viable possibilities for Christian living, or should it be prescriptive of the life-style a Christian ought to follow? Is it the task of the church to sanction behavior or to interpret the meaning of life? What is the place for the authority of the Bible concerning the question of life-style? Few persons who quest for understanding the family and the meaning of Christian living today escape struggling with these questions. Bowman has offered three convenient typologies for categorizing life-style variations: the absence of marriage, supplements to marriage, and modifications of marriage.[1] Before prescribing a

112

Christian approach to marriage or some possible approaches to the current issue, let us examine some of the better known alternatives.

ABSENCE OF MARRIAGE

For any number of reasons persons may choose not to marry, and circumstances may, in fact, prevent marriage. "To marry or not to marry"[2] is a real question for many persons today. There are those who feel a conventional marriage is entrapping due to its responsibilities, isolation, and longevity. Others fear heterosexual relationships and such fear drives them away from the intimacies of marriage. Still others repudiate marriage because they feel it is a part of the establishment or a relic of the past. Finally, others believe that the traditional nuclear family inhibits self-actualization, autonomy, gender identity, intimacy in a variety of interpersonal relations, openness in communication, and sexual variety.[3] There are three basic life-styles which subsist in the absence of marriage: choice of singleness, heterosexual cohabitation, and homosexual cohabitation.

The choice of singleness may result from any one of three circumstances. A person may choose singleness out of religious convictions or vows. Such is the choice of celibacy in the case of priests or nuns. Some persons are opposed to marriage because they feel it hampers their life-style of freedom and limits their career opportunities. A number of these persons have expressed the feeling that marriage is an institution which supports the establishment and maintains the status quo for it is in the family, they believe, that persons learn the dominance-submission game. Other single persons have simply postponed marriage until some future time in their lives. These persons are not opposed to marriage, but for the present prefer to remain single. They may not have found a suitable mate, but chances are they are not looking for one. Single persons who are friends from college or other relationships find many advantages in sharing apartment and living expenses while they pursue their single life-style interest.

Heterosexual cohabitation is a life-style that repudiates marriage in favor of a philosophy that people should be able to live together without the legality or permanence of marriage. Cohabitants claim that a marriage certificate is only a piece of paper and as such prohibits the completeness of the couple's commitment. They say true commitment is not to be found in license or certificates but in relationships. Four discernable themes of cohabitation have been identified.[4] The first theme, labeled the *Linus blanket,* is characterized by an overwhelming need to have a relationship with someone with little regard for whom or under what conditions. *Emancipation* is the theme of resistance to values taught by family and religion regarding participation in heterosexual relationships outside marriage. Restrictions are countered by internal pushes to loosen external controls. A third type, *convenience,* is characterized by short duration relationships which allow regular sexual contact and often the luxury of domestic living without the responsibilities of committed relationships. Finally, some persons cohabit as a kind of *testing* of the relationship. Relationships here exist as quasi-kinds of commitments in which the couple seeks to learn more about themselves and their functioning in intimate settings. Such relationships may lead to the commitment of marriage or termination.

Homosexual cohabitation is a life-style of living and having sexual relations with a person of one's own sex. According to the Kinsey studies 25% of the male population of the U.S. had more than incidental homosexual experience or reactions for at least three years between the ages of 16 and 50; only 10% were more or less exclusively homosexual during a similar period of time and 4% were exclusively homosexual throughout their lives. This data indicates that persons may have both heterosexual and homosexual responses during their lifetime, that there is a good deal more homosexual behavior than lasting homosexual identification, and a period of significant homosexual responses does not necessarily determine one's future sexual orientation.[5] Some homosexual persons choose to marry, but most individuals with homosexual preference remain unmarried by choice. In recent years since homosexual persons are freer to identify themselves, some have demanded the right to marry each other and a few have had wedding ceremonies. The absence of legal status for such relationships has become a major issue with those involved in the Gay Liberation movement.

SUPPLEMENTS TO MARRIAGE

A life-style that appears to be on the increase is one in which marriage and some alternate form exist simultaneously, a life-style of extramarital sexual relations. This life-style comes in any number of sexual expressions: adultery, prostitution and massage, group sex, various contracts of open marriage, and others.

Most people who enter marriage enter it with the expectation of sexual exclusiveness. Adultery is generally condemned by the population and those who engage in it do not generally offer it as an appropriate life-style. It is grounds for divorce in all states. However, extramarital sex in the form of adultery is as old as marriage itself. In recent years it appears that society and marital partners have become more tolerant of this life-style. It has become the fashionable or "in thing" in many circles to "have an affair." It is still true, however, that many a husband or wife, on learning about his or her spouse's infidelity, feels enraged, hurt, betrayed, and unloved. It has been estimated that infidelity is the cause for one third of all divorces, but in the majority of cases spouses never know of their mate's unfaithfulness.[6]

Extramarital sex may also be procured on the market place. Two of the most common forms of "play for pay" are prostitution and massage. Prostitution, the granting of nonmarital sex for renumeration, is said to be the world's oldest profession. The multibillion dollar industry comes in a variety of forms from the "high class hooker," to the hotel call girl, to the out-of-town business man's gratuity, to the street corner pick-up. Unfortunately the pimps are the profiteers in the business and the women the victims in one way or another.

A newer form of marketed sex is the massage parlor which has become a common sight throughout America in recent years. The massage is differentiated from the traditional form of prostitution in that the masseuses set limits on what sex they are willing to perform. The basic pattern of the massage puts a male customer in a room with a female masseuse, both in some state of undress, which sets the stage for the massage to begin. The masseuse may give a "straight" massage or give as many sexual "extras" as her client is willing to pay for and she is willing to give. Masseuses often break their own limits due to pressures to conform to customer desires and to build up clientele. Sexual services which are offered as extras range from forms of manual stimulation to sexual intercourse.[7]

While most present day extramarital sex takes the form of adultery or market payment and remains hidden beneath the disguise of conventional marital behavior, a small minority of husbands and wives grant each other the privilege of outside relationships. A few couples take separate vacations or allow each other a night out per week. It is understood that extramarital relationships are confined to those times only. Reasons given for such open contracts or understandings are that they keep the marital relationship moving forward and unimpaired. But what's out of one's sight may not be out of one's mind. Even so, extramarital frolic is one thing when it is out of sight, but another thing when in full view as in group sex.

Group sex, also called co-marital sex, swinging, and mate swapping, refers to extramarital sex in which both partners participate simultaneously and by mutual consent. Such groups range in size and usually use a selective process through which to recruit new members. Some groups have been associated for years, but generally the membership is fluid as there are many dropouts. Disillusionment is not uncommon. Although sex for the sake of sex is the primary object of swinging, a secondary objective may be that of socializing. Groups are ordinarily composed of married couples and the unmarried are generally not invited. A prevailing rule among swingers is the philosophy of personal detachment. No matter how free sex may be, there are to be no emotional attachments between partners resulting from swinging. Any form of sexual behavior or exchange is to occur without love, affection, or meaning. Swinging has sometimes been called a genital life-style.[8] The number of couples who engage in the mate swapping life-style can at best be roughly estimated, but some estimates place the figure at more than two and a half million.[9]

MODIFICATIONS, ALTERATIONS, AND INNOVATIONS

Life-styles which modify marriage and family living have been given considerable attention in recent years. Some of these modified models which we shall mention only briefly include: trial marriage, communes, single parenthood, voluntary childlessness, models for the elderly, and others. Herbert Otto, editor of *The Family in Search of a Future,* has brought together some fifteen diverse and often controversial life-styles which are either presently practiced or possibilities for modifications of marriage in the future.[10]

Trial marriage may be thought of as a testing or experimental relationship in which a man and a woman consent to live together as married persons without any permanent legally binding contracts. Other labels given to trial marriage are "apprenticeship marriage," "renewable marriage," and marriage in "two-steps."[11] The rationale given for trial marriage is that it allows potential spouses to come to know one another in the most intimate ways, a possibility unavailable in traditional marriage forms. The assumption is that persons cannot really know the other or cannot be sure of long range commitments until they have had the opportunity to share life with the other in the most intimate of ways. Margaret Mead has delineated such an arrangement in terms of two-step marriages.[12] She discussed the first step in terms of "individual marriage," a licensed union with only ethical, not economic, obligations. Individual marriage would be binding on the couple only as long as they wished to be committed to each other, but would not apply to them as future parents. The second step, "parental marriage," would have its own license, ceremony, and contract, would always be preceded by individual marriage, and would be explicitly directed towards the founding of a family.

Serial marriage, sometimes referred to as "serial polygamy," or "progressive monogamy," is a life-style somewhat akin to trial marriage. Here is the life-style which has grown out of the rising rate of divorce and remarriage in which an individual has a series of spouses, one at a time. It appears we have begun to play a gigantic game of marital chairs as those who fail to find the promised panacea in one marriage seek a quick divorce and soon try again. More than one out of three of those who marry this year will divorce and three out of four of those will remarry within the next three years. These figures indicate that there is a growing acceptance of temporary marriage and short-lived commitments.

Communes represent a broad spectrum of modifications of marriage because they reveal a variety of life-styles within and between themselves. Group marriage is a life-style of collective parenting, sexual sharing, communal ownership, and communal goals. It is an extended family on a large scale, as distinguished from the extended family of blood kin. Communes are usually formed by groups of persons who either wish to escape from society or react to it. They may include a variety of types of persons from the well to the poorly educated; may be highly or loosely organized; may be autocratic or democratic; may be productive and self-sustaining or dependent on outside economic sources; may be religious or non-religious; and may be congenial or in conflict with their neighbors. On the whole, communalists are young people and, of course, youth itself is a fleeting thing. Since these persons are not generally preparing for life in mass society, the question arises as to how they shall manage when they fall into the age group which in their minds represents the establishment?

A single-parent family is by definition a family consisting of one parent and one or more dependent children living in the same household. One-parent families may occur through death of a spouse, separation or divorce, children out-of-wedlock, or more recently adoption. According to the U.S. Census Bureau there are 4.5 million families with children under 18 which are headed by single parents. Approximately 90 percent of these are headed by women with the remaining 10 percent by men. These figures in themselves seem cold and impersonal. We need to develop greater awareness and sensitivity to the pains, struggles, and trials that are associated with single-parenthood. Single-parenthood is almost always a burden in some respects as it is impossible for one person to carry the responsibilities and offer the nurturance of two parents. Two-parent families can offer sustaining succorance in the ways of companionship, love and affection, support, comfort in times of stress and need, and a visible presence by "standing in one's corner." While children may offer some support, they are generally not able to fill this need. What may be more overwhelming than anything else is that there is no other person present to fill this human need. Many single-parents express the pain of being and feeling all alone.

Voluntary childlessness constitutes an alternate form of marriage because dominant cultural definitions of the meaning of marriage assume that wanting and having children are natural and normal. It has been assumed that children are part of the meaning of marriage and as such are intrinsic sources of satisfaction. There are immense social pressures from the extended family, work associates, friends, and the media to bear children. Some childless wives perceive a variety of negative sanctions towards them for their antinatalist sentiments. It appears that generally the concept of voluntary childlessness is not an intention at the time of marriage. Childless couples usually postpone the event of children only to decide at some future time that they either enjoy their present life-styles too much to have them interrupted by the event of children or that they are too old to begin such an endeavor. Still, some wives do reverse the motherhood mystique and proclaim that childlessness is as normal as motherhood, that pregnancy and childbirth are at best unpleasant and at worst difficult and dangerous, that child care is burdensome and unrewarding, and that motherhood is restraining rather than fulfilling. There is a feeling that if motherhood does not preclude the achievement of self-actualization and career success, it at least makes these goals problematic and entrapping. Veevers has cited the dominant themes of the child-free life-style as commitment to careers, quest for experience, the absence of generativity, and the idealization of the husband-wife relationship.[13]

The demography of old age has posed a special problem concerning the family structure of the aged. While the aged have increased in number and proportion in the population, the sex ratio has become progressively imbalanced with an ever growing surfeit of widows. There are certain characteristics which are more common among people who have reached this age: loss of family and friends, lack of flexibility of income, lack of opportunity for productive and rewarding work, more frequent incidents of illness requiring long periods of recovery, loss of mental and physical stimulation, and societal pressure to conform to pre-cast patterns of activity and behavior.[14] These problems which are primarily social in nature coupled with the dissolution of the conjugal family through the loss of spouse indicate the need for emotional support and intimacy which nurture the spirit of a person at a time in life when the need is very great. This need has created several life-styles among the aged. Some older persons answer the need through cohabitation cognizant of the fact that legal marriage would penalize them in terms of needed Social Security benefits. Victor Kassel foresees a coming life-style of polygyny for the aged, a life-style already in practice among many.[15]

CONCLUSIONS

We have examined a number of alternate life-styles. Some are chosen by their adherents; others are thrust upon persons and perhaps they would escape them if they could. Many are single-parents out of circumstance, not out of choice. Some of the life-styles of the elderly that may be thought of as variant are more a matter of loneliness, isolation, and the human need for intimacy, than a matter of conscious choice or any desire to experiment. Let us now move from description to prescription and let us begin by saying that life-styles that are experimental by purpose and design need to be closely examined. While they provide sensational material by their extremism, defiance of convention, and general shock treatment, their importance has greatly been exaggerated. Periodic exchange of marriage partners has been on the American scene for a long time; adultery is an age-old practice; and sexual experimentation is as old as mankind. The only thing that may be new is that experimental forms are more openly practiced and more widely accepted.

Statements which assert that newer patterns are indications that marriage is a dying institution about to be replaced by something new and radically different are simply not supported by the facts. As David and Vera Mace have stated, "Monogamous marriage and the nuclear family are very old and durable institutions, which have shown remarkable flexibility in adapting to a great variety of human environments."[16] Many well meaning people have become confused regarding the church's task and alternate life-styles. In their loving concern for all, they have sought to be offensive to none, even though the gospel itself is sometimes offensive. In their efforts they have sought to adapt the church's ethic to whatever life-style may come along regardless of how the life-style may differ from the teachings of the Scriptures. There appears to be a fear that the church will somehow "lose out" if it does not amalgamate its expectations for behavior to fit the norms of the culture. This kind of thinking creates a setting in which the culture becomes the transforming agent rather than the church and it also creates a lack of tension between the church and the world. If the church ever loses out, it will do so because it abandons its ideals, not because it keeps a firm moral position. But the church is also a very old and durable institution. There is a need for the church to provide a supportive ministry to the monogamous relationships of marriage and the family. It could begin such a ministry by recommitting itself to the worth and intrinsic goodness of these relationships. A second step could be to reaffirm the Scriptures as the sufficient rule for faith and practice. The question of the authority of the Bible seems central in much contemporary debate regarding the church's approach to human sexuality and some variant life-styles. The church may thirdly provide a program of enrichment for marriage and family life. Since such programs have become very popular, they should be easily accessible to the church. The church needs to understand that all persons who live variant life-styles are not there by choice; it therefore needs a program of support, care, and understanding for marriage and family life. Finally, the church needs to offer a ministry of compassion and reconciliation to those persons who chose life-styles at variance with Christian understandings.

We in the church should recommit ourselves to the affirmation that sexual love in the context of marriage is the gift of God, although we cannot commit the modern heresy which claims that the meaning of married love is sex alone. We need to know and understand that when sex is practiced within the context of a loyal and committed relationship, love finds its true meaning and fulfillment. Because it is God's intention that sexual love be expressed in the context of committed marriage, it finds its authentic place here and is spoiled when practiced outside this context. Christian ethics must distinguish between love that is true and committed and infatuations that are temporary and non-binding. The fact that there is a growing acceptance of variant life-styles cannot chart the course of marital and sexual behavior for the church unless we accept the flimsy doctrine that what is average is what is acceptable. For those whose Lord is the God of the Christian faith there must be certain restraints and self-limitations which are enjoined by love, trust, and commitment.

NOTES

1. Henry A. Bowman, *Marriage for Moderns* (New York: McGraw-Hill, 1974).

2. Elizabeth Achtemeier, *The Committed Marriage* (Philadelphia: Westminster Press, 1976).

3. Betty E. Cogswell, "Variant Family Forms and Life-Styles: Rejection of the Traditional Nuclear Family," *The Family Coordinator,* Vol. 24 (October, 1975), pp. 391-406.

4. Carl A. Ridley, Dan J. Peterson, and Arthur W. Avery, "Cohabitation: Does It Make for a Better Marriage?" *The Family Coordinator,* Vol. 27 (April, 1978), pp. 129-136.

5. Philip W. Blumstein and Pepper Schwartz, "Bisexuality in Men," in Carol Warren, Ed., *Sexuality: Encounters, Identities, and Relationships* (Beverly Hills: Sage, 1977).

6. Morton Hunt, "The Future of Marriage," in Carl E. Williams and John F. Crosby, Eds., *Choice and Challenge* (Dubuque, Iowa: Brown, 1974).

7. Paul K. Rasmussen and Lauren L. Kuhn, "The New Masseuse: Play for Pay," in Carol Warren, Ed., *Sexuality: Encounters, Identities, and Relationships* (Beverly Hills: Sage, 1977).

8. Bowman, *op. cit.*

9. Duane Denfeld and Michael Gordon, "Mate Swapping: The Family That Swings Together Clings Together," in Arlene S. Skolnick and Jerome H. Skolnick, Eds., *Family in Transition* (Boston: Little, Brown and Company, 1971).

10. Herbert A. Otto, Ed., *The Family in Search of a Future* (New York: Appleton-Century-Crofts, 1970).

11. Jessie Bernard, *The Future of Marriage* (New York: Bantam Books, 1973).

12. Margaret Mead, "Marriage in Two Steps," in Herbert A. Otto, Ed., *The Family in Search of a Future* (New York: Appleton-Century-Crofts, 1970).

13. J. E. Veevers, "The Moral Careers of Voluntary Childless Wives: Notes on the Defense of a Variant World View," *The Family Coordinator* Vol. 24 (October, 1975), pp. 473-487.

14. Donald F. Clingan, *Aging Persons in the Community of Faith* (St. Louis: Christian Board of Publication, 1977).

15. Victor Kassel, "Polygyny After Sixty," in Herbert A. Otto, Ed., *The Family in Search of a Future* (New York: Appleton-Century-Crofts, 1970).

16. David and Vera Mace, *We Can Have Better Marriages* (Nashville: Abingdon, 1974).

11 Good News for the Homosexual

by Robert M. Nuermberger

Christian churches are genuinely remiss for failing to deal justly and mercifully with homosexuals. Too many times the churches turn away from dialogue, either out of ignorance or fear, or from a judgmental attitude, not recognizing that the homosexual issue is one of the most fruitful issues today in terms of forcing the church at large to deal with Scripture, total evangelizing and healing. It seems that whenever the churches have become too closely identified with the cultures of their times, that God permits problems and social issues to arise to drive the church back to pure doctrine, definition of itself, reaffirmation of Scripture as the revealed Word of God, and to basic Biblical concepts. God never allows the church at large to be too complacent, nor to be at rest.

Homosexual people are, after all, people. Some of them are God's own chosen people, the true Israel, faithful followers of Jesus, confessing to a new birth in Christ. They need the comfort of the Body of Christ. They desperately need friendship. They are often capable of great warmth and tenderness, and do not run from personal relationships. Like the woman caught in adultery and the prodigal son, they know how to give and to receive affection. They need to be treated like any other Christian who struggles to be sanctified, agonizes over his sins and needs counseling.

Unfortunately, many homosexuals are demanding much more than being treated as equals before the law and the judgments of God. They want to be seen as *guiltless* in respect to their homosexuality. They do not want to be thought of as sinning, but as created by God as homosexuals, i.e., as "constitutionally homosexual."

Let me say here that the position I take is that of the "loyal opposition." I do not want to be seen as hateful toward my homosexual

Robert M. Nuermberger is Director of the Christian Counseling Service Inc. in Chattanooga, Tennessee, and has a Ph.D. in Pastoral Counseling. This chapter is adapted from his article in *Christian Life* magazine October, 1978, "Can Believers Be Practicing Homosexuals Without Sinning?"

brothers and sisters, but rather as one who yearns to see them free, and as extending the right hand of fellowship in Christ. On the other hand, I stand unalterably opposed to the arguments that the Bible fails to speak clearly about homosexuality and that homosexuality is right and normal.

Homosexuality is rapidly becoming a cult with the Metropolitan Community Churches as its theological vanguard. In order to develop a viable theological stance on homosexuality, the nation is being softened up by a veritable propaganda campaign typified by such phrases as: "liberation," "toleration," "unfounded fears," "prejudicial stereotypes," "lack of understanding," "rigid conformity to legalism," "a healthy view of sex," "sex as God really intended it," "consenting adults," "freedom to be oneself," "Christians who are homosexually oriented," "repression," "individual liberty," "the goodness of coupleness," "the sanctity of intimate, committed personal relationships," "responsible love," and of course, "gay."

Where conflicts arise throughout the centuries over the nature of God, salvation, or moral issues such as homosexuality, the heart of the controversy is Scripture. The inspiration, sufficiency and authority of Scripture has been challenged since the age of the Apostles when Paul wrote Galatians to quell the Judaizers who confused law and grace, and John penned his Gospel and epistles to deal with the Gnostics who denied that the Christ truly came in human flesh. If the position is once accepted that the Bible does not really speak to the issue of homosexuality, then all other issues become extraneous for the church for the simple reason that the church has only one standard for its faith and practice, one unique book from which it can prophesy to the world, thus calling the world to repentance, and to obedience to the King of Kings.

HOMOSEXUALITY AS CONSTITUTIONAL

One key to the entire controversy over homosexuality is whether some persons are constitutionally homosexual, i.e., created by God as homosexual, and whether or not the Bible has anything to say about it. If it can be established that some are homosexually oriented from birth and cannot help their condition, and that the Bible does not speak on this issue, then it naturally follows that the churches will be forced to change their condemnation of homosexuality as sin; homosexuals will no longer be expected to feel guilty or to change their sexual desires. They will also be approved by the church and society as normal people, fully accepted into the congregations, hold offices, and be ordained as ministers of the Gospel without shame or fear of rejection.

A preliminary study on the Church and Homosexuality produced by a committee of The Presbyterian Church in the United States (colloquially known as "The Southern Presbyterian Church") has a section dealing with the causes and character of homosexuality. It says,

> Some sociologists believe that cultural prejudices about what is masculine and feminine may result in the rejection and alienation of a person who does not "fit in" or "measure up" and lead him or her to find acceptance and self-worth in homosexual relationships. Like heterosexual patterns of sexuality, homosexual patterns vary, and both can probably be accounted for only by a combination of psychological, medical and sociological factors (p. 11).

This study further uses the Kinsey report as its basis for holding that there are degrees of homosexuality and heterosexuality, that "most of us are thus to some extent both homo- and hetero-sexual," and that the closer a person is to having an exclusive homosexual orientation, the less possible it would be for that person to change.

The author of a paper I recently received, "Homosexuality: the Evangelical Puzzle," insists that some people are born homosexuals, that some of these have accepted Christ as Saviour, that the "born-again experience" really doesn't change their homosexuality, that homosexual orientation usually begins quite early in life, and that they are neutral or antagonistic toward heterosexuality, only being truly comfortable as homosexuals. Since all of this is true, he says, it must follow that it is right for Christians to be homosexual, and consequently the churches must re-examine their interpretation of Scripture to make it fit the real facts, thus approving of homosexuality.

Christian homosexuals realize that the constitutional-orientation argument is very powerful, and that if they can manage to convince the general population that this position is true, then the battle is essentially won. So far, they have the backing of the American Psychiatric Association which has removed the category of homosexuality from its index of diseases and mental aberrations. Obviously, if a child is born with a defect, then he cannot possibly be held responsible for this defect, and society may have to help him adjust to it.

However, the concept that homosexuality is constitutional rests on the flimsiest of evidence and a great deal of conjecture. The fields of psychiatry and psychology are in chaos regarding the nature of man and how to resolve his problems. There are many theories about whether homosexuality is abnormal or normal, is a disease, or is detrimental. Empirical experiments and tests have completely failed to show any relationship between chemical composition of the body and homosexual or heterosexual orientation. There is no genetic evidence; chromosome studies have not shown any abnormalities in homosexuals. Glandular studies have proved that there are no differences between homosexuals and heterosexuals. Non-genetic hermaphrodites (persons who may have some male and some female organs or characteristics) are not prone toward homosexuality. Studies of genes and neuro-endocrine circuits reveal nothing.

For Christian homosexuals, the final hope would seem to be socio-logical studies. We are told that the relationship of a child to his parents may cause homosexuality. Usually, the theory is that if a boy became homosexual it is probably due to a hostile, rejecting, unaffectionate father, or a seductive, possessive mother who levered her son against the males in her family. While it is interesting to carry on such specu-lation, it is also quite fruitless. The same negative factors in a family produce strongly heterosexual boys and girls, some of whom become sexually permissive with members of the opposite sex, and some who do not. And there are too many homosexuals who have affectionate parents, understanding fathers, and non-possessive mothers.

The biological, psychiatric, and sociological evidence is nowhere to be found. For the Christian homosexual the real evidence must come from the Bible, from theology and philosophy. But here especial-ly, they are on soft ground.

The Christian homosexual will readily admit that if a person is born with a heterosexual orientation and chooses to reject this for a homosexual orientation, then he has sinned, having fallen under the condemnation of Romans 1:26,27. But, they argue, that if a person is born homosexual, then he cannot be held responsible, nor expected to change. What is their evidence for such an orientation? The bottom line is personal experience! They point out that many homosexuals have often agonized over their homosexuality, prayed on their knees hours on end, have had the "baptism of the Spirit," sought counseling, and have never found genuine relief until they finally accepted themselves as constitutional homosexuals and stopped trying to change what they now see as God-given and good.

A number of things are wrong with this argument. First, it begins with, and is firmly imbedded in, personal experience; in short, feelings. Secondly, it completely fails to take into account all the means of grace that God has granted to the church. Thirdly, it undermines and denies the sufficiency and authority of Scripture as the only source of faith and practice. Fourth, it assumes that an agonizing problem that doesn't apparently change through prayer and pain must be "God-given." Fifth, it ultimately denies the sovereignty of God because it assumes that God cannot change constitutional problems.

The fact is that man does have a constitution toward homosexuality. The Bible calls it our sin-nature. The author of "Homosexuality: the Evangelical Puzzle" says,

> The problem arises when we are repeatedly faced with born-again
> Christians who are *yet homosexually oriented.* (Emphasis is mine.)

Because man has a nature dead in trespasses and sins, that statement is understandably true. But then, you could just as easily insert almost anything into that sentence. We could say, "The problem arises when we are repeatedly faced with born-again Christians who are yet *cheating* on their income tax, committing adultery, alcoholics, slandering their fellow Christians, gluttonous, and so on. Of course Christians misbehave, especially when they are not grounded in the Word of God, living in fellowship with other believers, or are still young in the faith and God has not yet dealt with some of their problems. Sanctification is a life-long process.

DO HOMOSEXUALS REALLY CHANGE?

Christian homosexuals emphatically state that homosexuals cannot change their sexual orientation. This is not based on facts, but on rationalization, and is a vain attempt to justify homosexuality as right. The outstanding Christian psychiatrist from Atlanta, Dr. James Mallory, asserts that many homosexuals do change, even when treated by non-Christian counselors (*Christian Life*, Oct. '77, p. 73). And the "cure rate" among Christian counselors is extremely high. I personally have seen almost every homosexual who has come to me for counseling change his life-style. Many are now married, and happily heterosexual.

One of the most subtle arguments is given by the author of "the Evangelical Puzzle" who says, "Without discounting the sincerity of these individuals and organizations who claim to be 'changing' homosexuals, it is important to realize that most 'changes' from homosexuality are really instances of changes of homosexual inactivity, not changes of heterosexuality." In reply, if we change the orientation of a man from being an active murderer to becoming nonviolent, it is not altogether a bad thing! We may not be able to *totally* eradicate anger, violent feelings or thoughts within him, since that is a lifetime process and might not be finally accomplished until his glorification, assuming that he is a Christian. But if our homosexual friends will admit that a change in sexual preference is evidence of a true change in the nature of a person, then I think a good case can be made by many counselors that most homosexuals who seek counseling have been "cured."

It is necessary to maintain a constant walk with Christ and daily crucifixion. In my estimation, when an individual recognizes that according to Scripture homosexuality is sin, that he wants to get out of the gay community, that he is tired of depression, fragmentation, disillusionment and lovelessness, that he yearns to lead a life of holiness with Christ as his Master over all sexuality, then the possibilities of his deliverance are exceedingly high and there is no reason he cannot escape homosexuality as a life style and orientation. To argue anything less is to deny the cleansing power of the Blood of Christ and to make a mockery of the Gospel.

Christians should recognize that every member of the Body of Christ is to be received with compassion and counseled, as the Body ministry is for all. The churches must allow the homosexual, the adulterer, or whomever, to openly confess their sins to each other and to receive help from the Body of Christ; otherwise it is failing in its task of healing and reconciliation.

To argue that loving the homosexual and understanding the homosexual must necessarily lead to *approving* of his homosexuality is a misunderstanding and confusion of the worst order, and only serves to perpetuate the problem. To love the individual does not mean that I must accept his sin as good, but it does mean that I have to stand along side of him and help him through his struggles until he abandons his homosexuality just as I have to struggle with the adulterer until he gives up his adultery, or the murderer until he becomes peaceful.

The author of "the Evangelical Puzzle" tries to bolster his position by saying that surveys taken of homosexuals do not indicate that people who are constitutional homosexuals have changed into heterosexuals. The argument is that "In a society where at least eight million Americans are homosexuals, why is it nearly impossible to find former homosexuals who through Christ have found 'deliverance' from their homosexuality?" This is a false statement. Homosexuals have found deliverance. The problem is that the counseling ministries to homosexuals are relatively new, and inroads have not yet been made into that community of any phenomenal extent, but the testimony is that homosexuals can and do get out of the gay community.

HOMOSEXUAL ACT AND HOMOSEXUAL ORIENTATION

In a major address before the Christian Association of Psychological Studies in June of 1977, one of the pioneers in Pastoral Counseling, Dr. Seward Hiltner, stated that the biblical writers did not understand the concept of homosexual orientation. He held the position that homosexuality was misidentified simply because the writers of Bible times did not have access to our knowledge of psychological and biological facts. Hiltner said,

> At least in its reference to homosexuality, therefore, the Bible does not speak at all to the principal way in which homosexuality must be understood today (*The Bulletin,* official publication of The Christian Association for Psychological Studies, vol. 3, 1977, No. 4, p. 4).

He concludes by suggesting that psychologists will have to be depended upon "in constructing the theology that is now needed in relation to this question" (p. 5).

Dr. Greg Bahnsen of the Reformed Theological Seminary, Jackson, Mississippi, disagrees. In *A Biblical Study of Homosexuality,* a mimeographed paper copyrighted by Dr. Bahnsen, he says that science cannot establish or alter ethical norms delivered by the Sovereign Lord. The implication is that psychologists cannot be depended upon to construct our theology, rather that theology will judge psychology. Bahnsen says that even if we grant that the Bible never distinguishes homosexual acts from homosexual orientation, we may not draw the conclusion that the *Bible writers knew nothing about orientation.* The distinction may not be morally relevant. Scripture condemns both *orientation* and *act* because both emanate from a sinful nature. Jesus dogmatically asserted that from the heart proceeded evil actions, thoughts, murders, adulteries, fornication, thefts, false witness, and blasphemies (Matt. 15:19).

BIBLICAL AUTHORITY VS. CULTURAL RELATIVISM

For the believer who desires to be obedient to His Master, the basis of understanding anything rests upon.

1) the nature of an infinite, Holy God who created and maintains the universe,
2) the revelation of God Himself to us in the Bible, and
3) the fact that apart from the Bible, we have no sure source of knowledge about God, life, or ethics.

The Christian homosexual position when carefully examined can be exposed for what it is at its very core: an attack upon the integrity, sufficiency, and authority of Scripture, which for the Christian Church is an attack upon the very nature of our Holy God.

I have used an argument many times with university students who are confused about Scripture, an argument which for me makes good sense, although it can never change a person's basic assumptions that he holds in the face of all logic and fact. The argument goes something like this:

1. Either *a supreme God exists,* or *He does not exist.* If He does not exist, then man is not responsible to God, but only to himself, and man is free to design his own life as he sees fit.
2. If a supreme God exists, then He is either *personal,* or He is *non-personal.* That is, He has personality with all its ability to initiate action, communicate, think, plan, and feel. If God exists, but is non-personal, then "It" is simply a blind, irrational force without a positive or negative direction, and man is not responsible to it.
3. If a supreme God exists who is personal, then He is either *good* or *evil.* If He is evil, or some mixture of good and evil like the Greek gods, then man has to protect himself from this dangerous God to the best of his ability, and in any event, man could well be better than this God. In this case, man would be responsible only to himself.
4. If God is supreme, personal, and holy, then He has either *spoken* to man or *not spoken.* If God has not spoken to man, then man is not responsible to God.
5. If God has spoken, then He has either spoken *clearly* so that man

can understand, or He has *not spoken clearly,* in which case, God cannot ethically require man to understand.

6. But if there is a supreme, personal, holy God who has spoken clearly to man, then man is *fully responsible* to listen and to obey. Romans 1:18 ff. says that God has spoken clearly and man is without excuse.

Applied to the Christian homosexual position, this says that our God is fully aware of homosexuality, whether by act or orientation, and that He has clearly spoken on this issue.

The establishment of Scripture as the only infallible rule of faith and practice is the only solid ground for hope for the homosexual. While it unalterably opposes and condemns homosexuality as sin, it also affords the homosexual his great hope for deliverance from the snare of sin and holds out before him the possibility of attaining a true sexual identity. Diluting the Scripture of these truths will only rob the homosexual of his confidence in a sovereign God who alone can bring him peace.

There are two assumptions made by the Christian homosexual position that attack the authority of Scripture: its view of cultural relativism which in turn is based upon its philosophy of fact. We shall deal with the latter first.

A. PHILOSOPHY OF FACT

We must realize that, one way or another, all of us have developed a philosophy about "facts." Most of us were educated in a humanistic school system that carefully taught us to see God as just another "fact" that could be ignored, and really should not be discussed during school hours. "Religion," including Christianity, was viewed merely as another source of knowledge, though not nearly as important as "science." We were led to believe that there was a sharp dichotomy between faith and science. Science was objective, incontrovertible, its methods sacrosanct, its conclusions arrived at with cool logic and precision; whereas faith belonged to the subjective part of man, did not rest on facts, was irrational or at least non-rational, belonged to the individual's private world, and in the end did not make any difference as to how successful we were in life. Science was safe, but faith was a blind leap into the unknown. This philosophy was so carefully instilled in us day-by-day over the years that most of us were embarrassed to confess that we were Christians. The scientist now became God, and the real God and His revealed Book were relegated to the myths of antiquity.

The Bible says something quite different. It categorically states that the entire universe was created by God and virtually cries out that God exists and that He is all-powerful (Romans 1:18-20). All facts have been created by God and are for His glory; man's job is to interpret facts correctly. The problem is that unless man is regenerated and under the authority of God's Word, he cannot correctly interpret the facts around him; therefore unregenerate man, and the Christian who refuses to accept the authority of the Bible as God's revealed Word, is bound to misinterpret the facts around him. Both will be bound to interpret the facts according to humanistic philosophy.

The problem with Christian advocates of homosexuality is that they base their interpretations of homosexuality entirely on two assumptions which they see as facts: (1) that experience defines truth, and (2) that cultural relativism is a truth.

B. CULTURAL RELATIVISM

Cultural relativism is the view that what was true in former cultures is not necessarily true today, or in common thought, "One man's truth is another man's poison." To some degree, we all believe that certain opinions do change, that not all people think alike, and that we even change our own opinions on right and wrong over a period of time. Some "truths" are relative to their times. But I find that the Christian homosexual attitude regarding Old Testament concepts completely fails to distinguish between moral truths and those ceremonial requirements that establish Israel as a separated people in every detail of their lives. One proponent of Christian homosexuality sweeps away God's view of homosexuality expressed in Leviticus 18:22 and 20:13 as worthy of death because it happens to come in the same book as restrictions regarding eating shellfish and other animals. Others hold that Paul's view of homosexuality must be seen in the same light as his views regarding men wearing long hair in I Corinthians 11.

Cultural relativism is squarely founded upon personal experience as the ground of truth; its "truth" is determined by the will of the majority and the demands of the age.

Thinking Christians cannot accept this experiential-relativistic philosophy, but totally reject it as the ground of truth. There is only one ground of truth; God is Truth and creates truth. The Christian can only presume that all facts are God's created truths, and apart from God's creation there are no facts. Furthermore, unless God reveals Himself and interprets the facts by revelation, we have no possibility of knowing truth but are completely in the dark. Only God knows the mind exhaustively and comprehensively because God is infinite, eternal, and unchangeable in his nature and attributes. Only He can see the whole picture, and therefore only He can tell you what any part of that picture means or how it should be interpreted. It was on this basis that the reformers of the 16th and 17th centuries developed the concept that Scripture interprets Scripture, that is, that if Scripture is unclear in one area, it must be made clear by another passage. Only that position establishes the Bible as the Word of God, and only that position takes the Bible seriously. The Christian homosexual position that argues from experience and relativism does not take the Bible seriously as the revealed Word of God which defines truth, but rather forces the Bible to say what it wants it to say and therefore so dilutes the Scripture as to make it say nothing definitively in regard to any value of life.

Jesus was not a victim or proponent of cultural relativism, nor did He shrink back from proclaiming God's Word as absolute. Jesus didn't argue that "Deuteronomy was adequate enough in Moses' time, but since 1400 years have changed the circumstances, it cannot speak to me today." Rather, He said, "I came to fulfill the Law and the Prophets," and often quoted Scripture as the basis of knowing right and wrong.

THE TWISTING OF ROMANS 1:26,27.

The cultural relativistic assumptions of the Christian homosexual position is most clearly seen when applied to its interpretation of Romans 1:26,27. The Christian homosexual position here is that this passage does not apply to constitutional homosexuals, but only to constitutional heterosexuals who abandoned their heterosexuality in favor of homosexuality. That interpretation makes *disobedience,* not homosexuality, sinful.

This is a marvelous rationalization because it takes the homosexual off the hook. He no longer has to see homosexuality as sin because he has made the Bible argue that it is *not* sin. The problem with his argument is that he has inadvertently forced the Bible to also say that the rest of Romans does not pertain to the homosexual.

Verses 18-32 show God's wrath revealed against men who wickedly suppress the truth by their wickedness.

Now then, if all of this pertains only to heterosexuals, and not to those "whom God made homosexuals," then it naturally follows by the simplest logic, that verses 28-32 also do not apply to homosexuals. Using that kind of logic it follows that homosexuals are not guilty of these things, and that furthermore, these things are *wrong* for the heterosexual but *right* for the homosexual. Obviously, this would be patently ridiculous! The Christian homosexual will react to the above argument by proclaiming that he is what God made him, and that that is obviously the wrong way to interpret Scripture. If so, then I charge that the Christian homosexual wants to interpret Scripture to his own convenience. He wants to bend it to his ends and will not be subject to the Author of the Scripture but subjects the Scripture to the authority of himself, and thus reflects what Paul argues in verse 27, that because of homosexuality men "received unto themselves the due penalty for perversion." The penalty for moral perversion is intellectual perversion, and the most obvious consequence is the perversion of Scripture and the tearing down of the authority of Scripture, which also constitutes an attack on the nature, the veracity and the holiness of God.

In the face of such a strong position, the Christian homosexual will rise up in wrath. He hears condemnation and rejection coming from the orthodox wing of the church. He believes that other Christians do not love him and extend unto him Christian fellowship as a Christian brother. Let it be said in reply, that the position I am taking is to uphold the integrity of God's revealed Word against the attempt of any to get out from under its authority, for it speaks to all men in all ages and defines what sin is, and specifically states that God is angry with sin and will judge it in whatever form it appears because God is no respecter of persons.

On the other hand, my argument is not a reflection of hatred of the homosexual as a person. On the contrary, the very Word of God also states that every sinner should be received graciously and lovingly and he should be accepted by the church if he repents from his sins and turns from his evil ways. But even if he does not turn from his evil ways, he is still to be loved and extended compassion, but his evil will not be condoned.

SODOM: GENESIS 19

The Christian homosexual position thoroughly rejects interpreting the inhabitants of Sodom as homosexuals. The author of "Puzzle" argues that (1) the "Biblical references on Sodom nowhere mention homosexuality," (2) that the issue in Sodom was lack of hospitality, (3) that the word "to know" simply meant to "get acquainted," and that (4) "responsible committed relationships between people" are certainly not dealt with in Genesis.

Now it is agreed that when God prophesied against Sodom and Gomorrah in Is. 1:10, Jer. 23:14, and Ezek. 16:46-58, and when Jesus mentions them in Matt. 10:14-15 and Luke 10:10-12, homosexuality is not mentioned, for the focus is on their pride and idolatry. However, it is noteworthy that the writer omits the main point: the names of these cities were synonymous with the grossest forms of evil imaginable, and that when God wished to provide a model for evil, all He had to do was to name the cities.

But it takes a real spiritual blindness not to see that the sin of Sodom for which among others it was judged was homosexuality. While in general the word *yadha,* "to know," often does not mean "sexual knowledge," but perhaps a deep intimacy of spirit, the contexts clearly define its meaning.

Yadha happens to be used as "sexual knowledge" especially in the context of Genesis. Gen. 4:1, Adam *knew* his wife and she conceived Cain. Gen. 4:17, Cain *knew* his wife and she conceived Enoch. Refer also to Gen. 4:25 and 38:26. In the context of Genesis, "to know" *often means* to have sexual relations, whatever it might mean elsewhere in Scripture. And it is in Genesis that we find the Sodom story.

A careful reading of Genesis 19 leads one to the conclusion that hospitality is not the meaning, nor is acquaintance. In fact, the men of the city (repeated twice for emphasis) were ready to break down the door in order to get at the angels to "know them." That's a strange way certainly to get acquainted!

But if Genesis leaves us in doubt about God's view of homosexuality, consider the parallel passage in Judges 19 and 20. The sons of Belial (19:22 ff.) set upon the house of the old man at Gibeah, beating on the door and demanding the Levite so that "we may know him." The old man did the same thing as Lot; he offered them his daughter and the Levite's concubine for their sexual pleasure in order to protect the Levite. So the Gibeahites "knew her and abused her all night." As a consequence of this evil, God permitted 400,000 troops to destroy the town.

Yes, the Sodomites and the Gibeahites were prepared to violate the rules of hospitality, but the way they chose was homosexual, and both towns were destroyed. God's wrath descends whenever sin becomes ungovernable.

GOD'S ORDER

Scripture clearly proclaims God as holy, desiring us to be like Him in His holiness, and that He is the Lawgiver who establishes order in the universe. The order that God established regarding sexuality is that man (generic) is created both male and female, Gen. 1:27,28.

Maleness reflects some of the attributes of God. Femaleness reflects other attributes, such as God's protective qualities, as His bearing us as children. The marriage relationship reflects other attributes, perhaps the relationship of the Trinity where there are three persons, but one God. Maleness alone cannot reflect all that God desires to reveal of Himself in nature and spiritual communion. Man is not homo-sexual.

The focus on homosexual "rights" and "responsible commitments" emphasizes genital sexual activity. The Christian homosexual position would be useless unless genital activity was the purpose; human needs must be served, and they are willing to bend the Scriptures to get it. At its core, homosexuality is rebellion against God's authority and established order, and idolatry of the worst variety.

CONCLUSION

God must be seen as a God of wrath, justice, and righteousness Who operates according to precise law, and Who is also a God of infinite compassion, mercy and love Who receives the sinner through the atonement of Christ, and actively pursues his continual sanctification until the day of Christ.

The church must take a stand on these issues if it is going to make an impact on the world. My concern is that many homosexuals in this country either had a Christian heritage which they reject, or genuinely profess faith in Jesus Christ as Saviour and still struggle with homosexual longings. Christ is not the Lord of their sexual life and yet many of them want this. We only do them service when we tell them that they can get out of "gayness." The Christian who tries to build a theory condoning homosexuality is guilty of sinning against his brother by keeping him trapped in his sin and removing from him all hope of deliverance. Our position must be uncompromising with these issues but magnificent in its love.

Until the Christian gays abandon their commitment to cultural relativism and humanism for comfort and justification, repent of their apostasy, and return to the Scriptures *alone* as their rule of faith and practice, they will stand under the judgement of God. It will be to them even as in the days when God said to Jeremiah concerning an apostate Judah,

How can you say, 'We are wise, and the law of the Lord is with us'? But behold, the lying pen of the scribes has made it into a lie. The wise men are put to shame, they are dismayed and caught; Behold, they have rejected the word of the Lord, and what kind of wisdom do they have?" (Jer. 8:8,9, NAS).

12 Christian and Homosexual: A Contradiction

by William P. Wilson
and Robert Abarno

INTRODUCTION

The four etiologic theories of homosexuality are noted by Freedman, et al.[1] They include the "Deviant–but–natural" theory; i.e., innately man is neither heterosexual nor homosexual with conditioning and biosocial patterning as determinants. The second theory is genetic. Those who hold this view see homosexuality as a constitutionally or genetically determined disease, disorder or defect. Thirdly, Freudian theory conceptualizes male homosexuality as a combined biogenetic and psychosocial disorder. Fourthly, there are those who believe that the disease is determined solely by early life experiences. Bieber[2] is the primary advocate of this position. His observations demonstrate the presence of adverse intrafamilial influences, so that homosexuality evolves as a consequence of these deleterious experiences.

Irrespective of the scientific views of its etiology, Christians view the problem of homosexuality in a Christian as a contradiction. This is especially true in light of the Biblical admonition found in Romans 1:28 ff., "Because men refuse to keep in mind the true knowledge about God [and serve creation instead of the Creator], he has given them over to corrupted minds." There is, however, a viable option, a conscious choice or decision. These corrupted minds can be changed (Romans 12:2).

Homosexuality, then, from a Biblical view implies that it is a learned pattern, not genetic. Romans 1:21 ff., "They know God, but they do not give him the honor that belongs to him, nor do they thank him. ... Because men are such fools, God has given them over to do the filthy things their hearts desire, and they do shameful things with

William P. Wilson, M.D., is Professor and Head of the Division of Biological Psychiatry, Department of Psychiatry, Duke University Medical Center, and Director of the Program for the Study of Christianity in Medicine; Robert Abarno is Research Associate and Coordinator of the Program for the Study of Christianity in Medicine. This chapter is adapted from their article in The Bulletin (Vol. 4, No. 2, Summer 1978) of the Christian Association for Psychological Studies.

each other" (*The New Testament in Today's English Version*). Therefore, we can say that many learned behaviors, i.e., homosexuality, prostitution, gluttony, and alcoholism, are controllable and changeable. For the Christian, inappropriate behavior is a spiritual disease; functionally, a disturbance of desire and object choice.

PATIENT MATERIALS AND METHODS

The patient material in this study consisted of six male homosexuals referred to us for treatment by Christian laymen, ministers, and physicians. None of the patients had previously known any of the other patients or his sexual preference. Each was examined psychiatrically prior to being treated psychotherapeutically. We obtained a detailed history and determined the mental status. Inquiry was made into his early life experiences. We were especially interested here in the intra-familial relationships of child and father and mother. We also obtained a detailed description of the patient's sex life. In this we noted experiences of early sexual arousal, masturbatory practices, first homosexual or heterosexual experiences. First awareness of sex objects preference and the patients sexual fantasy life were also noted. Further inquiry was made into the patient's homosexual life. These included: how he made contacts, his preferred activity (fellatorism and/or sodomy) and the life-style that he lived.

Further documentation of all historical information was also obtained when possible from at least one other significant informant.

Since our therapeutic orientation is Christian, the patient knew that we would treat him with Christian psychotherapeutic techniques in both individual and group therapy. Our therapeutic endeavors did, however, include further examination of each patient's familial environment:

1. Stability of parents' marriage.
2. Presence of love and order.
3. Discipline, its typology.
4. Roles.
5. Value systems taught.
6. Spiritual atmosphere in the home.

We also inquired into the patient's Christian life, i.e., his salvation experience and Christian nurture, as well as his understanding of Christian commitment. The following tests were employed to evaluate the effect or lack of effect of Christian experience, and subsequent Christian psychotherapy.

1. Repentance: Does the Christian homosexual want to be healed? John 5:3-6; Psalms 37:3,4.
2. Transformation: Does the Christian homosexual want to be transformed? Romans 12:2.

3. Faith: Does the homosexual really expect God to change him? Philippians 3:21; 4:8,9.
4. Prayer: The fervent prayer of a righteous man availeth much. James 5:13 ff.
5. Will: "Nevertheless, not my will, but thine be done." Luke 22:42. To do God's will for his life.

Christian psychotherapy was oriented toward increasing the degree of commitment, to allow God to change the individual. This was accomplished through prayer, inquiry into and presentation of Biblical truth, and utilization of the power of the Holy Spirit. Standard psychotherapeutic techniques with a depth psychology orientation were also employed in individual and group therapy to intervene in conflict areas.

RESULTS
Topical
The mean age of the patients was 23.6 years. Two of the patients are married (each for the first time), the four remaining patients are single, never married (no divorces). None of the patients cohabited with a female prior to marriage nor did the single patients cohabit with a female.

One patient is a junior high school teacher, one an insurance salesman, another is an ad layout man. Three patients are students (two undergraduates, one graduate). One patient is in socioeconomic class 1, the other five patients are class 3.

Sexual
Five of the six patients in this investigation were active homosexuals. One patient was celibate but was homosexual in orientation, mannerisms, gait, etc.

The two married homosexuals during their marriage were more than occasionally heterosexual. All patients reported homosexual masturbatory fantasies. The first homosexual experience occurred at a mean age of 13.7 years with a range of 11-18 years. Three had the first homosexual encounter with friends, two had a casual first episode, and one had his first encounter with his cousin.

Two patients were exclusively fellators, one exclusively a sodomist, two were engaged in both fellatio and sodomy. One patient was celibate but had frequent homosexual masturbatory fantasies with conscious sexual desire for males.

Four of the six patients are not involved in homosexual activity. Two married patients are maintaining their marital status. One continues to have intercourse with his wife. One patient who previously was a latent homosexual is no longer having homosexual masturbatory fantasies and has been dating a female for four months. One patient previously active, although covertly, has had only one homosexual experience since therapy began in August 1977. Two patients remain active homosexuals; one has sporadic experiences, the other is active and presently engaged in a homosexual relationship which began in early December 1977.

Psychopathology

These patients were remarkably similar in their psychopathology. All patients reported pervasive anxiety and recurring depression; four patients appeared to be angry. Paranoia common to homosexuals seemed to be an underlying psychological state.[3] Suicidal ideation was reported by all patients with two patients describing a specific plan.

The two patients who are currently active in homosexual relationships continue to manifest extreme anxiety. Both are unreliable in attendance at individual and group therapy. Both are extremely defensive and have reported continued psychological conflicts in daily functioning. However, neither patient has been willing or able to resolve his dependency on individual therapy. Depression is manifest in these patients' inability to function efficiently at work and/or at school, because of lack of interest and energy. Four patients evidence minimal psychopathology. Mild anxiety is evident but depression has been relieved with a noticeable elevation of mood, interest, and energy. Changes in sleep and appetite which were present are no longer of clinical significance in these four patients.

Family Life

Gross distortions in family relationships were found. Four of the patients came from homes where there was definite evidence of marital instability. This was manifest in separations, divorce, arguing, violence, alcoholism, and infidelity. In one instance there was excessive closeness of the parents with exclusion of the child from the relationship. We have been unable to evaluate the marital stability of the parents of one patient. In all homes the mother, father, child love relationships were profoundly disturbed or distorted. In all except one home the discipline was harsh, excessive, and/or uncompromising. In many instances it was also inconsistent.

Roles were disturbed in all homes in that the mother was either weak and compliant, sickly, or emotionally disturbed. All fathers were harsh and uncompromising in their attitudes and cold toward their male child. All fathers were hard workers and successful in their vocations.

Values were usually appropriately taught in word but often not in deed.

There was little religious influence in the early lives of our patients.

All patients have had significant conflict with their families. The two patients who are still homosexually active have not resolved to any degree their conflicts with significant family members. Neither of these patients have revealed their homosexuality to their parents and both became extremely anxious when two other patients reported that they had confronted their fathers. In response to the excellent results of these meetings and the positive results reported by those who did confront their parent, the two active homosexuals withdrew further and appeared more anxious and depressed. The remaining two patients now maintain a non-conflictual relationship with their significant family members. (Their homosexuality is known to the family but has never been acknowledged or discussed.)

Christian Life

All of the patients have experienced regeneration through faith in Jesus Christ. One who is homosexually active is not leading an active Christian life. This patient appears to be angry with God and is not seeking to relate to him. This subject holds little hope for healing. The other active homosexual, when confronted, revealed that he has never repented, does not seek to be transformed, does not by faith expect God to change him but paradoxically believes that God can change him. This patient's prayer life continues but is admittedly deficient in power and sincerity. Currently, his will is not to change despite the fact he claims to be a Christian. This source of conflict, i.e., his Christianity vs. homosexuality, appears to have been magnified in direct proportion to his recent (12/77) increasing homosexual involvement. It is particularly interesting to note that this patient had been involved in full-time Christian service just prior to beginning therapy.

Another patient is minimally active in his Christian life and experience but when confronted admitted his only reason for being heterosexual would be for his family and not because he is a Christian. However, his abstinence from homosexual activity appears to be as a result of his father's renewed concern. The patient and his father's newly acquired ability to communicate and his mother's recent suicidal gesture appear to have initiated self-examination of his previously held attitude of hostility. This patient continues to pray and in the light of recent family developments seems to be seeking God's will for his life. We will comment on these psychodynamics in the following discussion.

The other three patients, when confronted report with calmness and confidence that they have repented, have been transformed, have faith, have prayed earnestly privately and in therapy, and have asked for God's will for their lives, i.e.,

P-2: "My reason for living is to serve God."

P-3: "Until I agonized before God in prayer, I did not have peace. Now God has answered my prayers. I am going to remain in my marriage and stay active in my church."

P-4: On two occasions in group this patient said with sincerity and deep feeling, "God will heal me, I know it!"

Results of Therapy

Three of the patients of this study have abandoned a homosexual life-style and/or homosexual fantasies. These patients are currently involved in prayer, Bible study, and are regularly attending and participating in the work and mission of Biblically-based Christian churches. For these patients, Christian and homosexual is a contradiction! One patient is not currently active as a homosexual but is uncommitted to a Biblically-based Christian life-style. This patient does not have regular involvement in a Christian church. Two patients are active as homosexuals and are uncommitted as Christians.

DISCUSSION

Our findings strongly support the theory that obligatory homosexuality is a learned behavior that occurs in part because of massive childhood fears. Anxiety in these patients apparently has been pervasive from early childhood and persists as a primary psychopathological state. Superimposed on this state is a failure of normal male sexual differentiation which occurs as a result of abnormal father-mother-child relationships. This consists of an imposition of female role expectations by the father and mother. The emergence of obligatory homosexuality appears to us to result from the early complex negative patterning proposed by Socarides.[4]

The negative patterning observed in three of our patients can be described as follows. Each of our patients experienced an overly close relationship with the mother during early life. In each instance, however, there was deep marital conflict that had preceded the patient's birth. In all three of these cases the mother was often absent from the home or incapacitated by illness. Because of this incapacitation the female role was imposed on the patient by one or both parents in order that he might assume the duties of the inadequate mother.

To illustrate this role assumption is the story related by one of our patients who reported acting out his mother's role in a recent incident with his father. This patient was shocked by the sudden realization of his role assumption. He became extremely anxious and then hostile, when he realized his father had imposed a mother/female role on him while shopping with a younger sibling. The father actually behaved in this reported incident as if his son was his wife. The measure of long-term symbiotic conditioning was evident in the way in which father reacted to the patient; not as a father to a son, but as an irate husband to a petulant wife.

During the course of our study, this patient's mother made a planned suicide gesture. She was hospitalized and as a result, we were able to make an in depth investigation of the dynamics involved in the intra-familial relationships between mother, father, and the patient. Several hours of investigation were also conducted with the patient's siblings. Our observations seemed to confirm Bieber, *et. al.,*[5] and Socarides[6] hypotheses that intrafamilial early patterning, i.e., learned maladaptation, massive childhood fears and inadequate patterning lead to obligatory (true) homosexuality.

The foregoing is presented to emphasize the profundity of the dynamic forces that have produced the homosexual's orientation. The lack of differentiation from the symbiotic relationship with the mother gives rise to not only the sexual object choice but also determines the development of mannerisms, gait, speech patterns, and value systems. It is with this knowledge that we approach the homosexual in treatment. Our choices are: to accept the homosexual's disease and try to help him live with his "thorn in the flesh," or we can say that he is not sick and therefore we should accept him as he is, or we can undertake to unravel the dynamics of his illness and try to treat it. This latter choice is the only one available to the Christian therapist.

Marmor[7] in a review made the point that homosexuals with the best chance of changing are those with strong motivation. In our experience motivation to change is not commonly seen. However, we recognized that a homosexual who came into the Christian life might be highly motivated, if he has been presented and has accepted Biblical truths. This acceptance should result in a high level of motivation.

In our conceptualization of Christian psychotherapy regeneration is a *sine-qua-non* for a high level of motivation. Regeneration also results in a high level of cooperation—a second factor listed by Marmor as necessary for change. The fact that the patients in this study reported that being homosexual and Christian was a contradiction was reflected in the conflict they felt about continuing their homosexual life-style. It was interesting that all stated that a Christian orientation to psychotherapeutic intervention was the only approach acceptable to them. Because we saw ourselves only as instruments of their healing and were nonjudgmental in our approach we obtained a high level of cooperation.

Because the homosexual feels rejected and alienated from society, the forgiving community that we represent was appealing to him. He understood that God judged his behavior and that we could not therefore condemn him as a person but could condemn his homosexual behavior. This understanding was helpful to reinforcing his cooperation.

Being instruments of the Holy Spirit we were moved to help the homosexual understand the process by which God would heal him. Important to all of the patients was a clear understanding of the nature of repentance. We, therefore, helped them to understand that at salvation they had had to develop a sorrow toward God on account of sin accompanied by a repugnance toward sin, and that they had had to humbly surrender their will to God in order to serve him. Our evaluation of their level of surrender was determined by the content and sincerity of their prayers. We have recognized that prayer[8] is a primary instrument of healing and that the patient must engage in an active personal and corporate prayer life, if he is to be healed. We do therefore begin and end each session with prayer, and pray on all occasions where it seems indicated. Our reasons for evaluating the patient's prayer is based on the scripture which says that "one reason you don't have what you want, is that you don't ask God for it" (James 4:3 LB). Sincerity is revealed in prayer emphatically. With an understanding of his state of repentance, therefore, we help the patient continue his repentance and thus his salvation by using techniques of confrontation, admonition, exhortation, and encouragement.

The results of our therapy have been encouraging to us and we believe that the Christian therapist has an added dimension of therapy to offer the homosexual. He offers through the mode of change,[9] that is reconciliation with God, an infinitely greater opportunity for healing. The Christian therapist has available the power of the Holy Spirit, the efficacy of prayer, and the truth of the Word to increase his therapeutic armamentarium.

Finally, we believe that involvement in the greater Christian community as reflected in engagement in corporate worship experiences is also therapeutic. It is in this setting that the homosexual can find further acceptance and healing.

CONCLUSIONS

Six male homosexuals have been examined and treated using Christian psychotherapeutic techniques. It was observed that the dynamic formulations of Bieber are applicable in all six of our patients. All were believing Christians who had not gained victory over their problems. Therapy resulted in a change in sexual object choice and orientation in three patients. Two others continue to be active homosexuals remaining in conflict. One other is celibate but has not changed his orientation. It is concluded that Christian and homosexual is a contradiction and is recognized as such by the Christian homosexual.

NOTES

1. Freedman, A., *et. al., Comprehensive Textbook of Psychiatry* (Baltimore: The Williams and Wilkins Co., 1972).

2. Bieber, I., *et. al., Homosexuality* (New York: Basic Books Inc., 1962).

3. Socarides, C., "Homosexuality and Medicine," *JAMA,* Vol. 217, No. 7 (May 1970): 1199.

4. *Ibid.*

5. Freedman, p. 415.

6. Socarides, p. 1201.

7. Marmor, J., "Homosexuality in Males," *Psychiatric Annals,* Vol. 1, No. 4 (December 1971): 44.

8. Wilson, W. P., *et. al.,* "Therapeutic Prayer," Duke University Medical Center, 1976.

9. Wilson, W. P., "Christian Psychotherapy," Duke University Medical Center, 1977.

13 A Saturday Morning Dialogue

by Jim Kasper
and Mike Bussee

Part I: Equipping The Church

INTRODUCTION

Mike: Let's begin. We should say that this seminar is not designed to train churches to round up homosexuals and change them. That's not at all what we're talking about. We're talking about equipping the church to deal with people who are experiencing conflict between their homosexuality and their Christianity and are wanting that conflict resolved. Over the past four years that our ministry has been in existence, we've probably dealt face-to-face with about 500 people who were seeking change at some level. About 98% of those people were already Christians.

Jim: So it is possible to be gay and Christian at the same time. The issue is: is that permissible? And so far we feel it is not. These people are in a collision course. They can't adjust their sexual choice with their faith and that's when they come to see us. And the parents come to see us. Besides the one-to-one counseling, we do literature and a lot of phone counseling—3,000 calls per month from the Hotline Center. We account for 8%. And we also do a lot of work with parents. We have a Thursday night group that meets with them specifically just to assuage some of their fears and to learn from other parents how they get through this crisis. A lot of parents feel super-guilt when they discover their kid is homosexual. "What did I do wrong?" "I should have done this."

Mike: The history of our ministry, EXIT, began back in 1973. We started out very small. We didn't expect to do this at all. The Hotline

---

Jim Kaspar and Mike Bussee of EXIT, an outreach of Melodyland Hotline Center in Anaheim, California, presented this dialogue April 8, 1978 before The Philadelphia Convocation On Human Sexuality. The Convocation, sponsored by the United Church People for Biblical Witness, met in Old First United Church of Christ; the dialogue has been edited because of its length.

143

Center is just a 24-hour crisis intervention line and we started to get calls from homosexual persons. Jim, because he had this background, started to teach a seminar to our counselors to train them to deal more intelligently and compassionately with the callers. From there he started teaching seminars. The word got out and he started teaching seminars at other churches. People started coming to us for counseling and we found ourselves in the thick of it before we knew what hit us, really. And now our primary ministry is counseling. About half our work is counseling, half of it is speaking to churches and to groups such as yours.

An interesting development is that, in 1976, EXIT hosted a conference in Anaheim that brought together representatives of ministries similar to ours from across the country and we formed an international coalition of Christian ministries offering change called EXODUS. There's an address that you can write to listed at the end of this dialogue. The main purposes of EXODUS are, basically, for the ministries to use each other as referrals, to keep each other alerted to new materials that are out, and just to keep in touch and encourage one another.

Jim: And these agencies are distributed generally coast to coast. Okay, our lives. Mike and I represent two different facets of the gay community. Not all gays exercise their gayness in the same way. Not all gays do the same thing.

My case is as a gay person who came out—that's a term you should learn. To come out as opposed to being in the closet. To come out means you're known. You declare, "I am gay." There's a lot of power that happens with that. It's almost like declaring your Christian faith to non-believers. "I am a Christian." It does something. You take that on as an identity. Well, that's what I did.

In New York, when I came out about 10 years ago, I was very active in the gay community there, and I liked it. For me, homosexuality was a very positive, reinforcing experience. People liked me for who I was, and the gay friends who were around me liked me because I appeared to have my act together. I would have been called a "happy gay," and I certainly felt happy with what I knew at that time. And then, in California (I was transferred and looking for a job) I met an old college buddy of mine named Tom who had just become a Christian. He was only three months old, very young, and I could tell there was something different in his life, but I didn't know what. All I can remember about Tom is his very liberal sexual ideas. In college we tried quite a few things together and I thought, "Great, I'll have my chance with him." Tom really wasn't a homosexual or a heterosexual. He was tri-sexual. He'd try anything, and I thought I'd try something, too.

I met Tom, and he was different. And whatever he would say about his Christian experience, I would counter with a better argument— because I was smarter than him. But every time he bounced back with a smile. I couldn't dent what he had. Tom had a quality of life that I didn't have. As good as it was for me, an open, practicing gay, it still wasn't what he had. I became a Christian on that basis, not to escape homosexuality, but rather to acquire what Tom had. That's a significant order of events. God won my heart first. It wasn't until a year and a half later that He started dealing with my homosexuality.

I was still practicing homosexual things as a brand-new Christian. I know this will really set a lot of you back. That was true. I have to admit that. Now, why? Does that mean that I wasn't really a Christian or that God couldn't change me? No, all those things were true. It's just that I didn't know anything about the armor of God. After 90 days as a brand-new Christian my warranty kind of ran out and I had sexual pressures again in my life and I went right back to homosexuality. That's the way I'd solved it before. But it wasn't as great as I remembered. Something had already changed in my mind. So God won my heart first and then a year and a half later when I was able to trust Him with other things as big as my homosexuality, He began changing those ideas.

Remember this as Christian workers, as Christian leaders. The key issue is not homosexuality, rather, winning that person for Christ and letting Him be the action agent. This whole seminar is designed on those lines. Now I was open, out. Mike was different.

Mike: Jim represented your typical gay who had come out, happy homosexual, who probably would have just really gotten on your nerves because you couldn't . . .

Jim: I still do!

Mike: He gets on mine! I represented probably the majority of homosexuals in that I was still in the closet. I was secretive about my homosexuality. I didn't want parents, friends, girlfriends to find out. Unlike Jim, who was happy with his homosexuality, I was pretty miserable, and pretty quilt-ridden and wanted out very badly. And wherever I turned I heard either that it was cool and I should just adjust to it, or that maybe I could possibly get out of it if I had 10 years and $50,000 and could go into extensive psychotherapy, and neither of those two options sounded very attractive to me. And I looked, and I searched pretty desperately for somebody who said, "Yeah, it's possible for people to make real changes in their lives and to get out of homosexuality." I didn't find anything like that until I had read every book in the library on homosexuality, starting when I was about age 13, which is when I realized I was a homosexual.

It was William Aaron's book that really hit me because one of the opening lines is, "Once gay, always gay, is a lie," period, and it set me back and I read the whole book in about 45 minutes. I was so eager. I'm going to draw a diagram that helps us in counseling. It might also help you to show this whole structure, this whole continuum of involvement.

Jim: This is a diagram that will show you the progression of behavior in many gays' lives. Not all gays do the same thing and on the scale; when you meet somebody, it's easier for you to visualize where they might be.

Mike: Right. Most people sometime during their development, usually around 10 or 11, engage in some sort of homosexual behavior, experimentation. It's very, very common.

Jim: Sex play.

Mike: It's what Jim referred to as tri-sexuality. Most people never go beyond that in terms of the homosexual continuum. They go on to other things. They develop normally heterosexually. Some people, for some reason, me included, went further on that continuum. I began to identify myself as homosexual. I said, "I am homosexual," and that was a monumental statement when I said it because I wasn't just describing an aspect of my life. I was describing the sum total of everything I was, did, thought, believed. When I said, "I am a homosexual," it was sort of like the Lord saying, "I am that I am." It was a description of who I was. It was sort of a paradoxical thing. It was sort of a relief to finally say that to myself—"Well, I guess I'm homosexual." And it was also a despairing kind of thing like—"Well, this is what I am. I'll never change."

Some people never go beyond that homosexual identity. Other people will feel a need to go on and get involved in a homosexual life-style, participate in a homosexual subculture, work for gay establishments, associate with other gays. Just before I became a Christian, along that continuum, I would have placed myself right about here (between identity and involvement).

Jim: I'd be farther on (at involvement in the gay life-style).

Mike: This little diagram is just kind of helpful. It's been helpful to us. When we get somebody who says, "I am homosexual," we don't take that at face value. We ask them what they mean by that, especially when the person is young. We really advise against this kind of labeling, especially of a young kid who says that he thinks he might be homosexual. We stay away from that word, "homosexual." In fact, we prefer to use the word homosexual as an adjective rather than a noun. Actually there's no such thing as a homosexual. There are people who are involved at various activities along a sexual continuum, but there's no such *thing* as a homosexual. I think that's kind of too all-inclusive. So we ask a person who says "I'm a homosexual," "where?" We try to get a picture in our own heads of where along this continuum the person is placing himself. And the way that we deal with the person in counseling will vary a whole lot. Sometimes after the seminars we've done, we've had people, even in their 40's, say, "Well, once when I was about 12 I had an experience with my cousin. Does this mean that I'm homosexual?" And that happens a whole lot. I was surprised by it because of that homosexual behavior which is very, very common. So keep that continuum in mind when you're approaching this whole issue of counseling.

THREE COMMON ERRORS

Jim: These are three common errors of the church. We have listed here three labels—in quotes—"mainliners," "liberals," "gay theologians." We do this as a collective idea. This is not meant to attack any denominational thing. There are three trends, three common thoughts these churches give off. The "mainliner" church would be the large denomination, generally. And the general trend of thought is this: "Clean up first, then come back." If they discover a homosexual in the church congregation, even in the church family, they ask them to go away. If they discover them in a college, a church college, they ask them to go away until it's taken care of. I'm not sure what taken care of means. The understanding of homosexuality is quite low among Christians. We have one mother who thought that homosexuality was sex at home, or that bisexuality was sex twice a week.

Mike: No kidding.

Jim: This is no kidding.

Mike: This is for real. The mainliner approach is the approach that is very fond of quoting Genesis 19 and delights in telling how God barbecues homosexuals and that sort of thing. I don't think it's openly malicious necessarily. I think it's out of ignorance or fear that the church has commonly reacted this way. Next you have what we call the "liberal" approach, and that's "We love you and we accept you just the way you are. Welcome." And that's it.

Jim: This is what's called "sloppy agape." And that's not really loving, if you think about it.

Mike: There's no dynamic or challenge for change there.

Jim: If a person comes in—"I've got a broken arm," and they say, "Oh, you've got a broken arm. Please come in." When gays are asking for help, they *are* asking for help, and it's not enough to love them as they are. As you'll see, challenge is necessary. That's an ingredient in love and we plan to communicate that today—challenge.

Mike: Then you have the gay theologians. Although there's a particular church, the Metropolitan Community Church, I think the theology, the arguments of the pro-gay theologians have penetrated the church at large pretty well. And a lot of the arguments make a whole lot of sense on the surface, but if you scratch a little bit deeper, you see that there's some pretty tricky scriptural somersaulting going on, and a lot of internal inconsistencies and illogics in most of what gay theology is about. We're not going to get into that. Read Kirk's book. Read Kent Philpott's book on gay theology. And we have a little paper on gay theology, too. There are some very obvious flaws, I think, in gay theology, if we accept the Scripture as actually the revealed character of God. If not, we're all sort of floundering anyway. But look into that. Basically the message of the gay church is, "Homosexuality is a gift of God. Accept it and praise Him for it, and live responsibly within that as much as is possible."

Jim: Now I participated recently in an interview with a gay pastor and this is one of the key issues: Is homosexuality still sin? He said, "Yes, it was, in the Old Testament, but that's culture-lock, time-lock. It doesn't apply any more." And then another theologian asked of him, "Does this mean that God has changed His mind?" He said, "Yes, that's entirely possible." That's how he believes it. So this is the crisis even your group is faced with: Has God changed His mind or is Scripture truly what it says, the revealed nature, the revealed character of Christ?

CORRECT APPROACH

Mike: The correct approach that we advocate is very similar to the way in which Christ dealt with the woman caught in adultery. Here was a woman involved in sexual sin. He didn't back down on God's standard of holiness that adultery was sin, but neither did He outright condemn her and berate her and dehumanize her and leave her on the street. There was a balance in what Christ did. He exhibited both the holiness and the love of God, and if the church lets down on one of those, we're not really sharing the gospel. Not really.

So Philpott has said there are four things the church could do in terms of communicating a helping attitude to the homosexual seeking help. "A" is Forgiveness. When Philpott is talking about forgiveness, he means keeping in mind that we're all basically in that same boat, that all of us have fallen short of the glory of God.

Jim: Read I Corinthians 6:9-10.

Mike: Typically on a scale of 1 to 10, with 10 being the worst of all possible sins, homosexuality has been rated about 13.5. There's that kind of grading that we tend to do. There are certain sins which are more socially acceptable, certain ones that we can excuse. But I really don't think that God does that with us. We all have fallen short and are in need of Him. We're going to point out I Corinthians 6:9-11 which says, "Do not be deceived. Neither fornicators nor idolators nor drunkards nor revilers nor swindlers," and it just about lumps all of us in there someplace, "will inherit the kingdom of God." Verse 11 was the verse I think that excited me more than any verse I had read in the Bible because it said, "And such *were* some of you." It was past tense. When I read it, it seemed like it was underlined and about three inches high, "*WERE* some of you," which said some very exciting things to me. That on the basis of forgiveness—that's point "A"—Paul was speaking openly of the fact that there were former drunkards, former revilers, former swindlers, former homosexuals in that first century church in Corinth. And I know the pro-gay argument that the little word translated "homosexual" really isn't "homosexual," but the thing that's exciting to me is that the only thing in the cosmos that is not subject to change is God Himself. Everything else can be affected by Him and changed by Him. If we start limiting that in any way, we've limited God and the power of God. So on the basis of their forgiveness, not on the basis of anything they have done, but on the basis of Christ's forgiveness, the church offering forgiveness, the forgiveness of Christ, these people have become new. Forgiveness, then acceptance. By acceptance we mean welcoming those people.

Jim: Welcoming into the body. That doesn't mean you excuse their sin—you know that Christ Himself didn't excuse the sin of the adulterous woman. Read from that passage, would you? This all links together.

Mike: He asked her, "Woman, is there no one left to condemn you," and she said, "No one, Lord." He says, "Neither do I condemn you." Condemn *her.* I don't know why as Christians we have problems with this, that it's possible to condemn the sin without condemning the person. And I don't know why that's so hard for us to get a handle on. But He said, "Neither do I condemn you. Go and sin no more." He didn't back down for an instant on this Biblical proclamation that adultery was sin. But He loved her and He forgave her and He gave her the command to go and sin no more. He welcomed her, He accepted her. I think probably the thing that helped me more than anything else in getting out of homosexuality was being welcomed by the Christians that I met and not being treated as though I had the "plague" because of my homosexual past. It knocked me off my feet—the kind of active love that was expressed to me in that acceptance and that welcoming.

Jim: The body is really meant to be like a hospital, a healing community, where people who are in the process of change day by day are welcome. I think it comes back again to the fear of anything generally sexual. I think it's good that you called this conference "Human Sexuality" overall, and haven't singled out homosexuality. That's perhaps the first error. Homosexuality is not a big deal to God. It's sin. That's enough. It's sin, and He can deal with it—if that person yields.

Mike: Okay, let's progress here. Okay, love. Here we just want to underline again that we're not talking about sloppy agape, but about a love that challenges, that supports, that encourages, that sort of love—the love that goes the second mile. That kind of thing. I don't need to say much more about that. If you want more about it. I Corinthians 13 is probably the best.

Jim: Love is a challenging thing, too, and it's also a confronting thing. You mentioned sloppy agape before. It's necessary sometimes to tell a person no, or try this. That isn't being unloving. If you said nothing ... that would be unloving. Sometimes you have to kind of support.

WHERE TO BEGIN

Jim: This is something we enjoy at Melodyland, our home church. We have a spiritual umbrella there, and we recommend that for all the groups. They need that. They need to be overseen by a pastor or somebody who has that spiritual wisdom. They shouldn't be on their own.

Mike: Also, we think it's a good idea when you're considering structuring a ministry to make it a part of the already existing outreach of the church, rather than set up some sort of special outreach. The Hotline had been set up as just a 24-hour crisis line for years before EXIT began to be part of it, and I think that was good, because people who are contacting the Hotline aren't automatically labeled as having a problem with homosexuality, because the Hotline deals in a variety of areas.

Jim: So we need to talk about it. We need to make the help known. Now it comes down to how to structure the ministry. There's a point here, you should all remember, as church leaders: count the cost. And there is a cost involved in any kind of ministry, even like this.

Mike: We kind of found ourselves as a minority within a minority. Gays are a minority. Ex-gays are the minority within the minority, and we kind of take flak from both sides. We get people in gay lib who are upset at us for saying that homosexuals can change, that there's another option besides just adjusting. We get that kind of anger. We also get the anger from the very fundamental, very conservative kinds of church groups who think that it's better just left unsaid. Keep it all under the rug. That's the kind of cost that needs to be counted. It's not a terrifically popular ministry. It's subject to a lot of suspicion. People tend to stand back and watch, almost hoping that we'll get back into homosexuality so they can prove us wrong. There's not a whole lot of support. I'm not just playing "poor me"—I'm just saying count the cost if you're considering some sort of ministry like that.

FORMS OF MINISTRY

Mike: Now we'd like to get into actually the kinds of ministries that are available, the kinds of ministries that have been tried by these various outreaches across the country, and their pros and cons. Let's talk about the pros and cons of phone counseling.

Jim: We do a lot of phone counseling and that's how most of our people call us. They often call anonymously or even invent a name for us. We insist on a name because you don't want to call them "it." And they do this, I think, to protect themselves. That's the advantage of phone counseling: they can remain anonymous. A lot of gays aren't sure they want to disclose to anyone. They're not sure what you're going to do with that information. They don't know if they can trust you. They don't know if what they say about themselves really is true. Phone counseling is helpful in that way. As much as we can, we try to lead them into one-to-one counseling. We do like to see people in person. We don't insist on it, but there are some good reasons for leading them to one-to-one. First of all, the person who comes in generally really means business. He's at a point of crisis where he really wants to hear something. He wants to have something adjusted. He wants to know what you've been doing in your own life. He wants to know what your Christian experience is like. Is it worth it? Is it worth the change he might have to go through?

Mike: Next is groups. Most of the ministries have tried groups and have been very, very effective with them. The obvious advantage of groups is that they can tend to help counteract that feeling of isloation and loss that a person feels when they decide to leave homosexuality, leave that supportive life-style and subculture.

Jim: You have to consider how frightening that is for some gays. For some, all they have are gay friends. They live in a gay neighborhood. To change is quite a thing. A lot of their self-identity seems to be lost. What's going to replace it? Hopefully a group setting.

Mike: Groups have been very effective as long as they represented sort of the church in microcosm. The obvious danger with groups is that they can become sort of like a gay social club, and Frank Worthen, who does a lot of work with groups up in the San Francisco Bay area, invented a term called the Gayalog. And the Gayalog is when the people come together and talk *only* about homosexuality and go into long dissertations about their experiences last weekend and that sort of thing. That's why in our groups, and in Frank's groups and other groups that have started around the country, we try to have a balance of people from various backgrounds. Most of the people in the group are coming from a homosexual background. But we try to maybe include a young married couple or just a single, heterosexual guy in the group so that it can provide that sort of balance. One of the things that was most helpful to me in getting out of homosexuality was seeing that a lot of the things that I labeled homosexual weren't homosexual at all. They were common human problems.

Jim: They were experiential.

Mike: I labeled loneliness as homosexual. I labeled other kinds of emotions as being homosexual, and it was refreshing for me to find out that other human beings encountered those same sorts of frustrations and feelings and doubts and to feel that I was not all alone. That was one of the obvious strong points of the group. Street and bar ministry has been tried. In general, I don't like street evangelism because most of it's rude.

Jim: Explain.

Mike: I don't know how it's done here on the East Coast, but on the West Coast it's typically somebody rushing up and stuffing a tract in somebody's hand. We call it "hit and run" evangelism. It's very impersonal. It just comes off kind of rude and non-caring. Street and bar ministry is not in-depth. It's more or less a touch-point, a way of maybe starting a relationship with somebody who might be looking for a way out. It was remarkable when we were doing the sharing on the street how many of the people we talked to were Christians who felt like, "Uh oh," who were maybe despairing over being there, feeling that they really shouldn't be there anyway, and then to meet another Christian who's willing to talk to them on the street—it was just kind of humorous to watch, sometimes.

Media and ads should maybe be divided in half. Media and ads have not usually been very helpful except when the media can be, say, articles in Christian magazines which have been very helpful in terms of talking about ministry. We've been on television a few times and we got a lot of letters and responses from that, serious requests for help, for information, requests from parents for help. Ads have been tried by some ministries and it doesn't really work because it smacks of that kind of commercialism—you know, we're selling ex-gayism. Most publications are very reluctant to take an ad like that, anyway.

Jim: Yes. The gay publications are reluctant. Now. Correspondence. Other than phone counseling or seeing people in person, this is perhaps the most active area of ministering, people writing you letters and you organizing some kind of return, some kind of followthrough. It's also the most responsible area because it requires a good system of filing and retrieval. We have a good one if you'd like to know about it: Numerical Access. But it also means workers—people who are really dedicated to doing that kind of clerical work, following through on literature requests, on a Bible study, on a local referral to their area. It's an important ministry but it means you have to be responsible with it.

Mike: We get about, oh, 300-350 letters a month, and that increases all the time. It's good for those people who live in Outer Mongolia or other areas where there isn't a ministry close to them. At least they can maintain some kind of contact through the mail, and it's been helpful in that way. It gets depressing when there's a backlog and all those letters are crying out for some sort of response. So that's something to consider when you're considering a correspondence ministry.

Literature and tapes. There's finally some good literature coming out on homosexuality, and I don't see anything wrong with writing back to a person and saying, "Well, I've never personally experienced a homosexual life-style myself, but I would be willing to correspond with you and help you. Here's some literature written by people who have that might be helpful to you." The person who ministered to me the most didn't know a thing about homosexuality and I was kind of glad, because then I could have talked about homosexuality and then he could have talked about homosexuality. Instead we talked about me. We talked about him. It was that kind of personal interchange, not necessarily his knowledge or expertise in dealing with homosexuality, but his willingness to stick with me that was most helpful. Literature and tapes—tapes. If you've got the tape duplicator it's fine. But if it breaks down, you get nasty letters like, "Three months ago I ordered a tape from you."

Jim: We're still getting those letters. And then, of course, public seminars—that's evident. We distinguish between public seminars like this and rallies. Rallies generally don't help. An ex-gay rally isn't going to incite too much interest. It will incite a lot of interest in those who want to speak against homosexuality, and that's not helpful. That's not productive.

QUESTIONS AND ANSWERS

Mike: Are there questions on anything we've said so far?

Question. Has most of your work been with males? There seems to be a prejudice in that area.

Mike: Yeah. It's an obvious prejudice, too, since Jim and I know the male homosexual background. I would say about 90% of our work is with men who have written to us for help, and I don't know what explains that. I don't know if it's that the women are reluctant to write to us.

Jim: I have some insight on that. A lot of women have a misunderstanding of men. They don't know what to do with them. In some cases they're absolutely afraid of them. To come to two male counselors is perhaps too much for many. Some will write letters instead. That's a little more protective, a little more distant, and they can still get some of the information they want.

There are some distinctions between gay men and gay females. I can give you some. In terms of relationships, gay men have much shorter relationships. Often one-nighters are sufficient. Men are kind of like proud roosters. They like to be independent. They don't like to settle down. I know there is a trend and a teaching where they should come together for monogamous relationships, but that's an ideal. That really isn't working effectively. If they admit that, that's how it really is. Women, on the other hand, tend to have longer relationships. In fact, after a while, a lot of lesbians will put aside the sexual activity completely because their relationships are built more on emotional and feeling responses, one for the other. They're more concerned that way.

Mike: I know it sounds like a stereotype, but in practice that's what seems to happen a lot—the way the requests and the interactions we get seem to support that.

Jim: It's not unusual for gals to stay together three years or five years.

Question. Are there effective Christian ministries relating to women?

Mike: Yes. There's one ministry that has three former lesbians on staff in Minneapolis, Minnesota. It's called Outpost. You can write to EXODUS to get the address of that referral. It's Box 4222, Minneapolis, MN, 55414.

Jim: There are fewer ministries for women and I have another insight on that. I think it's more difficult to detect lesbianism than homosexuality. In other words, women can get away with it.

Mike: It's more socially acceptable, for one thing.

Jim: It seems to be that way. If you walk down a mall and see two gals holding hands and walking together, that's not a big thing. But if you see two guys holding hands, or three guys, it gets really questionable then.

Question. Comment on Ed Davis of the L.A. Police Department, the gay rights movement, Anita Bryant, and TV programs depicting the gay life-style.

Jim: I think most of your questions will be answered in the second part. We could defer, and then ask them again if you're not satisfied.

Mike: Could I answer just briefly?

Jim: Yes.

Mike: I think largely because of the gay rights movement, we have had the freedom to speak, that we kind of followed on their coat tails, and they were kind of the ice-breakers and the ground-breakers that brought the homosexual issue enough out in the open that we could speak about it without being stoned, probably. And I think much of what gay lib says has a lot of value, and I agree with a whole lot of it. I agree that gays have very often been treated as second-class human beings because of their sin, and I personally—I'm not speaking for EXIT or for Jim or for Melodyland or anyone else—but I personally am in favor of not gay civil rights but human rights, and I don't think that a person's sexual object choice should be grounds for denying someone rights that are theoretically, at least, constitutionally guaranteed.

Jim: You get the occasional impression that gays are asking for more rights than the other co-workers would have, but that's not the issue.

Mike: I'm also opposed to those kinds of laws that would require affirmative action hiring of gays and give *special* legal categories to homosexuals—I don't agree with that.

Ed Davis I don't know too much about—he's a character—that's all I can say.

Anita Bryant, I think, was a very sincere, alarmed Christian mother who, for the most part, was pretty misinformed about homosexuality, had a lot of the facts mixed up about it, especially when it came to things like child molestation. She was convinced—I think she still is convinced—that homosexuals are typically child molesters, and should be watched very carefully in that regard.

Jim: On this point, it might be good to inject here that, statistically, heterosexual molestation is 13 to 1, as opposed to homosexual molestation. That means that a heterosexual molesting someone within his family unit, and possibly even in their own home.

Mike: 75% of the reported cases of child abuse in southern California— in 75% of the cases the man was a relative of the girl that was molested, and in 75% of those cases the molestation occurred in the parents' home while the parents were gone.

Jim: That's no defense for that. All that behavior is felonious. In fact, the gay community is very anti, very much against those who are molesters because this is bad publicity. This is bad press. It's not timed right for what they want to do with their gay movement. Mike and I do the same thing that the gays seem to do. We affirm them as people. We distinguish our approach because we think what they're doing is scripturally wrong, without basis, and so the gays feel we're divisive because we're promising a false hope. Gays aren't supposed to change. It's a gift from God. That's what they say. They should adjust to what they're doing. We say it's entirely possible to change if that gay person wants it, and if the church will give the answer. The church has the answer, if it were not afraid to give it. That's the whole idea of our education program.

Mike: The issue in Dade County, if I understand it correctly, too, came down to an issue of religious freedom in that the Dade County ordinance would have made it illegal for churches and private religious organizations to refuse to hire on the basis of homosexuality, which seems to me to bridge the First Amendment rights to freedom of religion, and in that respect I'm very glad that the law itself was re-pealed, but there was a lot of emotional flak and mud-throwing on both sides, which I thought was totally unnecessary and which made minis-try very, very difficult. It made it difficult for us and for others, es-pecially those on the streets, because when we'd identify ourselves as Christians, they'd back off, expecting a very heavy condemnatory kind of thing to be laid on the person. One of the young men who does bar ministry said that he would have to spend his first half-hour trying to convince this person he was not with Anita Bryant before he could actually start talking about help. So in that way the emotionalism— the issue—is what I got upset about, the way it took on such grandiose proportions and became the big national . . .

Jim: You should read her book. It's very thought-provoking. I think she was very sincere, not always sincerely correct, and I think she was victimized by a cruel press. Read her book and you'll see how she was badly misquoted very often. Let's progress.

Mike: On TV series. I'd say I'm getting tired of it. I think there's more for plot material than finding out that somebody is homosexual. I'm just getting tired of it. There've been some good programs that have dealt with it, dealt pretty sanely and humanely, but it's beginning to be the thing. I mean, you've gotta have at least one issue where someone discovers that someone close to them is a homosexual. And I'm longing for comedies and some other kinds of human interest plots. It's the thing right now. There were some really interesting programs. There was one called "The Autobiography of Quentin Crisp: The Naked Servant," which was really interesting. Also, I think it was "That Certain Summer" with Hal Holbrook—I really liked that. It was very well done. There's some good stuff that's come out, but I think there's also some sort of cheap exploitations so that you can have a show on homosexuality.

Part II: Reaching the People

PRESENTING ATTITUDES

Mike: We've done part I, which was kind of equipping the church. We talked first in terms of getting attitudes in order and, secondly, about some practical considerations for actually structuring a ministry. Now we're going to be speaking to the issue. Okay, you've got your attitudes in order; you've got a ministry established; and now you've got a person asking for help. Now what? What do you do? What can you expect, first of all, in terms of the person? How will he come across—he or she?

Jim: These are often the presenting things that you'll get from people. This happens a lot when you're talking with someone in a counseling situation. They present an idea but there's really a deeper problem. Somebody will come in and say, "My husband is just unloving to me." That's the presenting problem. The real problem is that he's alcoholic and they don't want to face it, or that he has something else in his character.

Mike: We'll be talking about those presenting attitudes. What kind of attitudes can you expect when someone comes to you for help or contacts your ministry? We've encountered all of these.

Jim: Hey, a lot of gays are openly hostile because they wonder where *you're* at. Are you anti-gay; are you anti-person? You'll have to establish that with them.

Mike: We'll get people who are very angered by the fact that we're saying that there's a way out of homosexuality. Well, we've been accused of being deprogrammers and in the gay press there've been things written about the back rooms where there are tables with chains. Really, they should see my office! But you will get the openly hostile person, and we do. Why might the person be openly hostile? Because of prior hurts; because maybe he suspects that you are anti-person because you are anti-gay. The response is to, as much as possible, keep your cool, explain what your ministry is really about, and identify with them. Say, "Yeah, I can understand how you might be hostile given a lot of the stuff that's happened to the gay community. I'd be pretty angry, too."

Jim: We draw them out into a communication, in our conversation, so they can vent their anger on you. It's just anger—that's all—don't take it personally—and see how they've come to evolve to this place.

Mike: Right. Next is the person who's skeptical.

Jim: Skeptical of you really—looking for a flaw.

Mike: Just waiting for something to snag you on. We'll get people like this. Again, why might they be skeptical? Because they've been hurt in the past or disappointed in the past and because there have been an awful lot of very flaky things suggested to homosexuals.

Jim: Here's a really good one.

Mike: One man in Europe was claiming that he had helped people to change through injecting pulverized lamb's embryos into their blood-stream. Certain organizations we know of will send special prayer cloths through the mail. That kind of thing. Again, the way to respond to the person who is skeptical is to say, "I can understand how you might be. I would be awfully skeptical, too."

Jim: False promises produce skepticism, too. For example, "Come to Christ and you'll never have a homosexual temptation again." Well, Christ doesn't promise that kind of life to any Christian. He says with that time of temptation there's an escape. He's able to provide it. Christians go through ups and downs.

Mike: Then we'll get the game players. The game player wants to know all the gory details about what our previous homosexual life-style was like. And the motivations for that are just maybe boredom. It's kind of fun to call up your local ex-gay and try to embarrass him with certain kinds of questions. We've had obscene calls. Again, we try to respond to all of those calls, remembering that the person, even the obscene caller and the game player, is a person with a need. I've had some really good counseling experiences come out of the person who came off really filthy with their opening remarks and then I've said something like, "It must be kind of sad to have nothing to do but say dirty things over the phone," without getting all upset about it, and I got into a really good conversation and subsequent personal counseling with this young man who came off like that. On the other hand, you need to use your discretion, if it's just getting out of hand. We occasionally hang up, and that's all right to do, too.

Jim: Well, a lot of it is just shock to put you off and see where you're at.

Mike: To test your sincerity, to see if you're going to hang in there.

Jim: He's still a person.

Mike: Then you'll get people who are frightened to disclose. And the classic opener is, "I have a friend who. . ." Now that's also very understandable. I remember doing that when I was asking people about things or writing to an organization to find what they are about. Rather than blow the person's cover, what we usually do in counseling is go along with it and talk in the third person—talk about the friend. You know, "Well, what should my friend do?" "Well, if I were your friend, I'd feel pretty frightened about talking about it," and that sort of thing. And then occasionally we'll do a tricky thing and that's throw in a "How long have you felt this way?", and the person, before he even realizes it, will say, "Oh, it's been about three—I've felt this way—whoops!", you know. And then it's broken down. But there's a real reason—it's protective to say that, and don't immediately blow the person's cover. Allow them to go on. We've had people where I've known the person was talking about himself and he's maybe gone on for a couple of months talking about "he" and then he gave me the big news and he thought I'd be all shocked.

Jim: And then we have the person who is seeking help. Sometimes they're really desperate. You'll sense that in their voice. They really want to know, "Have you got something—a challenge that can really affect my life?" and you just flow with that just as you would with any other counseling situation. If we can leave anything with you today, it would have to be this: Don't let homosexuality become a special issue in your mind. It isn't. It's simply a life sin problem and it has the same solution as the other things. It needs the same kind of supporting church to guide these people through, the same kind of acceptance of that person as a person, and yet countering whatever is not in God's design.

WHAT DO THEY WANT?

Mike: Right. Now when a person says they really want help that's often not enough. What kind of help do they want? The person may be sincerely seeking help. What kind of help? We've had people such as the happy gay—the person who wants us to help him to be a happy homosexual.

Jim: They want us to help them feel better about it.

Mike: They want suggestions on how to improve their homosexual relationships, or where they can meet homosexual partners. In all these cases, why is the person contacting you now? There's some sort of precipitating event. Very often when we get a call, it's because they've just broken up with a lover, their parents have just found out, someone at their job has found out and they're afraid of losing it, just a disappointing love affair. Those are usually the precipitating events.

I cannot in good conscience help a person to be a happy homosexual, and just adjust to what I consider to be, scripturally, sin; but that doesn't mean that I can't help that person where he is then. He may be lonely; he may be hurting; whatever, and I can minister to those needs as best as I can. And I can tell him, "I'm sorry, I can't help you in that way. Can we talk about what's bothering you? Can we talk about the other things?" and lead him out that way. The happy homosexual. Then you get the person sometimes who wants you to help him do some blame shifting, and they'll start with, "Well, when I was three years old," and they'll give you the whole story, and what they want you to do is help them find somebody to stick the blame on. All this becomes pretty evident by their speaking style.

Jim: It's quite impressive how much of this is thought out ahead of time in their head. We've had ten page letters giving us a whole archeological dig all the way through the past, "from age 3 this happened to me; my parents shouldn't have done this; my dad wasn't available; he wasn't a good model; and I was molested by a school teacher; and this happened, and that happened." This is very important for you as a counselor to realize, that archeological digs—what happened back then—really isn't helpful. Even the experts can't agree often on what causes homosexuality. It's a can of worms.

What really is more significant is, right now, what motivates the person to stay with their homosexuality. Consider this: there has to be some kind of payoff for it to remain attractive. Alcoholism is a good example. It's not cheap to be an alcoholic. You have to have the money to buy the booze. You have to find it. You have to find some place to go and hide to conceal it, hopefully, if that's important to you. There's a lot of time invested there. It has a payoff. It does something for them physiologically, mentally, otherwise. The same for homosexuality. A lot of basic human needs are met by gayness—feeling good about self, belonging to others, knowing they like you, group reception, all those inclusive things that are just called human needs.

Mike: This was a very significant point in my life. For a long time I blamed my homosexuality on my dad. If he had only been more affectionate, if only he had been more accepting, if he'd been less critical, if he had done this. What I was kind of playing was sort of a "poor me" kind of thing, and it almost guaranteed that my life was going to stay the way it was or get worse. And I was trying to figure out, "Why am I homosexual?" I finally came to the conclusion that I would never know exactly why I got involved in homosexuality. And even if I did, what was I going to do about it once I found out? What I needed to look at was not what's caused my homosexuality, but what's it doing for me *now*. That's the motivation—cause versus motivation. What's motivating me to continue it *now,* and maybe Christ can meet those present needs better than my homosexuality can. And when I was convinced that He could, I was willing to relinquish my homosexuality to Him.

Jim: This is the correct posture for the counselor, too, to examine why they're doing it now, because that's where they are. That's where you are. And then they can really see very often how they're rationalizing that homosexual behavior—how they're making it seem more acceptable to others right now.

Mike: Then we have what we call bandaid therapy and these are people who are sincerely in need, too. But we'll get people who will call maybe every 10 days, who have just maybe slipped back and who want kind of a pat on the head, an okay sort of thing, just send them out again, and that whole thing. A patch-up job.

Jim: That really attacks my patience quite often. I usually give them to Mike and he takes care of them.

Mike: Then you get people who are really seeking some sort of radical change. Now, like Jim, I did not become a Christian to get out of my homosexuality. I became a Christian to become a Christian. Jesus is more than a cure-all for sin, and I didn't accept Him as my Savior just to get out of that particular sin. I accepted Him as my Savior because I was convinced that He was who He said He was. That's very, very different. Then, about a year later, after He had really won my trust and changed me in other ways He kind of shined this big spotlight on my homosexuality and said, "Now this. Now we're going to work on this." And it wasn't a feeling of guilt that I had. I kind of felt like, "Oh, good, finally something's going to happen." This is the kind of experience I had. Something's going to start changing, and I was kind of excited and frightened about it. When we're talking about radical change, we're talking about a person not suppressing homosexuality. I'm not suppressing my homosexuality. If anything, I'm more aware of the motivation for why it was there, and I'm more aware of the temptations when they come and I'm less engaged in trying to rationalize them away. When we're talking about change we're not talking about suppressing homosexuality but a yielding of it upward. Not a pushing it downward but a yielding of it upward, and that's a relief. The repression just gets very, very tense until, like a pressure cooker, it explodes. But if I can yield it in a process, a continual process, to God and depend on Him and His strength, then I'm not suppressing it. It's a real big difference. When we're talking about radical change, we're talking about a person who's willing to submit their sexuality to God on that entire continuum—behavior, identity, and life-style. Change the behavior, accept a new identity, and form a new life-style. And that's scary as can be, if it's been all that you've known.

THE EX-GAY EXPERIENCE

Mike: We're ready to talk about the ex-gay experience. I wrote this up, not as a formula for how to change homosexuals, but I was trying to bring together experiences that people in the process of change seem to go through and seem to report a lot and tried to put them in some kind of order. I'd like you to read them. We're not going in depth over it, but usually there's a turning point event. A place where the person says, "Has it been worth it?" Something happens and they begin to re-examine their homosexuality. For Jim, it was meeting that person who seemed to have a quality of life better than his own.

Jim: Right.

Mike: They kind of got the whole thought process going. For me, it was a depressing relationship that was getting more and more routine and getting more and more de-personalized and getting more and more deeply involved until I couldn't take it any more. That was my turning point event. Acceptance of Christ as Savior—pretty obvious. Baptism of the Holy Spirit is kind of interesting—and this isn't to push charismata, but it's interesting. Most of the ministries that I know of from a Christian perspective that are offering this kind of counseling have a charismatic base. Next comes a breakaway event and that person is willing to say, "Okay," and they let go—they break away.

Jim: This is a scary event when it happens. He realizes that himself, often without anyone telling him, and he is at a point where he needs assurance from the church family, the body of Christ, wherever he is, that he will have a cushion—some place to go. He's giving up this for this brand new thing. The ex-gay reality, and he needs that supportive community.

Mike: I remember when I made that breakaway from homosexuality. It went into the next point which is a burn-out syndrome. I remember telling my friends that I felt like I had had open-heart surgery without any anesthetic—like somebody had just ripped something out of my chest—and I felt kind of a vacuum there that my homosexuality had filled for a long time. The burn-out syndrome for some people—just a total absence of sexual interest—wanting to get away from sex in general. I don't want to be heterosexual; I don't want to be homosexual; I don't want to be bisexual; I don't want to be sexual, period, for a while. For too long my life had centered around sexuality. This is what I experienced: just wanting to retreat from all things sexual for a while, and maybe explore other parts of my identity besides the sexual one. For other people the burn-out syndrome is characterized by the worse temptations of their life and more opportunities than they've ever had.

Jim: I went through what I call a resting period. I've been ex-gay since '70 and for that middle four years I really didn't have much problem with homosexual temptation. Occasional things. But then people started asking, "Well, gee, Jim, what are you? Are you celibate; are you ex-gay; are you non-sexual; when are you going to get married;" and all of a sudden these doubts came on me and I really didn't know where I was. That rest, that peace I was feeling, had gone and I realized I was being victimized a little bit by the expectancies people were placing on me. I'm in a position right now where I'm really very interested in marriage. I'm convinced that women are here to stay. There's evidence all around me. That was frightening for me at first. They represented unknown territory. Now it's different. But six years ago I couldn't have thought that. I'm very fortunate, having had a good church family around me, that gave me time to change.

Mike and I usually stress two things about the process of change. It's a position and it's a process. We are all immediately new creatures in Christ—that is the position we have before Him. We are fully justified, fully sanctified, fully washed. Then there's a day by day progression in dealing with whatever comes to you, whether it's temptation or the happy times or the spending of money. That should happen more often.

Mike: It's growing into the likeness of Christ. It's one of those fundamental Christian paradoxes that we're complete. God sees us as complete and blameless and without spot or wrinkle or any such thing. But we don't see ourselves that way yet. We're still locked in time and still going through change processes day by day. Each of us are. So being ex-gay is both a position and a process. I'm still changing. Things are still changing in my life. After that there becomes sometimes an aching need to tell someone, for disclosure, to tell someone. And it wasn't to tell someone about my homosexuality, but to tell someone that things were changing. We advise our counselees to do selective disclosure. They should not stand up at Wednesday night fellowship and announce it to the church body, because we've had people who've done that, but to find someone who they trust and they love and are pretty much assured that they will accept it well. Most of the people we've talked to have pointed to one special friend of the same sex—a Christian friend of the same sex. I had a young man named Michael. Michael was heterosexual, never been involved in homosexuality at all. I told him and when I told him, I started to cry. Michael hugged me and held onto me for about 45 minutes and said, "It's all right." That's all he said, "It's all right." And it was amazing what that did, after all that time because I was in a closet of keeping it secret. I don't know if you've had an event like that, but that need for disclosure is something I assume we have in common.

Jim: I had a straight friend. This is significant for the church to realize. It's the straight friends who are most helpful to ex-gays. There wasn't another ex-gay for me to appeal to, back then.

Mike: You were it!

Jim: No, there were many, but they weren't, shall we say, as well known back then. They're coast to coast. But the straight friends represent a certain buffer zone—a certain measurement a lot of ex-gays need just to stay strong, just to be available. I hope by now, in the course of the seminar, that you realize that you don't have to be ex-gay to deal with homosexuals. You can be who you are, and again, I'll stress it. It's the quality of your Christian life that will speak to him. He'll want what you have.

Mike: Then comes a new identity. For quite a while after I got out of homosexuality, after I quit practicing, I considered myself a Christian homosexual because I was still experiencing ongoing temptations and I never felt really at peace with that. It kind of felt like Christian adulterer, Christian robber, you know. It didn't sound right, and when I read I Corinthians 6:11, it said, "Such *were* some of you," I realized there was a need for me to take on a new identity, to declare, "I used to be like that." Well, gee, what do I call that? That's where we kind of coined the word ex-gay for lack of a better term. But there was something very positive about saying, "I used to be homosexual," and talking about it as my past. I am new now. Things are changing in me now. That used to be true of me, and I'm still struggling with it on some levels, but I'm changing. I'm really changing. Accepting a new identity and maybe even taking on the label ex-gay can be helpful at that point, and as a counselor I re-enforce that idea of past. I talk to them about their past.

Then there is that sense of community or mainstreaming. The real healing goes on when the person is fully accepted within the mainline body of the church. The best example I know of is a little church up in Oakland, California, where there are probably 15 or 20 people in their congregation who are known to be former homosexuals.

Jim: Many on staff.

Mike: Some of them are on church staff. They're worship leaders,

Sunday school teachers.

Jim: That's not because they're badges for the church to wear. "These are our resident ex-gays"—it's not that. They have a capacity to handle the jobs given to them, but they were mainstreamed. They were included in the body of Christ. Now we mentioned the groups earlier. That's a good way to help ex-gays come out of some of the change process, but only if you have those controls that we indicated, and a mixed group with a very distinct spiritual covering.

Mike: With the group only as a sort of a bridge into the mainline body of the church. Relating to the opposite sex. I was asked during the break, "When you say ex-gay, when you say change, do you mean change to heterosexuality? Do you mean becoming a heterosexual?" The answer to that is no. At least, not immediately. One of my counselees expressed it to me very well. He said, "I don't want to be straight. I just want to be unbent." Okay? That was a whole new way of thinking.

Jim: I wonder what straight represented to him.

Mike: I know what it represented to me. The divorce rate in Orange County is, you know, one marriage out of two ends in divorce, and what I had seen of heterosexual role modeling wasn't that hot, and I wasn't really that interested in it. I was just interested in leaving my past behind. There was that kind of neutral area. I wasn't really asexual but I just didn't really have a label for it.

The heterosexual interest for me unfolded kind of naturally, if I can say that, organically, without any effort on my part. I wasn't striving to become heterosexually interested in the opposite sex. I really wasn't at all. The first thing the Lord did was point out that the opposite sex were human beings to be related to on that level. And maybe they could even be friends. The closest girlfriend I had—we began to get closer and closer and I found out, much to my surprise, I was in love with her. And it wasn't even something I was attempting to do, and it frightened me to find that I could become so emotionally attached to her, and even physically attracted to her. What we're saying here is that heterosexuality should not be presented to the homosexual counselee as the goal to attain.

Jim: We had one incident with a pastor who really misunderstood this. Somebody sent this guy to this pastor and he was counseled for his homosexuality. This man thought what he needed was a heterosexual initiation, so he gave the man $25 and told him where to find the nearest prostitute. In his mind the opposite of homosexuality was heterosexuality. We're realizing as counselors that's not really the case.

Homosexuality breeds an irresponsible use of sex, and sexuality really is a God-given gift. He has it for us. It is meant to be part of our lives. What we've done with it has abused it so what a lot of us gays have to learn—I should say—what they have to unlearn—is a misuse of sex before they can take on a whole new set of responsibilities involved in heterosexuality.

Mike: Are you understanding this point? It's really a crucial one. It's an important one in that whole counseling process. I had to learn a lot of things about sexuality in general, about me, about what sex was really about, and other kinds of things. I remember praying earnestly that God would give me heterosexual lust because I thought that would be a sure sign that things had changed and I would look at girls to see if I got a biochemical buzz when they walked by, and nothing happened. Then I would berate myself and I'd think, "Well, I'm not really changing," and that sort of thing. Within that relationship that I have with my wife, within that marriage relationship, sex took on a whole different meaning, and rather than something I was trying to get, and rather than being a performance as it had been before, it was something I was giving. It was something I was expressing. For the first time in my life I could actually pray during sex, which is a totally new experience. It became an expression of love, just another kind of communication of love to her. And the whole expectancy that I had placed on it—all the role expectancies and everything else—just sort of melted away and I was free to love her and it was really nice. I am noticing now, as the change process goes on, that there are women who will definitely turn my head, which is brand new for me and kind of surprising. I don't want to get into that.

Jim: I want to hear some more about that. That's good.

Mike: No!

Jim: And our last point . . .

Mike: The last point is casting off the label. This kind of frightened us. We'd get to the point that our ex-gay counselees—who maybe were married or still single (Jim's single and doing very well) got to the point that they didn't want to be ex-gays any more, and I thought, "oh, no, they're backsliding. They're getting back into their homosexuality." What they were really doing is saying, "I don't even want to be identified with my past anymore." And they would throw off the ex-gay label and move out of town and get a new job and a new congregation where nobody knew about it, where it wasn't an issue, past, present, or future. I used to see it as a negative thing, and I've seen that that's probably the final stage in growth. I'm experiencing a lot of that myself now—a desire to get away from it and get into other things because there's a whole lot more to me than just my homosexual past, and I'd like to have the chance and space to express that.

HOW YOU CAN HELP

Jim: Let's continue our outline here. What you can do to help.

Mike: What you can do to help. We almost forgot to put this one down because this is what we actually do in counseling. This is the closest thing we've got to a method and it's not really a method. We overlooked it for a long time in our seminars because we did it without thinking about it. But these are the things we actually do in counseling. First, we despecialize. In our own mind and in the mind of the person, we try to despecialize homosexuality as the "biggie" and we may talk maybe about homosexuality the first time we get together with the counselee and from then on mention it once or twice and end up really talking about their life and the present motivation for their life and that sort of thing.

Jim: The ex-gay has to realize that God saved all of him—his sum total—all his value systems, all his life goals, all of his sexuality. And God is going to deal in all those areas, not just his former gayness.

Mike: It's interesting. The first thing the Lord really started dealing with me on and pointed out needed to change, was my lying, not my sexuality, but my compulsive lying. I had gotten to the point that I would lie for no reason—just to lie. And that changed first. Second was a disrespect for my parents which changed, which really surprised my mom, because when she used to call me, she'd say, "Michael." I'd say, "Yeah", or "What do you want?" And I started responding to her, "Yes, ma'am?", and she thought I was being sarcastic. She got very angry at me for saying "yes, ma'am". It took her a while to get used to it. There were other things that changed. Jim often talks about the way he spent money. The Lord dealt with that.

Jim: Yeah. That was the first thing He did. Personal finances and how I treated other people. Often I'd have a use for them and I'd expend them and they would go away. But that had to change. The third thing that He dealt with was how I drove my car. He's still dealing with that. The fourth thing was my homosexuality. God waited until that long because I was a very slow learner, actually. It took me a year and a half to really want to trust Him. Finally, I released that part to Him, too.

Mike: So despecializing is one of the best things you can do without undercutting the value of the person. You can despecialize how big homosexuality seems to him. The next thing is pretty obvious. Allow him to disclose. You are very likely the very first person who has calmly listened to the disclosure.

Jim: Disclose yourself. Forget this idea of the clinical distance or the thoughtful pastor stroking his chin. He's a friend talking to you, and you have some answers for him.

Mike: And share your own life. The thing that was really refreshing to me is I would go to my friend Michael and say, "Michael, I'm really being tempted sexually," and he'd look at me with a big grin and say, "You, too, huh?" Even though he was tempted by other things, the experience of temptation itself and the struggle with temptation was something we had in common, and it was nice for me to know, and the fact that he was willing to disclose helped me a lot.

Jim: And the emotions and the fears that you'll see in the discussion are probably very much what you can identify with. Maybe not the homosexuality, but that isn't the issue anyway. We're dealing with the whole person. You can identify with that.

Mike: Keep confidentiality. Don't spread it around. Obvious things. Counseling ethics. One important thing is—we'll get letters from parents who will say: "I have a son who's living in San Francisco. Would you please send him some literature?" Absolutely not. The second person request we refuse. We'll send the literature maybe to the mother saying, "If you would like to send it on to your son with a little note from you personally, feel free to." We avoid that invasion of privacy. Encourage. I think probably most of what we do is just encouraging the person, identifying with them, saying, "Yeah, I know what that's like," and offering encouragement and support, and the kind of prompting to go on, to move on. That's a big part of the work.

Restore. That's if the person has actually backslidden or sinned, and we take that Scripture from Galatians 6:1. It says, "If a brother is over-taken by a trespass, those of you who are more spiritually mature should restore such a one with a spirit of gentleness, taking heed to yourself, lest ye too be tempted." The word "restore" there is a Greek term—it's a medical term—that means "to set a dislocated bone." I think it's a beautiful picture, that the Christian who's fallen back into sin is still a part of the body. The arm that's out of joint—it's still a part of the body. It's just dislocated. It's causing a lot of pain to itself. It's causing a lot of pain to the body, and it needs someone to lovingly put it back in place. "Restore such a one with a spirit of gentleness."

Pointing the way to Christ is pretty obvious. All of what we're doing is pointing the person to Christ. I certainly don't have any power to change homosexuals. I never claimed that I did. In fact, if anything, I feel really inadequate to deal in this area. What I can do is point the person who is talking to me to the Person Who helped me, and that's the best thing I can do.

Jim: Restore patience. We have a reference here of I Thessalonians 5:14. Sometimes what we do is not always rebuking people. Sometimes we really are exercising patience with them. And the verse—I Thessalonians 5:14—reads this way: "And I urge you, brethren, admonish the unruly, encourage the fainthearted, help the weak, be patient with all men." That's the one verse.

Mike: I don't know how many of you are familiar with Jay Adams' book, *Competent to Counsel.* He builds his entire scheme of counseling around a Greek word, *nouthetic,* which means to admonish and to confront with the standards of Scripture, and it has some validity. I Thessalonians 5:14 says, "admonish the unruly, encourage the fainthearted, help the weak." The first part of that, "admonish the unruly," is that word, *nouthetic.* And sometimes that's necessary—to admonish somebody who's got the ability, who's got the resources available to him but won't use them. He's being stubborn. There's a time in counseling for admonishing. Most of what you'll do will be encouraging the fainthearted, people who have tried and met with failure. Encourage the fainthearted. Finally, help the weak. That's people who do not have the capacity, who do not have the resources available to them. Sometimes we've had people who, besides their homosexuality, were really addicted to drugs or had no place to stay or those kinds of things, and there were real physical needs that needed help. So help the weak—the person without the resources. The final line is "be patient with all." I say that, not really for your benefit, but for mine to remind myself to be patient. This kind of work is kind of trying.

Jim: Let's put it away once and for all. Once gay, always gay, is a lie. The person can change from his homosexuality if he wants to, and the church has the answer if it were not afraid to give it. We've attempted to equip the church with the answers and to experientially show you what we have come through as counselors and as ex-gays. I think you have it in yourself, even before coming to a seminar like this. But the whole idea is to get re-education first, take it back to your local churches, have them be re-educated, and then open yourselves for ministry to the homosexual. He's really looking for it and he needs it. Mike and I will close with this one corny line, but it's true: Once we were gay, but now we're happy. And we thank you.

BIBLIOGRAPHY

Aaron, William, *Straight: A Heterosexual Talks About His Homosexual Past* (New York: Doubleday and Co. Inc., 1972).

Drakeford, John, *A Christian View of Homosexuality* (Nashville: Broadman Press, 1977).

Kirk, Jerry, *The Homosexual Crisis in the Mainline Church* (Nashville: Thomas Nelson Inc., 1978).

Philpott, Kent, *The Gay Theology* (Plainfield NJ: Logos International, 1977).

Philpott, Kent, *The Third Sex?* (Plainfield NJ: Logos International, 1975).

Schonauer, Betty, *et. al., Healing for the Homosexual* (Oklahoma City: Presbyterian Charismatic Communion Inc., 1978).

REFERRALS

Exodus International Inc., Box 4272, Minneapolis, MN. 55414.

14 Civil Rights for Homosexual Persons

by Martin Duffy

General Synod 10 in 1975 voted a pronouncement which proclaimed that all persons are entitled to full civil liberties and equal protection under the law and that a person's sexual preference is not grounds for the denial of civil liberties. It declared support for the enactment of federal, state and local legislation guaranteeing civil liberties without regard to affectional or sexual preferences and called upon the churches, Associations, Conferences and Instrumentalities to work for the enactment of such legislation.

Three comments are in order. First, the pronouncement expressed the traditional concern of the United Church of Christ for people's civil and human rights. It was undergirded by compassion for people who have often faced contempt, persecution and denial of opportunity from both Christians and society at large. Second, the pronouncement was remarkable for severing social concern from moral judgment. Both the preamble and the pronouncement itself explicitly refused to take a position on the morality of "same-gender relationships." This evasion was remarkable since moral guidance is expected from the church and never before had our denomination severed its social concern (e.g. for black people and women) from the relevant Biblical and moral teachings. Third, the pronouncement was marred by linguistic and logical imprecision. "Without discrimination related to affectional or sexual preferences" would seem to provide legal protection to pedophiliacs, for instance, certainly not the authors' or the Synod's intention. And the pronouncement did not logically relate the rights of homosexual persons with the rights and freedoms of others or with the general welfare. These weaknesses, together with the "new morality" suggested in the 1977 *Human Sexuality* report, have prompted the United Church People for Biblical Witness to formulate a policy on the civil rights of homosexual persons.

Martin Duffy served on the U.C.C. Equal Opportunities Commission and as Vice-President of the U.C.C. Ministers for Racial and Social Justice; he has been active in civil and human rights movements for many years.

UNITED CHURCH PEOPLE POSITION

The National Steering Committee, meeting in St. Louis, July 12-14, 1978, adopted a Policy Statement which includes the following paragraph on homosexuality:

to deal specifically with issues of homosexuality:

a. to advocate the rejection of proposals for ordaining practicing homosexual persons and for church recognition of homosexual unions;

b. to encourage ministries of compassion, healing and justice for homosexual persons (and all sexually disordered persons);

c. to affirm the civil rights of homosexual persons as human beings, balanced by considerations of the welfare of society, public morality, and respect for the rights of others as stated in Article 29 of the United Nations Declaration of Human Rights in 1949.

This position was adopted after lengthy and sometimes tense discussions. The consensus of the group was that it would support civil rights of homosexual persons as human beings, not as a special interest group or minority, and that these rights have to be balanced by considerations stated in the United Nations Declaration of Human Rights. The text of Article 29 (2) reads: "In the exercise of his rights and freedoms, everyone shall be subject to such limitations as are determined by law solely for the purpose of securing due recognition and respect for the rights and freedoms of others and of meeting the just requirements of morality, public order and the general welfare in a democratic society."

We decided to retain the term civil rights because of its significant history in United States law requiring equal protection and justice for all, and in the social ministry of the United Church of Christ. Complete agreement on this point or on any of the points discussed will not be found within our group but our general line of reasoning follows. We do not believe that homosexual persons should be persecuted, villified, denied equal protection of the law or the opportunity to earn their daily bread because they are homosexual. At the same time, we believe that the civil rights of homosexual persons should not be exercised or protected in ways that substantially injure the general welfare, the rights and freedoms of others or the moral order upon which all freedom and justice depends. We favor recent court decisions and sections in the Federal Code protecting homosexual persons from arbitrary dismissal and harassment. We oppose granting homosexual persons minority status under Affirmative Action programs since (1) this would define a minority by *behavior* rather than *birth,* and (2) could result in forcible violations of the moral values of society. We believe that there are some positions which can properly be denied to self-avowed, practicing homosexuals on the grounds that such employment represents a threat to the general welfare and moral order of society. Elementary school teachers, for instance, play an important role in the character formation of the children in their charge. We cannot therefore support federal, state and local laws guaranteeing civil rights without regard to sexual and affectional preference unless such laws are carefully defined and balanced with considerations insuring protection for society as well as for the individual. Some of these points will be discussed in the sections below.

CIVIL RIGHTS

The terms *civil rights, civil liberties* and *human rights* are often used synonymously. *Webster's Third International Dictionary* refers *civil liberties* to the broad freedoms established in the Bill of Rights, including freedom from arbitrary government interference. *Webster's* defines *civil rights:* "1. *specif.* the rights secured to citizens of the U.S. by the 13th and 14th Amendments . . . and certain Acts passed by Congress . . . abolishing the civil incidents of involuntary servitude. 2. rights that guarantee to all citizens equal opportunities (as for employment, schooling, housing, or voting) regardless of race, religion, sex, or national origin." In the United States, then, the term *civil rights* has a specific meaning and history stemming from the treatment of black people after the Civil War. Government protection and interference in state and local affairs was necessary to insure all citizens the equal protection of the laws and to break down barriers of custom and prejudice that robbed people of equal opportunity.

In addition to black people, civil rights advocates have espoused the cause of women, American Indians, Orientals, Spanish speaking groups, Catholics and Jews. In recent years civil rights concerns have been expressed for the poor, for welfare clients and for homosexual persons. Through advocacy, organization and protest the purview of civil rights has been greatly expanded, as have the laws and governmental agencies which enforce them. Major Civil Rights Acts were passed by Congress in 1957, 1960, 1964, 1965, 1968 and 1970. These acts enforced the right to vote, forwarded the desegregation of public facilities and schools, insured equal access to public accommodations, forbid discrimination in the sale or rental of housing, guaranteed equal employment opportunity and created the Civil Rights Commission and the Equal Employment Opportunity Commission (J. M. Burke, *Civil Rights,* New York, 1974). Although the General Synod 10 pronouncement used the term *civil liberties,* its language refers to civil rights concerns, as can be seen in the sentence, "Discrimination . . . in employment, housing, public accommodations . . . has inflicted an incalculable burden of fear into the lives of persons in society and in the church. . . ." While the great civil rights advance in our lifetime has been accompanied by social upheaval and personal anguish, Christians should be profoundly grateful for its relative success. Members of the United Church of Christ can be proud that our church has been in the forefront of the struggle.

Few would deny that homosexual persons have suffered discrimination in the areas cited above. Some believe that homosexuals deserve what they get since they are indulging in sinful behavior. Each Christian should ponder whether he desires similar societal punishments for his own sinful behavior. And he should explore the full meaning of the compassion of Christ for sinful humanity. Homosexual persons also run afoul of the law or administrative rulings in such areas as citizenship, marriage, child custody, probation and finance. Not every instance has to be seen as a case of discrimination. In child custody cases, a parent's homosexuality is one of a number of factors that bears upon the child's welfare. But, again, each Christian is responsible to consider the deep anguish of persons trapped in these conflicts, often without conscious choice of their own.

There are at least three avenues for ending the injustices inflicted upon homosexual persons and insuring their civil rights, with due regard for the rights and freedoms of others. We can favor a growing trend of public tolerance and understanding abetted by recent federal court and executive rulings. The trend of federal court decisions is that homosexuality is not grounds for summary dismissal from government service unless a connection can be shown between homosexuality and efficiency of service. In 1976 the federal government issued this guideline:

> The Commission and agencies have been enjoined not to find a person unsuitable for Federal employment solely because that person is homosexual or has engaged in homosexual acts . . . a person may be dismissed or found unsuitable . . . where the evidence establishes that such person's sexual conduct affects job fitness (5 C.F.R. Sec. 731.202–1976, cited by Francis H. Hare, Jr. in "The Law and the Homosexual," *Consultation on Homosexuality,* Spring City, PA: Presbyterians United for Biblical Concerns, p. 86).

This guideline makes excellent sense for state and local governments and for private companies as well since it applies a reasonable, universal rule and does not imply a double standard; heterosexual persons whose sexual conduct affects job fitness could be equally liable to dismissal.

A second approach is the adoption and enforcement of the kind of legislation proposed in the 1975 pronouncement. In my introduction I have pointed out two difficulties of this approach: (1) imprecise definition, and (2) a lack of logical relationship to the rights and freedoms of others and to the general welfare. These problems could possibly be overcome with more careful writing of the proposed laws. Another concern voiced by many is that such legislation would create a legal framework for defining homosexuals as a minority under Affirmative Action programs. I will treat this problem in the next section.

A third approach is decriminalizing homosexual acts between consenting adults. This has been done in England and a number of other European nations and in some of our own states. Removing criminal sanctions from homosexual acts would cut the ground from under much of the existing unequal treatment. It should be clear, however, that removing criminal sanctions does not imply removing moral sanctions or all civil sanctions. (Homosexuality could be used in divorce proceedings or considered as a factor in granting citizenship.) In fact the removal of criminal sanctions might remove a confusing burden from the church, allowing it to concentrate upon its mission of Biblical teaching, evangelism and healing. Perhaps this is a warfare better fought with spiritual than legal weapons. In the case of the woman taken in adultery (John 8:2-11), Jesus favored the approach of moral and spiritual healing over that of criminal sanctions.

AFFIRMATIVE ACTION

Affirmative Action programs are agreements reached between federal agencies and employers whereby the employer pledges to implement a detailed plan for hiring persons from minority groups which have suffered past discrimination or are underrepresented in the work force. Enforcement agencies are the Equal Employment Opportunities Commission acting under Title VII of the 1964 Civil Rights Act and the HEW Office of Civil Rights under various statutes and rulings (Title XI of the Higher Education Act mandates equal treatment of the sexes). Affirmative Action in some cases is satisfied by a serious effort to attract minority persons—chiefly blacks and women—and in other cases sets a quota or percentage figure of minority people to be employed. (According to the Supreme Court Bakke decision, the latter method can be used with employers only when a history of systematic exclusion has been determined.)

The journal *Society* reports, "The U.S. Commission of Civil Rights now states that the number of minority persons found in employment at every level must be 'equal to their proportions in the populations.' " It continues, "these minorities include blacks, persons with Spanish surnames, American Indians, Orientals, and now women," but not white ethnic groups, poor whites, Catholics or Jews (13:10, Jan. 1976). The Civil Rights Commission makes recommendations, not rulings, so that the above quotation indicates the general direction of Affirmative Action programs, not the legal requirement. The minorities listed indicate the decisions of the administrative agencies; they do not include any religious groups although religion is one of the criteria in the 1964 Civil Rights Act. The minorities selected represent the best judgment of the agencies and the list could obviously be expanded. None of the Civil Rights laws spell out Affirmative Action; these programs are interpretations of the statutes by enforcement agencies but have been given the force of law by court decisions upholding particular agreements.

In meetings of the United Church People for Biblical Witness with its constituency across the nation, concern has been expressed whether the 1975 General Synod pronouncement favors Affirmative Action programs for homosexual persons. A letter from a member of a U.C.C. church in Webster Groves, Missouri, raises these concerns: (1) a self-proclaimed homosexual works for a personal service business; clients then refuse to do business with the firm because they do not wish to support open immorality; consequently the owner's business is destroyed; (2) a homosexual person teaches or serves as a pastor or adopts children; this is publicly known and the powerful influence of example leads young people to accept as normal behavior what may destroy the family and end the human race. Another question that has been raised is whether religious organizations could be forced to hire practicing homosexual persons contrary to their beliefs.

I do not believe that under existing laws and programs these prospective abuses can be legally enforced. Richard F. Lovelace in his excellent book, *Homosexuality and the Church,* quotes the United Presbyterian Task Force Background Report:

> Under civil rights laws, no church, church-related school, or church-related institution need hire any heterosexual or homosexual person in violation of its religious scruples (as guaranteed by the First Amendment to the Constitution) . . . . No firm or establishment need employ a heterosexual or homosexual person whose behavior on the job offends customers and calls into question the company's reputation" (Old Tappen, N.J.: Fleming H. Revell Co., 1978, p. 139).

The question is the effect new laws will have. I agree with Dr. Lovelace when he says that the First Amendment rights of churches and church-related institutions must be protected and that "the church should oppose any legislation which indiscriminately enforces the employment of openly avowed, practicing homosexuals in professions where this violates the civil rights of others." And I repeat what I have previously said. Affirmative Action programs on behalf of homosexual persons would set a dangerous precedent by defining a minority in terms of *behavior* rather than *birth;* they could result in forcible violations of the moral values of society.

LIMITATIONS ON CIVIL RIGHTS

All civil and human rights have certain inherent limitations. These limitations have been cogently stated in the UN Universal Declaration of Human Rights. Article 29 (2), quoted above, speaks of "such limitations as are determined by law solely for the purpose of securing due recognition and respect of the rights and freedoms of others and of meeting the just requirements of morality, public order and the general welfare in a democratic society." This charter recognizes that every society rests upon a fundamental moral order. The legal and judicial systems of a society have to coexist in some kind of rational correspondence with its underlying moral order. In our culture, the Judeo-Christian ethic has for centuries provided the fundamental moral order which gives meaning and direction to our legal and judicial tradition. This tradition has consistently moved toward the securing of human rights with equal justice for all. It has done so because of the moral order which gives it direction and meaning and any serious breach between our moral order and our legal tradition can only help to destroy the latter. This is why the refusal of our 1975 Synod pronouncement to make a moral judgment on homosexuality has such serious consequences. Until such a judgment is reached, the whole matter of justice for homosexual persons cannot be thought through.

Article 16 (3) of the Universal Declaration of Human Rights says that "The family is the natural and fundamental group unit of society and is entitled to protection by the society and the State." This principle has been agreed upon by nations and cultures from around the world. It correlates with the words "public order and the general welfare" in Article 29. Society has the right and the duty to protect the family and legal actions on behalf of homosexual persons have to be limited by this obligation.

The social philosopher Ernest van den Haag maintains that society has the right to defend and protect its traditions and institutions and the moral values they convey. Although he supports equal rights for homosexual persons in most forms of employment, he warns against it in areas like the elementary school:

> The issue is not protection of homosexual individuals against unwarranted loss, injury, humiliation, or inconvenience but the attempt to force society to grant approval to all preferences or forms of behavior, and thus to deny it the right to defend and protect its traditions and institutions—sexual, moral, aesthetic or social (cited by Dr. Lovelace in "The Active Homosexual Life-Style and the Church," *Consultation on Homosexuality*, p. 48).

None of the limitations on civil rights stated above detract from the Christian's duty to protect the civil rights of homosexual persons or to prevent, to the extent of his power, cruelty, persecution and slander. But the limitations which are inherent to all social and moral life should instruct the Christian about the nature and method of his effort.

APPENDIX: Statements and Documents

Appendix: Statements and Documents

ON TAKING SCRIPTURE SERIOUSLY
by Frederick W. Schroeder

The late Reinhold Niebuhr often stressed the importance of taking the Bible seriously; which, he said, is not the same as taking it literally. A literal interpretation of biblical stories and episodes that are garbed in picturesque or parabolic imagery raises more questions than it solves. Taking the Bible seriously is another matter. For instance, the story of the fall of man like the story of the tower of Babel speaks of human pride and pretensions, of man's attempt to transcend his creatureliness and to arrogate to himself the wisdom and the power of God. And the Jonah story is a powerful indictment of religious parochialism.

Taking the Bible seriously is to recognize that "all Scripture is inspired of God," as St. Paul wrote, "and is profitable for teaching, for reproof, for correction and for training in righteousness, that the man of God may be complete, equipped for every good work" (2 Tim. 3:16-17).

It should be noted that the apostle declared *all* Scripture to be inspired of God, not just some parts of it. All Scripture includes the Mosaic Code as well as the Sermon on the Mount, the social pronouncements of the prophets as well as the ethical strictures of the apostles. It is noteworthy, too, that in all matters of faith and conduct Scripture maintains a fine balance, matching grace with judgment, responsibility with rights, accountability with opportunity.

Protestants in particular ought to take Scripture seriously, for only in so doing are they true to their Reformation heritage. It was the clear testimony of Scripture that gave Luther the courage and the weapons to expose and oppose the aberrations of the church of his day. By the same token, it is on the clear testimony of Scripture that we must take

---

Frederick W. Schroeder of Elmhurst, Illinois, is the former President of Eden Theological Seminary.

our stand when the mores of a secularized culture threaten to demoralize the Christian way of life.

When one takes the Bible seriously one allows it to say what it has to say, and not what one wants it to say. So-called eisegesis (reading human predilections into the text) must not be permitted to replace exegesis (drawing out the meaning of the text). Equally fallacious is the attempt to dismiss biblical precepts and principles as being no more than the norms of a primitive culture that have had their day. To be sure the Bible speaks of religious and social customs which may or may not be applicable today. Cultural patterns change from age to age. The great moral imperatives of the law do not. They are unchanging and unchangeable; they are as valid and definitive today as they have been since the dawn of history. The Mosaic Code, for instance, incorporates the moral order of the universe. Idolatry, murder, adultery, robbery and theft are as much an infraction of that order today as they were when Moses brought the ten commandments down from Mt. Sinai.

All this has a bearing on the current controversy regarding the homosexual life-style. In the 1975 pronouncement on homosexuality (reprinted in *Human Sexuality: A Preliminary Study*) it is stated, "It is not within the province of this pronouncement to make an ethical judgment about same-gender relationships." Why not? Is it not a primary responsibility of the church to make ethical judgments? Silence on the morality of the homosexual life-style creates the impression that it is beyond reproach. But is it?

The pronouncement is vulnerable because it resorts to a highly selective use of Scripture. It leans heavily on what the prophets said about civil rights and social justice, whereas it is completely silent on what the New Testament has to say about homosexuality. The letter to the Romans (1:24-27) is very specific in this matter. It declares homosexualism to be both unnatural and immoral. No theological learning is necessary to recognize its abnormality. The anatomical difference between male and female speaks for itself on that score. So St. Paul was simply stating the obvious when he wrote that "women exchanged natural relations for unnatural, and men likewise gave up natural relations with women and were consumed with passion for one another." In his first letter to the Corinthians (6:9-10) he declares that homosexuals along with idolaters, adulterers, thieves and drunkards will not inherit the kingdom of God. These and similar statements scattered throughout the New Testament dare not be ignored.

Everything in Scripture is a part of what St. Paul called "the whole counsel of God" (Acts 20:27). By its very nature the church is obligated to teach and preach the whole counsel of God. No one can claim to take the Bible seriously without taking into account the law and the gospel, the pronouncements of the prophets and the teachings of the apostles.

STATEMENT ON SEXUALITY
Church of the Apostles
Lancaster, Penna.

Because we look to the Bible as a rule of faith and guide to our action and acknowledge the Lordship of Christ in all of life, we believe that the whole area of human sexuality needs to be biblically interpreted, more fully understood and addressed in our time.

We affirm these things in response to "Human Sexuality: A Preliminary Study."

We hold that a Christian ethic for sexuality is grounded in the order of creation. That order is affirmed in Genesis 1:27, "God created man in his own image, in the image of God he created him, male and female he created them." This order is further affirmed in Genesis 2:18-24, "Then the LORD God said, 'It is not good that the man should be alone.' " So the LORD God made woman and, "brought her to the man . . . Therefore a man leaves his father and his mother and cleaves to his wife, and they become one flesh." This order of creation for sexual relation is further confirmed by the teachings of Jesus, Matthew 19:4, "Have you not read that he who made them from the beginning made them male and female and said, 'For this reason a man shall leave his father and mother and be joined to his wife, and the two shall become one?' "

We acknowledge the sinfulness of all Men (generically "men" includes both sexes); Man has fallen short of God's intent in sexual relations. Sexuality is meant to result in the completion of a man and a woman. This is accomplished as love and affection are deepened and perpetuated in an exclusive sexual life within the marriage relationship. We recognize that man's sexual relations are adulterated. However, we are compelled to hold forth that ideal, strive for the full realization of God given potential, and confess that we have not attained it.

WHEREAS the Study and Resolutions allude to the acceptance of homosexuality as an alternate life-style,

WHEREAS the Preliminary Report and the 18 resolutions adopted by the General Synod of the United Church of Christ is biased in its selection and interpretation of material,

WHEREAS the Preliminary Report and the 18 resolutions were adopted by the 11th General Synod without first being studied and responses made by the Conferences, Associations and congregations,

WHEREAS certain resolutions are destructive of the peace and good order of congregations, Conferences and Associations particularly in their relations to the support of the General Synod;

This statement from the Church of the Apostles represents many similar statements we have received from churches across the nation in response to the Preliminary Study and the 18 Resolutions adopted by General Synod 11.

THEREFORE BE IT RESOLVED:

1) That heterosexual monogamous marriage and celibacy are the only God intended life-styles in sexual relations.
2) That we urge General Synod to affirm that:
   a. Sexuality is a God given Gift, and part of his created order.
   b. Homosexuality is a condition of disordered sexuality which reflects the sinfulness of human nature.
   c. Homosexual acts are contrary to the will of God and therefore not to be condoned.
3) That we call upon the 12th General Synod not to give any recognition to the Gay Caucus.
4) That the Executive Council of the General Synod reimplement resolution 1 of the Preliminary Study by requesting congregations, Associations and Conferences to study and respond to the Preliminary Study.
5) That the Executive Council make a report to the Conference, Associations and congregations of the results contained in the responses.
6) That upon the consensus drawn from the returned responses, a set of resolutions be prepared by the Conference and be submitted for consideration at the 12th General Synod.
7) That the Executive Council cease the implementaiton of resolutions 2 to 18.
8) That the Executive Council be instructed to prepare an addendum to the Preliminary Study on Family and Marriage. The Preliminary Report makes little reference to marriage and the family, a very unfortunate omission.
9) That we show concern and compassion for all sexually disordered persons, ministering to them and to all Christians with as much understanding as is possible in order that they may realize the fullest expression of sexuality within the Christian ethic.
10) That we give high priority to a ministry for fostering and strengthening marriage and the family.

EPILOGUE

We believe that the present unrest within the United Church of Christ over homosexuality is but a symptom of a deeper issue. That issue is how the local congregation can be more instrumental in determining the policies of the General Synod and the witness of the United Church of Christ. We affirm that ways must be found whereby the General Synod will be more sensitive to the work and the faith of the local congregation as together we seek to determine God's will in our time. The local church may never take the General Synod for granted;

neither may the General Synod take the local church for granted. It is, therefore, the responsibility of the local church to constantly study the issues, make appropriate responses, expressing through the Association and Conference approval or disapproval of the conduct and proceedings of the General Synod.

After learning the responses of other congregations, Associations and Conferences to the Preliminary Report on Sexuality and the action of the 12th General Synod, the Church of the Apostles will make an evaluation of the issues involved. Our evaluation and action may result in designated giving within or without the structures of the United Church of Christ. [United Church People for Biblical Witness does not encourage the withholding of funds from denominational programs.]

The General Synod and the local congregation need to be held in constant and creative tension. One organization offering hope for such creative dialogue is the United Church People for Biblical Witness, whose expressed purpose is to coordinate and facilitate local efforts for influencing the direction of the United Church of Christ in sexuality and other areas. And unless some other means emerges quickly for such dialogue, the above group deserves our immediate moral and financial support.

We affirm that the church is called to show a pastoral concern for all persons. The church is not a showcase for saints but a school for sinners. We affirm the right of all persons, including the homosexual, to be numbered among the fellowship of the church and to come to know the forgiveness of sin through Jesus Christ and the abundant life He promises. We affirm civil rights and the responsibilities they bear for all persons, consistent with the Biblical perspective and American Democracy.

We affirm that the church must proclaim the Word of God incisively to a society and culture which glorifies adulterated sexual gratifications. The church is called to speak on the issue of sexuality with insight, wisdom and forthright conviction based on God's word for our day. Let us speak not in hate or fear, but let us speak the truth out of love for the church and for all persons for whom Christ died. Whatever action we take, to paraphrase part of the marriage service, "Let us not enter into it unadvisedly or lightly, but reverently, responsibly, and in fear of God."

Finally, we acknowledge that human sexuality is not the only issue to be addressed in the light of the Christian ethic. Dishonesty in every sector of life (private, corporate, public), poverty, inadequate housing, unemployment, prejudices, racial discrimination, crime, ignorance, injustice, war, denuding the earth of its resources, etc., are contrary to God's order of Creation. These must equally be our concern.

Pastors: Glenn J. Rader

Nevin E. Schellenberger

THOUGHTS ON HUMAN SEXUALITY
FROM A BIBLICAL PERSPECTIVE
by Barbara J. Weller

After many years as a Christian who desires to live as a child of God, I have come to the conclusion that Scripture becomes terribly complicated when we try to escape its demands on our lives.[1] I have seen this happen in the whole area of sexuality in the United Church of Christ. While I believe that the church needs to constantly evaluate its teachings, I maintain that Scripture is very simple to understand if we are not trying to twist it to fit a predetermined mind-set.[2] This is especially true in the area of human sexuality. Reading through Scripture—both in the Old and New Testament—with the intent of learning what God has to say about sexuality, leaves us with a very clear understanding of the major points.

God is the Creator who knows all things. He realized when He created man with a sexual drive which would be the means of replenishing the earth that He was dealing with a very powerful appetite—not unlike the appetite for eating which would keep man alive. And so, just as God has spoken plainly about our gastronomic appetites to prevent us from misusing them, He has also spoken much in Scripture about our sexual appetites for the same purpose, to prevent us from misusing them.[3]

Beginning in Genesis,[4] God has made it very clear in His Word that sexual intercourse is to be reserved for marriage. At various times in the Bible, God allowed both polygamy and divorce, but always with the understanding that this was not His best for His children.[5] God's best for His children has always been one man and one woman, united for life and enjoying sexual intercourse exclusively with each other.[6] Paul has gone so far as to say in I Corinthians 7:3-5 that it is the duty of husbands and wives to provide pleasure for each other in this way to the utmost. But while God has always celebrated and encouraged sexual expression in marriage, He has always been equally clear that sexual intercourse outside of marriage is not what He intended for His children. And so in both the Old and New Testaments, fornication (which is sex *before* marriage) and adultery (which is sex *outside* of marriage) and divorce are always warned against in varying degrees because these actions do not represent God's best for His children.[7]

God created us. He created our sexual appetites. And He alone knows how we should use these appetites to make us happy. So He has given us the clear guidelines in Scripture that are stated above—one man and one woman enjoying the pleasures of sexual intercourse all

Barbara J. Weller of Souderton, Pennsylvania, is President of the Board of Directors of United Church People for Biblical Witness.

the days of their married life. Anything less than that (fornication, adultery, or divorce) is sin because it misses the mark that God has set for us. Of course, when God created us He knew that we would have trouble hitting the mark; and so He has always provided ways of repentance and forgiveness when we stray. In the Old Testament it was animal sacrifice. For us it is the acceptance of Jesus' sacrifice of Himself for our sins. There are few of us who have not been sexual sinners in one area or another, particularly when we consider Jesus' words that even to allow ourselves to lust is to miss God's best for us.[8] There are few of us who do not need to confess and accept forgiveness and repent, which means to turn around and begin to live as God has directed for our happiness.[9]

There is another area of sexuality dealt with in Scripture; and that is the area of same-sex relationships or homosexuality. Here again Scripture is very clear. First, we could consider all same-sex intercourse as fornication or adultery since, although God ordained heterosexual marriage in Genesis 2,[10] He never ordained same-sex marriages. Second, in *every* instance where homosexuality is mentioned in Scripture, it is mentioned in a negative way.[11]

Today we are hearing that facts of cultural sociology, psychology, and medicine override the clear voice of God in Scripture on these issues. But the truth is that in the history of medicine, psychology, and sociology, theories are fluid and constantly changing and, even today, there is disagreement among professionals about the facts of sexuality.

God's Word is not fluid; it does not change; and it is Truth.[12] If we, as Christians, are to determine God's thoughts in the area of sexuality, we need to do it by using Scripture.

God tells us in Romans 1 the origin of sexual irresponsibility. It is an outcome of man's sinfulness, of his turning away from God. Scripture does not tell us if the tendencies to homosexual *orientation* are inborn or learned;[13] but it does tell us in I Corinthians 6:9-11 that homosexual *behavior* can be healed through Jesus. We are not given specific ways to do this; but many formerly sexually irresponsible Christians (both homosexual and heterosexual) are willing to share their own experiences of being healed to help others. Some homosexuals can go on to change and lead normal married lives; others need to become sexually inactive to the glory of God.

Our culture tells us that to be denied the chance for sexual intercourse is the worst possible thing that could happen to anyone. But Scripture tells us in Matthew 19:10-12 and I Corinthians 7:1,7,32-40 that to turn over this area of our lives to God and to live in an unmarried state, without physically expressing our sexual selves, is a greater good than sexual immorality, whether heterosexual or homosexual. When Scripture expects all unmarried persons to live celibate lives, God is not asking any more of homosexuals than He asks of heterosexual persons who are unmarried or who, for one reason or another, are unable to have sexual intercourse in marriage. Many unmarried hetero-sexuals and homosexuals who are no longer sexually active attest to the fact that God knows what He is doing and that, for them, a sexually inactive life-style is a blessing and a greater pleasure than their old sexually active life-styles.

One final word must be said. In the whole area of sexuality, one sin (that is, missing God's best for us in some area) is no greater or lesser a sin than another.[14] We in the church cannot make homosexuals the lepers of the 20th Century while winking at fornication, adultery, and divorce. The church needs to begin a positive affirmation of lifetime marriage or lifetime celibacy to the glory of God. At the same time, the church needs to minister compassionately to all persons caught in the grip of sexual irresponsibility, whether heterosexual or homosexual. The Good News is that healing comes through Jesuş Christ.[15] Homo-sexuals or promiscuous heterosexuals will not be healed if they are shunned by the very Christians who could show them the Way and lovingly help them to walk in it.[16]

The church needs to minister to homosexuals the Word that there is hope for healing. The church needs to minister to divorced persons torn by guilt the Word that there is forgiveness and a chance to begin again. The church needs to minister to all marriages the Word that there are ways to make those marriages strong and fulfilling. The church needs to minister to unmarried young or older people the Word that there is strength in Christ to resist the culture around them. The church needs to minister to single persons the Word that in the fellowship of the Body of Christ they can find intimate, satisfying relationships without physical sex.

Especially in the age of situational ethics, the church needs to pro-claim the Good News that God has a way for us to be sexually responsi-ble, a way that can make us happier than we ever dreamed possible, a way that will help to heal many of the problems of our society. And that way is spelled out clearly in Scripture—one man and one woman enjoying the pleasures of sex exclusively with each other for a lifetime in marriage.

We cannot worm out of that with "new" cultural facts or with situational ethics. God's Word of condemnation to the Israelites in Judges 21:25 was that every man did what was right in his own eyes. God expects more of us as Christians. God expects us to do what is right in His eyes.[17]

NOTES

1. Proverbs 2.
2. Proverbs 3:5-8.
3. I Corinthians 6:12-20.
4. Genesis 2:24-25.
5. Matthew 19:8; Genesis 20; Genesis 16 (also read King David's story in II Samuel and I Kings 1 for evidence of troubles among his many wives).
6. Matthew 19:4-9.
7. Genesis 2:24; Proverbs 5:15-23; Matthew 5:31-32; 19:3-9; I Corinthians 7:1-5,10-16; Galatians 5:19-24; I Timothy 3:2-12.
8. Matthew 5:27.
9. Romans 3:23.
10. See also Matthew 19:4-6.
11. Genesis 19:1-10; Leviticus 18:22; 20:13; Deuteronomy 23:17; Romans 1:18, 26-27; I Corinthians 6:9-11; I Timothy 1:10; Jude vs. 7.
12. II Timothy 3:16-17; Matthew 5:17-19.
13. Matthew 19:10-12.
14. Romans 1:24-32; Galatians 5:16-21; James 2:10 (Note: however, see also I Corinthians 6:18).
15. I Corinthians 6:11.
16. Jude vs. 17-23.
17. I John 5:3.

THE MINORITY RESOLUTION RECOGNIZED
BY THE ELEVENTH GENERAL SYNOD

Whereas 34% of the delegates to the Eleventh General Synod voted negatively on "Recommendations in Regard To Human Sexuality Study"; and

Whereas "Human Sexuality: A Preliminary Study," the foundation for these Recommendations, was preliminary in nature; and

Whereas the Executive Council sent the Study to the Eleventh General Synod without recommendation, and sent it to delegates too late for sufficient time for study; and

Whereas we feel it is important that local churches have opportunity to examine, discuss, and respond to the Study; and

Whereas it appears there is a limited theological, biblical, and ethical viewpoint reflected in the Study which does not characterize the diverse perspectives of the United Church of Christ; and

Whereas there is a diversity of sociological and psychological perspectives not reflected in the Study; and

Whereas we appreciate the opportunity to engage in significant theological and ethical discussion; and appreciate the work done by those involved in preparing the Study to open this dialogue;

Therefore be it resolved:

(1) We call upon the local churches, Associations, and Conferences of the United Church of Christ to examine and discuss the Study and, prior to the Twelfth General Synod, respond to the Study through their Conference structures;

(2) We call upon the local churches, Associations, and Conferences to seek study materials on the subject reflecting biblical, theological, and ethical perspectives not reflected in the Study;

(3) The minority resolution be included in the study guide prepared by the United Church Board For Homeland Ministries and wherever the eighteen recommendations of the Eleventh General Synod are reported.

POLICY STATEMENT

United Church People for Biblical Witness, formed out of the minority caucus of GS 11 in response to the United Church of Christ Preliminary Human Sexuality Study, intends:

(1) to promote renewal of the church, faithfulness to our reformation heritage, and obedience to the authority of "the Scriptures of the Old and New Testaments . . . as the rule of Christian faith and practice" (Service of Ordination);

(2) to provide study materials on human sexuality issues reflecting biblical, theological, ethical, psychological, and sociological perspectives not reflected in the UCC preliminary study;

(3) to encourage genuine dialogue and debate within the United Church of Christ on the issues of the Human Sexuality Study with fairness to all points of view;

(4) to lift up the family as the fundamental unit of human society while affirming the special contributions that single persons can make in our church and society;

(5) to remind the church that the eighteen Recommendations in Regard to Human Sexuality adopted by the Eleventh General Synod, July, 1977, created the basis for implementation and action and that the intent of these recommendations needs to be clarified before the church takes further action upon them;

(6) to uphold a faithful biblical standard of ethical morality in all areas for clergy and lay people in the church;

(7) to deal specifically with issues of homosexuality:

a. to advocate the rejection of proposals for ordaining practicing homosexual persons and for church recognition of homosexual unions;

b. to encourage ministries of compassion, healing and justice for homosexual persons (and all sexually disordered persons);

c. to affirm the civil rights of homosexual persons as human beings, balanced by considerations of the welfare of society, public morality, and respect for the rights of others as stated in Article 29 of the United Nations Declaration of Human Rights in 1949.

This Policy Statement was adopted by the National Steering Committee of the United Church People for Biblical Witness, meeting in St. Louis, Missouri, July 12-14, 1978.

SUGGESTED READINGS

Suggested Readings

This reference list contains resources for continuing study of the issues treated throughout the book and, we trust, will make for informative, pleasurable reading. Readers will want to check through the list to cull out what meets their interest or need. Subject areas can be grouped fairly easily from the titles. The notes at the conclusion of each chapter should not be ignored for they provide additional source material on particular subjects. Please note the important bibliography on the ministry and ordination supplied by Dr. Shetler and listed separately at the conclusion of his chapter, "Ordination in the United Church of Christ." Jim Kaspar and Mike Bussee provided a short reading list on homosexuality which concludes their chapter, "A Saturday Morning Dialogue."

We recommend that study groups make every effort to obtain some of these suggested readings. Ranging in style from the popular to the highly technical, they set a high standard of scholarly and spiritual workmanship.

Achtemeier, E., *The Committed Marriage,* Philadelphia: The Westminster Press, 1976.

Adams J., *Christian Counselor's Manual,* Grand Rapids: Baker Book House, 1974.

Barth, K., *Church Dogmatics I,* eds. G. W. Bromiley and T. F. Torrance, Edinburgh: T. & T. Clark, 1956.

Bennett, J. C. et. al., *Storm Over Ethics,* United Church Press, 1967.

Berkouwer, G. C., *Holy Scripture,* trans. J. Rogers, Grand Rapids, Eerdmans, 1975.

Berkouwer, G. C., *The Second Vatican Council and the New Catholicism,* trans, L. B. Smedes, Grand Rapids, Eerdmans, 1965.

Bieber, I., *Sexual Inversion: The Multiple Roots of Homosexuality,* New York: Basic Books, Inc., 1965.

Bloesch, D. G., *Essentials of Evangelical Theology,* Vol. 1, San Francisco: Harper & Row, Publishers, 1978.

Bloesch, D. G., *The Invaded Church,* Waco, Texas: Word Inc., 1975.

Bonhoeffer, D., *The Cost of Discipleship,* Second Ed., trans. R. H. Fuller, SCM Press Ltd., 1959; also New York, The Macmillan Company, 1963.

Burke, J. M., *Civil Rights,* Second Ed., New York: R. R. Bowker Co., 1974.

Christenson, L., *The Christian Family,* Minneapolis: Bethany Fellowship, 1970.

Clinebell, H. J. Jr. and C. H., *The Intimate Marriage,* New York: Harper & Row, Publishers, 1970.

Cole, W. G., *Sex and Love in the Bible,* Association Press, 1959.

Consultation on Homosexuality, Spring City, Pa.: Presbyterians United For Biblical Concerns, 1977 (available for $3.50 from PUBC, 50 Buckwalter Rd., Spring City, Penna. 19475).

Davies, W. D., *Christian Origins and Judaism,* Philadelphia, Westminster Press, 1962.

Davies, W. D., *Introduction to Pharisaism,* Philadelphia: Fortress Press, 1967.

Denton, W., *Family Problems and What to Do About Them,* Philadelphia: Westminster Press, 1971.

De Rougemont, D., *Love in the Western World,* trans. M. Belgion, New York: Harper & Row, Publishers, 1956.

Encyclopedia of Sexual Behavior, Vol. I, ed. A. Ellis, New York: Hawthorne Books (see article by D. W. Cory).

Fairchild, R. W., *Christians in Families,* Covenant Life Curriculum, John Knox Press, 1964.

Frank, J. D., "Treatment of Homosexuals," *National Institute of Mental Health Task Force on Homosexuality: Final Report and Background Papers,* 1972.

Freedman, A. et. al., *Comprehensive Textbook of Psychiatry,* Baltimore: The Williams and Wilkins Co., 1972.

Glatzer, N. N., *Hillel the Elder: The Emergence of Classical Judaism,* Revised Ed., New York: Schocken Books, 1966.

Goldenson, R. M., *The Encyclopedia of Human Behavior,* 2 Vol., Garden City, N. Y.: Doubleday & Company, Inc., 1970.

Graham, B., *Find Freedom,* Grand Rapids: Zondervan, 1975. (see ch. 4).

Graham, B., *The Jesus Generation,* Minneapolis: World Wide Publications, 1971 (see ch. 5).

Grelot, P., *Man and Wife in Scripture,* New York: Herder & Herder, 1964.

The Interpreters Dictionary of The Bible, "Marriage," Vol. K-Q, p. 278, "Sex, Sexual Behavior," Vol. R-Z, p. 296, New York: Abingdon Press, 1962.

Katchadourian, H. A. and Lunde, D. T., *Fundamentals of Human Sexuality,* New York: Holt, Rinehart and Winston, Inc., 1972.

Kemeny, J. G., *A Philosopher Looks At Science,* New York: D. Van Nostrand Company, Inc., 1966.

Konvitz, M. R., *Bill of Rights Reader,* 5th Revised Ed., Ithaca, N. Y.: Cornell University Press, 1973.

LaHaye, T. and B., *The Act of Marriage,* Grand Rapids, Zondervan, 1976.

Lepp, I., *The Psychology of Loving,* Baltimore: Helicon, 1963.

Lewis, C. S., *The Abolition of Man,* New York: The Macmillan Company, 1947.

Lewis, C. S., *The Allegory of Love,* New York, Oxford University Press, 1958.

Lewis, C. S., *The Four Loves,* New York: Harcourt, Brace & World, 1960.

Lovelace, R. F., *Homosexuality and the Church,* Old Tappen, N. J.: Fleming H. Revell Company, 1978.

Mace, D. R., *Whom God Hath Joined,* Revised Ed., Philadelphia: The Westminster Press, 1973.

Mace, D. R. and V., *Marriage Enrichment in the Church,* Nashville: Broadman Press, 1976.

Mace, D. R. and V., *We Can Have Better Marriages,* New York: Abingdon Press, 1974.

May, W. E. and Harvey, J. F., *On Understanding Human Sexuality,* Synthesis Series, Chicago: Franciscan Herald Press, 1977.

Moore, G. F., *Judaism in the First Centuries of the Christian Era,* 2 vol., Cambridge, Harvard University Press, 1927.

Narramore, C., *Encyclopedia of Psychological Problems,* Grand Rapids, Zondervan, 1966.

Neusner, J., *First Century Judaism in Crisis,* Nashville: Abingdon Press, 1975.

Nygren, A., *Agape and Eros,* 1939.

Otto, H. A., *Marriage and Family Enrichment,* Nashville: Abingdon Press, 1976.

Religious Studies Review, Vol. 4, No. 1 (Jan. 1978), pp. 11-14 (comments on the UCC Preliminary Study).

The Report by the Committee to Study Homosexuality for the Council of the Christian Reformed Churches, Grand Rapids: Board of Publications of the Christian Reformed Church (available for $1.00 from Barbara J. Weller, 276 West Cherry Lane, Souderton, Penna. 18964).

Schechter, S., *Aspects of Rabbinic Theology,* New York, Schocken Books, 1961.

Schnakenburg, R., *The Moral Teaching of the New Testament,* New York: Herder & Herder, 1962.

Sexuality and the Human Community, Philadelphia: Office of General Assembly of the United Presbyterian Church in the United States of America, 1970.

Shedd, C. W., *Letters to Karen: On Keeping Love in Marriage,* Nashville: Abingdon Press, 1965.

Sorokin, P. A., *The Crisis of Our Age,* New York: E. P. Dutton & Co., Inc., 1941.

Tavard, G., *Holy Writ or Holy Church,* New York, Harper & Row, 1959.

Thielicke, H., *The Ethics of Sex,* trans. J. W. Doberstein, New York: Harper & Row, 1964.

Warfield, B. B., "Love in the New Testament," *Princeton Theological Review,* XVI, 1918, p. 153.

White, J., *EROS Defiled: The Christian and Sexual Sin,* Downers Grove, Ill.: InterVarsity Press.

Williams, D., *The Bond That Breaks: Will Homosexuality Split the Church?,* Los Angeles: BIM, 1978.